FRETFUL SLEEPERS
AND
OTHER ESSAYS

FRETFUL SLEEPERS
AND
OTHER ESSAYS

BILL PEARSON

HEINEMANN EDUCATIONAL BOOKS

Heinemann Educational Books Ltd
London Melbourne Toronto
Singapore Auckland Hong Kong
Nairobi New Delhi Ibadan
Johannesburg Kuala Lumpur

Published by Heinemann Educational Books (N.Z.) Ltd,
P.O. Box 36–064, Northcote, Auckland, 9, New Zealand
Printed by Dai Nippon Printing Co (H.K.) Ltd, Hong Kong

Contents

Acknowledgements

The author and publishers wish to acknowledge the following publications, in which these essays first appeared: *Collected Stories of Frank Sargeson* (Blackwood & Janet Paul), *Comment, Commonwealth Literature* (Heinemann Educational Books), *Here and Now, Image, Islands, Journal of the Polynesian Society, Landfall, Mate, New Zealand Listener, New Zealand Monthly Review.*

The author wishes also to acknowledge with gratitude the following for permission to reproduce poems in the essay 'The Recognition of Reality': Longman Paul and the poet for 'Not by Wind Ravaged' and 'Time and the Child', and an extract from 'Sea Call' from *No Ordinary Sun* by Hone Tuwhare; Pegasus Press Ltd and the Estate of A.R.D. Fairburn for 'I'm Older than You Please Listen' from the *Collected Poems* of A.R.D. Fairburn; Pegasus Press Ltd and Mrs Dorothea Mason for 'Song of Allegiance' from the *Collected Poems* of R.A.K. Mason.

Foreword

I have often been asked to collect these essays or to have one or other of them reprinted. 'Fretful Sleepers' has been clandestinely photocopied for class use at a teachers' training college, and a Maori advancement committee once asked me if I could disseminate my essay 'The Maori People' more widely.

The essays range more widely in topic than those of most literary critics; but most of them are concerned with the distinctiveness of living in New Zealand and with making meaningful imaginative play of that experience. For us the heightened self-awareness which is the breath of art entails some knowledge (and revaluation) of our double traditional heritage, European and Polynesian, some recognition of our changed relations with our neighbours in the Pacific islands and in South and East Asia so that we can discard attitudes and assumptions that we inherited from our late Victorian and Edwardian predecessors, and some understanding of our own society. The changing continuum of experience and attitudes and ideas, a sort of communal stream of consciousness, is the element in which works of art are conceived and to which they are in time delivered, and is too often dismissed as a chaos of 'non-literary considerations'.

I have wondered how much to revise the essays. I think it would have been a mistake to update them and my principle has been to revise only to clarify the original meaning or remove an obvious error or injustice or repetition. 'Under Pressure to Integrate' (originally called 'The Maori People') belongs so much to the context of the official Government policy towards Maoris at the time that updating would destroy much of its value. But I believe that the principles governing good race relations that are implied in the essay stand as strongly as they did when it was written, and I am sure that Maori aspirations have not changed, rather they have intensified. In 'Fretful Sleepers' I have removed a footnote where I was rash enough to make a prediction that did not come off. Although the last paragraphs of that essay refer to contemporary alarms I have left them intact since they convey something of the fears that leftists felt in the time of cold war in which it was written, and though parliamentary acts may change, I am not convinced that we have seen the last of the danger of censorship or persecution of artists.

Most of my reviews of fiction were written a year or more after the book being reviewed had been published, so that it had had a chance to be read widely beforehand. My aim has been to stimulate thought and I did not expect my evaluation of a novel to be taken as more than one intent view; not necessarily the view I would take now, because several of the writers have increased their stature since, enabling one to see their early work differently. If the reviews struck some readers as sharp it will be seen that I could admire but where I saw defects I felt obliged to speak plainly. One of them I was told had hurt the writer whose book I was considering and for that reason I would have preferred to leave it out, but it has been misrepresented as a jealous attack on a new talent and it is necessary to bring it forward so that readers can see for themselves. It is not wise to review in a small country and I gave it up.

I have included my earlier study of pakeha writing about Maoris in preference to my later and fuller one for two reasons. First, that some people have told me they found it more rewarding than the later one. Second, that the later one, 'The Maori and Literature 1938-1965', is available in two other books currently in print: *The Maori People in the 1960's*, edited by Erik Schwimmer (Longman Paul) and in *Essays in New Zealand Literature*, edited by Wystan Curnow (Heinemann Educational Books). In 'Attitudes to the Maori in Some Pakeha Fiction' I have revised one passage where (as Frank Sargeson has shown me) I read too much into the closing sentence of a story that I discuss. If before preparing these essays for the press I had thoroughly reconsidered Roderick Finlayson's stories, as I did immediately after for the edition of *Brown Man's Burden and Later Stories* about to be published by Auckland University Press, I would have further modified the comments that I make on them in two or three of the essays.

'The Recognition of Reality', originally delivered as an address to an audience who could not be expected to know a lot about our country or its literature, repeats ideas that originated in earlier essays but I have included it because it takes a broader perspective than they do and comprehends a number of my ideas.

Bill Pearson
July, 1973

Fretful Sleepers

A Sketch of New Zealand Behaviour and its Implications for the Artist

In this article I have to steer between two dangers, each represented by previous assessments of 'the New Zealand character'. The first is to use the first person plural as in Oliver Duff's *New Zealand Now*. When I read it my impression was that I'd been listening to a rotarian, the two of us puffing pipes by a fire, picking our noses, having a man-to-man talk over the whisky fumes. Like a conversation I overheard at New Zealand House: two middle-aged women: 'Everybody likes the New Zealanders. Oh yes, wherever you go, we're very popular.' The other said, six times at three-second intervals: 'Ye-es', then, 'M'm, I suppose we are, when you come to think of it. . . . Yes.' Mr Fairburn in *We New Zealanders* tickled and teased us in odd places without anyone feeling the worse for it. The other danger is to use a deadly or hostile third person plural as if we were the object of an anthropologist's research, as D'Arcy Cresswell did. Anna Kavan ('New Zealand: Answer to an Inquiry', *Horizon*, September 1943) tried hard to understand us; she was penetrating but she saw us from the outside looking on and a slight hysteria blinded her too. In this article I shall veer, saying *we* when I praise, *they* when I blame. The real difficulty, though, is to distinguish between what are permanent or emergent traits in New Zealanders, and what accidental or temporary adaptations, whether these are general, whether they belong to the West Coast where I grew up, whether I am only projecting my own faults. If I do this I am sticking my neck out and will take the consequences. Again I shall have to keep clear class backgrounds—whether I am talking of miners, clerks or businessmen. But since New Zealand is as homogeneous in its patterns of conduct as (I think) any other country, this is less important. By the time anyone has read this article, he will have objected a dozen times that I am not talking of New Zealanders but of men: these virtues and failings you will find the whole world over. That

This essay was first published in *Landfall*, September 1952, and reprinted with corrections in *Landfall Country*, ed. Charles Brasch (Caxton Press, 1960).

is true, but I am trying to sketch a character faithful in its emphases. To abstract what might be peculiar to New Zealanders would be to talk of a fiction.

I

It is a funny place to start—but writing away from New Zealand, I have no check on far-fetched deductions but a subjective one: what it felt like to grow up at home. When I was seven my mother told me if I was ever playing on the hill or in the paddocks at the bottom I was to watch out for miners' shafts hidden under long grass and blackberries. I was awed, partly at the prospect of disappearing, as it seemed, without hope of recovery, twelve feet into the earth, but as well at the blandness with which a responsible adult could tolerate the continuance of such dangers. I felt they should have done something about it. Who is *they*? It could be argued that to me as a child *they* simply meant *adults*; and at that time I did impute infallibility to adults. But it is not only in me: *they* crops up again and again unnoticed in the talk of New Zealanders, a convenient fiction that covers a gap in their thought or illustrates a dimly-felt need—for what? Whenever you pin down the *they*, you will find it is in one case the borough council, in another 'the goverment', in another the drainage board; but the speaker will have to think before he can identify them: he will probably say 'the authorities' or 'the powers that be'. *They* is the symbol for authority, protective and unquestioned and only noticed when something goes wrong.

The New Zealander delegates authority, then forgets it. He has shrugged off responsibility and wants to be left alone. There is no one more docile in the face of authority. He pleads rationalizations, 'doesn't want to make a fuss' or 'make a fool of himself', but generally he does what he is told, partly because everyone else is doing it, partly because he wants to be sociable and co-operate in a wishfully untroubled world. Only when things go visibly wrong does he recall his right to question the authority and change it. When he complains half his bitterness is that he has been made to complain because he hates complaint and can't complain with dignity. Anyone who questions too often is a 'moaner', yet in New Zealand the moaner is common. Things never run so smoothly as the New Zealander pretends. So he is suspicious of politics—the anti-conscription campaign and the Stockholm peace petition were suspect not out of fear of communism but because the man who tries to stop the drive to war is reminding everyone of the moral responsibility he gave away with his vote.

This is closely connected with another implication of my awe at my mother's warning: a middle-class conception of a universe well-plumbed and shockproof, where there aren't shafts for boys to fall into. That is at bottom of the ideal world of the New Zealander, one that 'runs by clockwork'. You get up at a regular hour, go to work, you marry and have a family, a house and garden, and you live on an even keel till you draw a pension and they bury you decently. The New Zealand way of life is ordained, but who ordains it?

God? But few New Zealanders care about him: they don't doubt he is there, he must be; a New Zealander who never says 'Christ' except unconsciously as an expletive will jump to confute an atheist. God is at the controls but he doesn't need the New Zealander's recognition. God disposes, man reposes. The universe is well-oiled and if you stick to your tracks you'll have a good journey in this life. After that? Well, if you've lived a respectable New Zealand life, what sort of God would he be to complain? We'll mostly end up in heaven, seemingly in one endless family reunion talking over old times. Of course this is a bourgeois eschatology: it is more explicit in the attitude of elderly, comfortable suburban womenfolk. But I think it applies to the public assumptions of more New Zealanders than go to church. Now when the well-oiled universe grinds, there wells a vague resentment: when life turns up a vigorous uncomfortable side, there is rebellion. The New Zealand woman feels disgust at seeing an epileptic fit: she talks of cancer as if it was, like v.d. or the illnesses of Erewhon, a reprehensible disease. Why? Because there isn't the corresponding balance of a known cure. It looks as if the Creator forgot something. The patient isn't to blame; has God played fair? So again of violent or tragic death. Someone must be to blame; these things don't happen without purpose ... : someone left a switch on, the driver had 'had drink'; and if not, then it shouldn't have been allowed—God is to blame. Under trial the New Zealand church-going woman is huffy: 'You're not the sort of God I was brought up to believe in.' She probably stops going to church, just to show him.

But, failing God, when the wrong affects more than one the solution is 'the government.' Even the champions of private enterprise expect government compensation when the crops fail. No people is easier material for governing. Though 'Hitler' and 'dictator' are common as terms of abuse (usually applied to a foreman who puts production before sociability) there is a lurking respect for the dictator because he has all the authority and gets things done without argument and compromise. When the Upper House went no one cared. It was only workers of the big unions, and the watersiders themselves, who were concerned at Mr Holland's emergency regulations, and a few intellectuals. Fascism has long been a danger potential in New Zealand. Of course fascism doesn't just occur: it is a deliberate strategy used by money-makers threatened with social discontent. But in countries nominally democratic, fascists have first to prepare the ground. In New Zealand the ground is already prepared, in these conditions: a docile sleepy electorate, veneration of war-heroes, willingness to persecute those who don't conform, gullibility in the face of headlines and radio peptalks.*

New Zealanders may well wake up one day to find a military dictator riding them and wonder how he got there. If the National Party was more astute it would have a V.C. as its party leader. You can't inherit freedom; yet most of our institutions are inherited and there is no common understanding that they were born of struggle. Even if the Upper House answered no need in New Zealand conditions, it is a check to power removed. Again there is a popular respect for summary justice. In Auckland during the war there were rumours that American soldiers sentenced to death by court-martial were taken to sea in launches, shot and dropped overboard. Whether the rumours were true or not, I don't know: what disturbs is the undertone of admiration with which they were repeated. The Yanks, one was told, didn't fuck around. There was a very real danger that the emergency organization of volunteers willing to assist police and provide scab labour in the 1951 dispute might have turned into a minor local Ku Klux Klan.

Not that New Zealanders would long tolerate a one-man government that hurt. I say that so long as the autocrat, like Peron, manipulated the sentiments of the people and governed broadly in the interests of the most powerful class, few would raise moral questions about the principle of dictatorship. Mr Holland, governing by radio, without a parliament, seems to have emerged from the waterfront dispute more popular than ever. The reason why the New Zealander is willing to invest his responsibility in a strong, benevolent ruler is that he himself is afraid of responsibility. He especially fears any position that raises him above 'the boys'. How many of us refused stripes in the army, just out of that fear. In the war, an airman turned police constable explained to me that he only joined the force to get out of going overseas and anyway he was indulgent to servicemen, looked after them when they were drunk rather than run them in. You may object, well he *did* join the force rather than risk his life. What I mean is that he felt no shame in owning to cowardice, but had to apologize for taking a job of potential hostility to his mates. Infantrymen who joined the Provost Corps would explain that really it was a good thing if chaps like them were M.P.'s because they would be easier on the boys than 'some other bastards' would be. They had to explain their decision as being in the interests of the boys they felt they had deserted. Possibly the boys aren't convinced and don't co-operate: the n.c.o. or provost becomes guilty and bitter and all the harder on them. Of course in civilian life there are other inducements to raising oneself—

---

* The Australians were far from docile in their reaction to the proposed anti-communist bill. It seems we are the most fertile testing-ground for legislation dreamt up not by the National Party but foreign diplomats: reactionary legislation is following the same pattern in four 'White Dominions.' We always were a social laboratory.

money, the demands of wife and family: these are accepted by society in its contrary idea that a man has to get ahead, look after himself. But the man who has raised himself, say from miner to deputy, or hand to foreman, is faintly haunted so long as he works with the men once equal to him. Off duty he probably takes care to drink with them; at work he will establish himself by confiding in the older hands who knew him before he rose, and being tough on the newer ones, who no doubt are 'a different stamp of material altogether, don't know what work is, most of them'.

II

Now the New Zealander, especially of the middle class, has a two-faced attitude to social climbing. We all dimly hope to rise, yet we are afraid of rising above the common level. We become righteously indignant when anyone tries to impose on us by reason of money or birth. 'Who does he think he is, Lord Muck?' Think of the sneers we have for the clipped polite speech of the English middle class—which we confuse with the speech of aristocracy—or for the visiting English aristocrat, the giggles of young girls at his manner, the cold shoulder of the worker. We can only stand it when he speaks from a platform: we fear direct human contact; he is the occasion of Rotarian oratory, a column in the press, but we are awkward in his presence as if our weaknesses were exposed. Because our vaunted pride in being as good as he is, is in fact a sense of inferiority. That is why so many New Zealanders, when they come to England, try to get to a royal garden party and conduct themselves like teen-agers in the presence of a film-star. Being middle-class we fear and sneer at royalty and aristocracy, yet we hanker after them because an aristocrat's goodwill confers security on our self-esteem. But on the other hand we feel superior to some workers, especially those of the strong left-wing unions—miners, watersiders and freezing workers; and, as tourists, to foreign menials, workers and peasants we adopt attitudes we wouldn't dare at home. I have heard New Zealanders in London say 'Cockney' and 'Irishman' in the same tone of voice as adults in my boyhood used to say 'night-man'. Generally the sense of inferiority makes us all the more determined to enforce the level: it is fear of social climbing that brings the dread conformity all artists in New Zealand have to contend with. This too is at back of our two-faced attitude to England. It is a boast to be *going* to England; but not to come back is desertion, like crashing your way into another class. We like to be told we are the Dominion most like England, yet an English educated accent makes us feel we are being imposed on. If it crops up in someone's talk that he has been to England his listener will at once suspect that he only raised the subject as an occasion of mentioning his travels. We sneer at English customs, yet from every visiting Englishman we exact words of praise and are offended if he criticizes us. We crave for commendation from those we feel inferior to. Remember how flattered we used to be to read those digest articles about New Zealand the Social Laboratory, the experiment watched by the whole world?

Most readers will remember the time they left their home towns to go to university, how when they went back in vacations (if they didn't fall prey to the temptation and feel superior) they looked double-hard at everyone they passed to avoid unconsciously snubbing anyone they knew. The word would get around, X is conceited, thinks himself someone just because he's at university—'Why, I can remember in the slump he didn't have shoes to his feet.' The home-town folk look for this and are disappointed if you don't give them the chance to condemn you because you are already *different*: you are at university. 'Being different' in New Zealand means 'trying to be superior'. I know of no other country where this is so. A friend of mine working as a builder's hand got along well with his workmates till the secret came out that he'd had a year at university. Defensive sneers met him after that, whenever he disagreed on anything: 'Don't think that just because you've been to 'varsity. . . . ' I worked a fortnight at a garage: the foreman couldn't resist telling the men I had an M.A. in English and dared me to 'improve their English.'* (He was a militant atheist and took pleasure in the offence given—to whom?—by their habitual swearing.) He wasn't serious, but a sprayer took me aside and solemnly warned me that if I had any ideas like that I was due to come a big thud.

There is no place in normal New Zealand society for the man who is different. The boy whose misfortune it is to be sent to a snob school like Christ's College or Wanganui Collegiate where a special dialect is taught, is immunized for life from contact with working men. He will always shy from them because he will sense their contempt for his speech. Even if by effort he makes permanent friendship with any of them he will always be apologized for: 'Course he talks la-di-da, but he's a real white joker once you get to know him.' It is not only difference suggesting social superiority the New Zealander fears, it is any variation from the norm. The man with a cleft palate, with a stutter, with short sight, will suffer. There will always be jokes behind his back; he will find it hard to make honest contact with other men because once he has been isolated, most men will talk to him only with tongue in cheek, humouring him at best, saving up a report for the boys in the bar. Even educated people feel they have to shout when they talk to foreigners, a habit as insulting as anticipating a stammerer. An Italian has trucked in a West Coast mine for twenty years: he is still alone, no girl would marry him, the fear of

---

* Many readers will be tempted to think I only mention this to advertise the degree.

his broken English and the contempt for his pleading eyes have been handed down from his first workmates, so that ropeboys just starting can feel cocky pride in shouting: 'Good day, you fucking rotten Skypoo bastard!' When I was a lad in Greymouth there was an inefficient teacher with holes in his socks, he hadn't much control over his class; the word got around and soon not only children but parents would point him out and laugh at him. There was a policeman, too, who had come off the worse in an argument with some local roughs: it seems he was hesitant, and he had a horse face. Soon the whole town was lusting after the chase, every few days there was a latest anecdote of indignity provoked by young bloods who had set out to ambush him and whet their wits on his helplessness. He couldn't go on his beat but someone whistled 'Horsey, keep your tail up'. In a month or two they shifted him, and the day he left someone rang up the railway station and ordered a horsebox. You can gain a reputation in New Zealand in a few backroom mumbles; you don't lose it in a lifetime.

The boycott is not always malicious: the tormentors need not know they hurt. The motive force is usually fear. It's not a pleasant thought; but it is true how afraid we all are of 'public opinion', 'what people will say'. Because always censoring and supervising our every act is the jury in the bar, the jury over the teacups, the jury in the editorial column. The jury makes weaklings of us all: we may kick against it, challenge it like D'Arcy Cresswell; if so we finish preoccupied with our act of defiance. Most of us give in, play the coward, and knowing it we become the puny little men leaning over the bar, pontificating in new juries, in the same way as this year's pullets pecked by old hens grow into next year's hens to peck the new batch of pullets.*

Some papers and organizations seem to exist for no other purpose than to enforce conformity: think of the Auckland *Observer*, some (though certainly not all) of the editorial policies of *Truth*, the public pronouncements of the executive of the R.S.A., the observations on public morals from the Women's Institute. Now that the Sedition Bill is law, it is an open question whether the jury habit will prove too strong for Mr Holland by criticizing the government in spite of the law, or whether (as I fear is more likely) it will co-operate with the law by making advance judgments on those people likely to be the victims of this law.

---

* The jury mentality is in our use of *should*. Ignoring the distinction between *shall* and *will* (which is observed in England but not New Zealand), *should* in England expresses probability: the English say *I should go* where we say *I'd go*. In New Zealand *should* expresses moral obligation, the same as the English *ought to*. Yet in New Zealand there is a new use coming into habit: *you should* meaning *there's an opportunity for you to*, as in *you should put the rent up*. It is symptom of an increasing attitude of unprincipled opportunism. *Can* means *may* in New Zealand. In the past this has meant no power without permission. It might be reversed and come to mean power is permission, might is right.

III

In public morality the New Zealander's guiding principle is: Do others do it? I doubt if a New Zealander has any other moral referee than public opinion: crimes he has been in youth educated against he will lose distaste for as soon as the wind changes. This is noticeable when a lot of New Zealanders go to another country of people with inferior standards of material comfort, as in a war. With our troops the home-grown moral standards were valid only among themselves: Egyptians and Italians were fair butt for a cruel, predatory and jocularly cynical approach. There is a legend, true I think, that when a Kiwi was beaten up in a brothel area, every Kiwi in Cairo assembled to riot his way through the Sharia-el-Birkeh and there wasn't a piece of furniture left whole in the district. Soldiers in search of more innocent sport would throw chairs at the orchestra in cheap cabarets; the sport of the A.S.C. was to up-end fruit-stalls with the tails of their trucks. The black market was, in Italy and Japan, accepted as a normal means of living without drawing on one's paybook. Of course British troops did these things and Australians, I believe, were worse, and of course such conduct is as old as the Vikings and older. Yet there is a special quality in the ease with which the New Zealander violates his home-town respectability, and admits it to be an expedient for getting by without trouble. A less violent example illustrates this: March 1950, in St Stephen's Hall in the Houses of Parliament, Westminster. Three old ladies from Dunedin waiting to be admitted to the gallery, because they wanted to hear Mr Churchill. A Swedish woman was the first to get a pass: she had been there before them, but they hadn't seen her. 'A foreigner! A foreigner getting into the British House of Commons before a British subject! A British policeman putting a foreigner before the British! Mr Churchill would give a lot to know about this!' 'She probably greased his palm or something.' 'Some of them are so low they'd stoop to anything.' The one who had said this called the policeman and tried to slip him, unobtrusively, a florin, 'just to get yourself some cigarettes or something'. The policeman protested loudly that it wasn't necessary, she flushed and prattled about cigarettes, possibly telling herself that of course she wouldn't stoop to foreign policy, and in the end he took the money, and they got in no sooner. The suspicion that a rival or enemy had done something she claimed to disapprove of was a challenge to do the same thing, to beat the rival at her own game. This is a dangerous mental habit and will help Mr Holland tremendously in his campaign to convince us that if you don't kill communists they will kill you.

We boast when under alcoholic liberation we violate our professed code of morals. Think of the animal comeback in the remark, common among New Zealand troops, usually said with a touch of flattery: 'He's a nice chap, he'd shit anywhere.' When a well-bred girl greets a man friend: 'Don't you speak to me!' she seems to imply that they both know that he's a rake and it's a secret to be proud of: of course, he isn't, but the idea is that the best people are rogues at heart, or rather, secret rogues are the nicest people to know. Among young people greetings like 'Hophead', 'Ram', 'Burglar', 'Sheik', 'Stopout', are accepted as flattery: 'burglar' I heard only in the army. We are in other ways as hypocritical. We claim to be social democrats at heart—or did two years ago—but we have a great respect for the man who can get away with it. In public we condemn the profiteer, in private we connive and rather admire him and envy him his opportunities. It is because we know our public sentiments are recognized to be subject to private reservation that we don't hesitate to do what we have condemned when we get the chance. So in public we always say the right thing, to which we are not committed. Any platform statement in New Zealand is suspect: the orator is only emptying his lungs to fill an occasion. When the Prime Minister spoke from the B.B.C. in January 1951, all he could produce was a tissue of naive clichés which here seemed odd because they weren't the British clichés. He was on his best behaviour, like a soldier sending home greetings on a Sunday-morning broadcast. (In fact Mr Holland did end with a message to all at some address or other.) Politicians and editors say one thing without expecting to be taken at their word: Mr Holland was reported in the London evening *Star* as saying: 'Britain will get all the meat we can send, even if we have to give it away, though that of course has never been suggested and is in fact quite out of the question.' He was simply saying the decent thing, only he corrected himself in case he should be taken at his word. So with us all: we profess decent neighbourly democratic ideas, but in practice we undermine them. And we feel no hypocrisy because we know everyone else does the same. It is usually the man who tries to live up to his word who is called hypocrite.

An English schoolmistress left New Zealand in 1948: she told reporters she was disgusted at the lack of morality in New Zealanders. Since we usually see morality as restraint on lust, most of us wondered what she meant. I think it was this: that few of us have the guts, at the challenge, to uphold any moral principle (except in sexual conduct) when it is flouted by a party of a greater number than ourselves. Think how easily the Rugby Union capitulated when the South Africans refused to have Maoris. (Though we pride ourselves that of course we have no colour bar, no one protested at first except some trade unions which were, most people assumed, just being trouble-makers; but when General Kippenberger spoke up, everyone sat up and listened because he was a war hero.) We proclaim the sanctity of property, yet we enjoy small thefts (say raiding a hotel meat-safe outside a country dance-hall): what group of New Zealanders could resist broaching an unguarded keg? We legislate to protect our forests and birds: we raid the bush for ponga fronds and lycopodium to decorate dance-halls, we knock down pigeons with stones and forestall protest with a sneer. We are the most puritan country in the world, yet we love a dirty story.*

If others do it, it is right; yet we spend half our energy disapproving the conduct of others. There is no emotion we feel so at home in as moral indignation. There is nothing unites us so much as having someone else to condemn; in fact we feel we are being sociable, doing our neighbour a good turn when we agree with him in condemning a third party. The talk of the housewife watching and reporting the conduct of her neighbours is an obverse assertion of her own virtue, a projection of the guilt she feels at having in herself motives to the conduct she condemns, a constant vigil over, and scratching of, her own emotions. If it is argued that villagers in every country are gossips I say they are not always malicious. There is not the same readiness to defame or ascribe disreputable motives. I know a Tyneside village where people talk small-talk about other people but their interest is kindly; as a New Zealander I found this unusual. So from fear of disapproval we don't want to do anything we couldn't freely admit to our friends. There is no emotion or sentiment we will allow ourselves unless it has sanction and precedent. When the man-in-the-pub speaks of his feelings he reduces them to a common denominator; he avoids distinction and definition in expression; tragedy is 'tough luck', disappointment 'a bit of a bastard'; another person's anger is usually falsified in some whimsical phrase, perhaps borrowed from another community—'took a dim view', 'did his scone', 'molte dispiace', 'went off the beam', 'off the deep end'. We fear precision and definition in most activities except engineering, sport and military drill. Even educated people fear to speak French with correct attention to nasals and fine vowels: they usually compromise with a 'near-enough-for-me' jargon unintelligible either to Frenchman or New Zealander, a compromise that contains its own apology: the man who does speak it correctly is thought to be 'putting on side'. For the writer who tries to follow faithfully the contours of New Zealand thought this means Mr Sargeson's tortuous account of the feelings of the little man, apologetic that he has feelings at all since they move him and emotion that takes him from identity with the crowd is something he distrusts. The New Zealander is afraid of voicing any confident thought or unsanctioned emotion. It is a common experience among youths presented with an unusual incident, when one, surer than the others, says 'I thought it was like. . . .' and with glad surprise the others declare, 'That's

---

* Mr Sargeson wrote in *Landfall* (March 1951): 'I, who think of myself as so very much a New Zealander, cannot find anything in myself to compare with her poise, her complete lack of pretence, her quick sympathy for all behaviour which proceeds from inner necessity, her superb indifference to personal criticism, her ability to resist every shoddy and commercial influence.' He laid open the fundamental weakness of the New Zealand character the chameleon-like lack of integrity. I don't mean honesty. I mean lack of a whole and unifying principle in one's make-up to which one has to be loyal or lose one's self esteem.

what I thought too!' Each would have kept his thought to himself, distrusting it, but is reassured to find that after all he is more like the others than he thought. The New Zealander suspects anyone who is sure with words, he thinks it is either glibness or showing off. (Could we take kindly to a Christopher Fry?) Once in a hotel lavatory an art student and I were talking of Peter McIntyre's drawings when a little man piped up that he was a returned man from the first war and he knew that we knew what we were talking about but there was no need to let the whole lavatory know it. We explained that the place had been empty when we entered, we hadn't seen him come in, and we left with his blessing. I can't speak for others: I know I hate talking anything but gossip in a bus or train or in the pictures: otherwise you sense the rest of the bus listening united in one unspoken sneer at half-cock. The New Zealander fears ideas that don't result in increased crop-yield or money or home comforts. The wise man never mentions his learning, after the same pattern as the popular ideal of the returned soldier who never mentions his battles.

IV

Now when most men in a community distrust their personal feelings there is a paucity of common experience. This is something the artist feels. There is no richness, no confidence any of us can fertilize our creations with. Beneath the life of the community we sense the sour, dumb struggling drive, we sense (like Colin McCahon) a strength in that drive the stronger for its being so innocently pent. It is doubtful if we can have a sensuous poet who does not develop his lushness by alienating himself from common men who would wound or coarsen it: he would tend to become esoteric and religious, or more intelligible but more austere; but the drive could be harnessed to an austere tragedy of the Greek pattern. Besides the deeper drive for security, for love, for happiness that is in all communities, there is a shallower drive for a common referential experience. To this need one can impute the gossip of the small town, the endless interest in things that bore the intellectual moored there. Whose paddock is this? Whose is that new car? Who lives in this house since Tom Dwyer went away, and how much did he sell it for? Accidents of circumstance in the comings and goings of people, those people themselves, become constants, universals, in a common framework of experience. The man who has left his home town loses contact with this experience: the stay-at-home is at a loss when he meets someone who doesn't know where Tom Dwyer lived. The search for common pegs on which to hang social intercourse takes strange forms among youths. Imported comic recordings become shapers of popular culture, of an influence unknown in the country they come from: think of the phrases and jokes that become social passwords—from Sandy Powell,

George Formby, Harry Tate, Danny Kaye, the peculiar call of *The Woodpecker Song*. Three years ago there were records first played fifteen years before, still played and still demanded: you can mimic the quips in new situations at a gathering of youngsters and the reference will be recognized. Another device among youngsters is the passing craze for foolish colloquy: sixteen years ago one of these went: 'Knock! Knock!' 'Who's there?' 'Tom.' 'Tom who?' 'Tom you were home in bed.' Another was the farewell: 'Abyssinia'—'Abyssinia Samoa'. Others are the reproductions of comic question-and-reply from current films featuring Eddie Cantor, the Marx Brothers, or Abbott and Costello. There was the rash of 'gopher-birds' that erupted all over our railway stations in 1946, the questions of Chad, the trail of Kilroy: all these fictions came from communities of men suddenly thrown together without any special social tradition outside King's Regulations or their American equivalent—Chad from the R.A.F., Kilroy from the U.S. army, the 'gopher-bird' from our army. In 1941 there was something mysteriously comradely among artillerymen at Wingatui in greeting one another *Whacko*! Girls caught on, and the cry became faintly suggestive of sexual expectation. It is a strange country where two girls and two soldiers could introduce themselves by the invocation of a meaningless word, then laugh with flushed embarrassment and end up going to a dance together. Yet all this conversational small-change is seized to fill a need in New Zealand—the need for a common experience to talk from, and the need for conventions to account for and place emotions unrecognized in the threadbare constitution of social behaviour.

So there is an aching need for art in our country. Of course there is creation—in thousands of vegetable gardens and at carpentry benches in back sheds; the creative urge always goes to make something immediately useful or money-saving. But we need an art to expose ourselves to ourselves, explain ourselves to ourselves, see ourselves in a perspective of place and time. But the New Zealander would shy from it because he is afraid to recognize himself. The youngster seizing on current song-hits, comic recordings and films and not-so-comic books—or the youngster of cults that build model aeroplanes, listen to hot jazz, or receive and transmit by short wave—is seizing a readymade and fake social binder out of fear of having to face the creation of one that belongs. A play that presented without sentimentality the patterns of New Zealand life would possibly bore an English audience: a New Zealand small town would 'tsk-tsk' it off the stage. Of course we are a cultural colony of Europe and always will be: the importation of our culture has always meant an accompanying unreality. The expectation of unreality has been confirmed by popular fiction, films and one-act plays. No artist can work without an audience willing to co-operate: if he is to be honest his audience must be honest; they must be prepared to speculate about themselves. This is something New Zealanders will not do.

For besides the unreality foreign and commercial, there has always been a leaning to dishonesty in local art. Take the verse of Hughie Smith, the Bard of Inangahua. He was really a bard, an entertainer in an isolated society in the days before wireless and cinema. He was in demand at smoke-concerts, reunions, hallowe'ens and Masonic meetings where he gave his compositions their first airings. Now most of his verse reads like Burns respectable and in dotage: grannie's hieland hame rosy in an exile's memory, West Coast landscapes self-consciously adopted by a man who had known better. The sentiments of the verse are prudent and public—'14-'18 jingoism, boozy West Coast cameraderie, watery tributes to bonnie lassies; even the lusty heyday of the ragtowns with their brothels and casinos and boatloads of dancing-girls from Sydney is diluted into a nostalgic wink at the waywardness of the boys. A better early Coast poet, Con O'Regan, is just as sentimental in his hankering for the gold-rush days. Perhaps this falsification is the result of the idea that what we say amongst ourselves we mustn't say in front of our daughters. But often Hughie Smith's audience was men only, hard-headed roughs too. Yet they expected the sentimentality: perhaps it was their only safety against feeling cast out from the Ireland or Scotland they could remember only from childhood.* But more likely the reason was that the men were assembled to drink and be happy, and the bard's job was to give them thoughts compatible with beery wellbeing. Unreality is in every local amateur effort at written expression. Think of the 'Over the Teacups' page of the *New Zealand Woman's Weekly,* or the local reporter's write-up, in any paper, of some amusing local incident: the writer tries to be humorous at all costs, but the humour is so tortuous and self-conscious, every slang word is in inverted commas, the point of the story is rubbed in with a bludgeon. In Gilbert Ward's booklets the wisecracking is self-conscious and defensive. Or take Hamilton Grieve's *Something in the Country Air*: you hear the voice of the infant mistress with a tongue that is the terror of children and headmaster and inspectors alike, expanding to tell an arch tale of a country courting, with acid nudges at 'romance' and the younger generation. Odd breaths of the countryside get through, but the characters are obscured by the defences—the pose of knowing all the answers, anticipation of the reader's prejudices, as in the enjoyment of a villainess's disappointment, evasive phrases like 'terra firma'. It all boils down to a paralysing self-consciousness, a fear to appear in public without fulfilling every expectation of the audience, a craving for protective camouflage.

The camouflage in the New Zealand character takes various forms. The rule may be summed up, do in private as you would in public. This is of course a wholesome principle: to deny it is to encourage hypocrisy.

---

* Strangely enough there has been less of this nostalgia about England. Some English customs and dialects are more foreign to us than Irish or Scots. Is it because the English settlers brought their class distinctions and prejudices with them, so didn't knit into a group?

Again I want to make clear that I am not pleading that romantic individualism which is so often the reaction of the sensitive undergraduate. I don't hold with 'self-expression' or 'the claims of the spirit' or other heart-warming slogans of the college lit. club. What I say is that each man has talent he could offer to the community; the vigour, direction and refinement of his emotions could enrich the life he and his neighbours live: there could be greater depth, more joy, heavier sorrow—all contained in, supported by a confident purpose. There is a dimension of experience the New Zealander does not know. Because he is afraid of that accursed self of his that might get off-side of his norm-ridden society. He will not even sing as he feels: he either assumes a mocking rhetorical tone (to let listeners know he does not take his voice seriously) or he consciously imitates the star who popularized the song—Dinah Shore or Tex Morton, down to the last catch in the throat: he is not singing so much as performing a tepid act of devotion to someone else's performance which is public property and must not be violated. Again, there are in the conversation of New Zealanders many stock fake situations which serve to cover real social relations: think of the uncalled-for occasions on which a fictional 'Oxford accent' is introduced to be made fun of, or cowboy-film American, or phoney Lancashire which makes do for the 'pommie accent': each expresses a recurrent sentiment—the 'Oxford accent' a militant sense of colonial inferiority, American the sneer at the skite, Lancashire the justification of colonial independence. These preoccupations obscure real relations with other people: the New Zealander does not see things as they are, he has too many foregone conclusions: so in his actions he defends himself against misinterpretation by certain mechanisms—singing with false gusto, writing in arch journalistic clichés, long discarded—if ever used—in British journalism. (After the stark spurts of news in the paper-rationed London 1½d. dailies, I found the Christchurch *Star-Sun's* accounts of 1950 floods and the Canterbury Centennial procession unreadable: you lost your way in the piled-up syntax—piles of participial phrases and clauses beginning with 'while'. The writer couldn't let the report speak for itself, he wanted to rub it into the reader that these were impressive events needing long words and redounding phrases. It was like reading those school essays we used to write, before Professor Gordon, in which every noun had to have at least one 'expressive' adjective, in which a bush fire was a fierce holocaust raging down stately corridors of ancient rimus.)

V

There are worse mortifications of self, as severe as a Jesuit's, the denial of real sensibilities and emotions for the sake of the almighty norm. An old man working on a gold dredge, who had lived in this part of the

Grey Valley all his life, pointed out to me an unusual colour effect of sun on bush on the hills. The foreman overheard and said to him: 'Garn! What's wrong with you.' Even two people alone have seldom the confidence to admit their relations: two friends parting will affect insensibility to each other's loss: intimacy a New Zealander can hardly bear and often innocently reacts against it, does penance for it, by arraigning his confidant before the public bar: intimacy is disloyalty to the rest of the gang. Even lovers tend to shirk sensitive contact: in the small town when it's known that Tom Peters and Daisy Hill are going together, they have a role to play and they play it in public and concentrate on the practical arrangements for the wedding. In town and country lovers strike poses before each other; they have no precedent for intimate contact apart from deceptive American films and *True Romances*. Their married relations are often clumsy and vegetable: paradoxically their intimacies are often performed in front of friends: when a wife says, before her husband, 'When I was ill he had to do the housework. Course he moaned like anything. But I never take any notice of him,' she is caressing him. Feeling lively they may indulge in half-hearted bedroom pursuit and tackle; enjoying it they will call each other 'mad' and they will not talk of it between themselves. Their private lives and loves develop best in shared suffering—illness, loss of job, eviction, death of a child: so far as they have private joys they live them with a faint sense of guilt, of disloyalty to friends and neighbours. The New Zealander more often grins than smiles.

His most common facial expression is a sneer. He has made the grade by doing violence to himself, by sneering at his impulses and sensibilities, so he can't help keeping that sneer always at hand ready for emergency. From his experience he senses all the pitfalls that threaten the youngster patterning himself after the almighty norm, so he is ready to warn other comers. 'Don't go that way, mate.' What is *that way*? Perhaps he said something about a sunset or the Alps—that way is effeminacy: perhaps he said something about peace—that way is 'being Bolshy': perhaps he took offence too readily at an imagined slight—that way is being 'anti-social'. The sneer is the protection of the ideal, the superego—or should one say, the infra-ego?—of the average chap. Let me describe him. He is manly—that is he is tough and not too talkative. He seldom shows emotion except anger and resentment: he drinks his beer fast but prides himself that, even full of beer, his reserve won't change. He can spend a rewarding evening drinking after hours, talking football and racehorses: he can't tell you why he drinks—for the company, he'll say; but why does he drink so fast? For fear of being thought slow to pay his round. Why then does he show no pleasure in drinking? Because his principle is moderation, not in the amount he drinks, but in his reaction to it. Before the 1948 referendum on drinking hours, a Dominion Breweries advertisement neatly expressed it: 'A good citizen is moderate in his thinking and in his actions. ... Be moderate.' Why have I settled on his drinking habits and stuck there? Because it is in the pub—and in his football club and on the racecourse—that an important part of his life is lived. His private life, at home, is in the vegetable garden and the workshop. For the rest, his home life is a perpetual requisition of jobs to be done, of watching what he says in front of the children: he has to go to the public house to have privacy. It is one place where his doings don't become the property of his wife's woman friends. It isn't only wowserism that keeps women out of the bars: when a woman enters a bar (except on the West Coast at Christmas) the men stop in their talk like surprised culprits. The bar is their stronghold and they want a place where they can swear loudly and boast without being held to their word.

Think of the unreality of our conduct before women and children. It is improper to use certain words in front of women: among youths if you don't use those words you are 'a bit wet', but if a woman comes near, unknown to you, and you still use any of them, the youths snigger, the men get prim and you blush and the woman—well, they say if she's a lady, she'll pretend not to hear, but she won't forget and she'll think the less of you for it. It is a funny country where the propriety of occasion for uttering a few sounds which have commonly lost all meaning can cause so much casuistry, guilt and apology.* In front of children we may not even mention beer: we morass ourselves in all sorts of subterfuges to pass the thought over the kids' heads. In the country, people in public positions, like parsons, teachers and senior civil servants have to sneak away to drink, to the scandal of the womenfolk, and the welcome of the men in the bar who are reassured by this deference of respectability to the pricks of the palate. The youth leering off to his first booze-up drinks as if he has been initiated into the mysteries of manhood. But some fathers can't be bothered with this hypocrisy: they swear and drink at home and their children grow up knowing the hypocrisy of others who are models before their children and only relax in the bar. These children come to see everything that comes from a parson or teacher, from a public platform or editorial column as hypocrisy: anything 'educational' is a hypocrisy pardonable as a means to social or economic climbing: religion they see as an organized racket. So they close their minds to all ideas of tolerance, justice, charity, consideration for others. They may in practice live according to these ideas, so far as social behaviour already observes them; but, except from the immunizing distance of a pulpit or platform, the articulation of these ideas irritates them. Anything that threatens instruction or 'improvement', selfconsciousness, imaginative effort, resolution or self-control—it may be the New Testament or Marx, Shakespeare or John Gilpin, symphonic music, a foreign film, an Anzac

---

* That the sounds have lost meaning is evident in a passage of Guthrie Wilson's *Brave Company* where in a soldier's thoughts, the word 'Christ' is interchangeable with one of the Anglo-Saxon unprintables, and the invocation is more protest than prayer.

Day speech or a verse in an autograph-book—they know it's 'all bull-shit'. Both to these children brought up swearing and seeing the old man drink and to those who know he does on the sly, reality boils down to a narrow materialism. There is one security in life—money, and the man who denies that he will not at least consider using any means to successfully chasing it is a hypocrite. For the young the purpose of money is to minister to physical sensations like the exultation of a fight, the sex act, or the passage of Monteith's down the uvula. Experience not a means to these ends is a waste of time. Of course young men grow out of these desires, but when they have so narrowed their ideas of valid conduct, what lies ahead but the New Zealand way of life, dumb and numb, null and dull, labouring out their days with irritating responsibilities to the newer and ultimate realities —wife and family and house and back garden, and the nagging unrecognized dissatisfactions that a Saturday afternoon in the pub after the football might yet appease? We retire early in New Zealand, settle down before we are thirty to a long quiet family life as uneventful as we can make it. We have our brief flutter among the bottles and in the dance-halls in our late teens and early twenties, and though the old women click their tongues, we know it is our right. A mother seldom lets her daughter marry her first boy friend, no matter how deeply they love, because 'she's only young once and she ought to have her fling. Time enough later to think of settling down.' Because once she settles down she isn't supposed to enjoy herself any more.

In the New Zealand metaphysic reality is something unpleasant and ugly and though we protect our women and children from it, we know in the long run it is unavoidable. We talk with prim shame of 'the facts of life': the Creator has been indecent. We disapprove of the profit motive since it takes men from identity with the crowd, but we think it can't be avoided. Young men have envied returned soldiers because they 'saw life in the raw'. It is significant that the weekly that features the uglier side of the news, calls itself *Truth*. (I know the name came from John Norton's Sydney *Truth* and that there are papers of the same name all over the world, but most of them are out to preach the 'truth' of a political sect.) People condemned the novels of John A. Lee out of puritanism but they did not doubt that he was lifting the screen from the indecent truth. The New Zealander suspects the idealist because he is giving a hopeful glamour to 'reality'. The only philosophy one could logically base on the New Zealand premiss is a tempered cynicism, often called 'realism'.

The New Zealander's fear of experience not immediate and not contributing to the accumulation of money or the satisfaction of blunted appetites, occurs daily when he reads the newspaper: he glances across the headlines of foreign news and it would have to be a declaration of war before he would pause. 'As usual, nothing in it,' he says and reads the Local and General and the sports page. In a small town his wife will go through the classified ads. to detect, from the phone number, who it is that's wanting to sell that sewing-machine or take a boarder. Yet we all read the paper, in order to be in touch with what everyone else reads. If a New Zealander goes to an exhibition or a museum he withholds his interest, grudgingly stumps around every stand for fear of missing something, but comes away saying with relief, 'There's fuck-all to see.' It was with a great sense of concession to duty that many soldiers went once to the pyramids or gaped around the Vatican Museum, hardly pausing, and went away, a duty done: 'Well now I can say I've seen it' and repaired to their beer.

(For writers an interesting corollary to a New Zealander's 'realism' is his response to the forceful use of words. I said he suspected clever, confident or intellectual use of words; but he admires a vigorous phraseology that caresses the rawness of 'reality' and its underlying oddity or sneer. A mechanic talking of a man baching while his wife was away, said: 'Oh, that's the cunt we found wrastlin his way out o' the jam tins.' Another, caught by a knock on his door while he was changing, his trousers round his ankles, his shirt over his head, said: 'You had me hobbled and blindfolded at the same time.' Osman Middleton knows how to exploit this vigour of language, even if he does give it an American twist.)

Now the reason for the New Zealander's fear of hypocrisy and his tempered cynicism is that he fears that if he professes to be, know, feel, or understand more than his neighbour, he is guilty of pretensions to social climbing. He is out to be no better than the next man. Thus a Catholic in New Zealand will resent even the most deferential discussion, in a public place, of his faith. He is trained to a loyalty higher than the almighty norm, yet he is loyal out of a stubbornness in the face of his own guilt at belonging to what he feels is in some ways an underground movement. Calling for his beer after Sunday mass he will not say where he has been and it is bad taste if you mention it. On the other hand the perpetual undercurrent, among Protestants and other unbelievers, of slanders and rumour of a Catholic conspiracy to catch all Protestant young men by marriage, comes from a fear of an institution whose doctrines are not readily inspectable and impeachable, in terms of 'reality', at the bar. The preoccupation with social climbing betrays a personal insecurity. How much of the gossip of New Zealanders is concerned solely with real or imagined slights given by their neighbours: 'sensitive' in New Zealand means susceptible to personal offence.

VI

Somewhere at the back of the outlook of the New Zealander is a dream, a dream of security in equality. Everybody acts the same, receives the same amount of the world's goods, everyone moves in the same direction.

Everyone has simple tastes, explainable desires which can be satisfied with proportionately simple effort. No one has any grievance and accidents don't happen. It is a version of a human dream, which I believe one half of the world is on the right road to bringing off as nearly as can be under the conditions of existence. The special quality of the New Zealander's version is that the evil is to disagree or be different. The chaos of existence is to be legislated into shape; the varieties of human quality and personality are to be levelled into conformity with the legislation. It is the development of individual talent that destroys the conformity: some men are left resenting their lack of another man's talent, so he must not use it, it is an unfair advantage. If life is (as the New Zealander assumes) a race, it is to be run by handicap. If nature can't be controlled then man must be: social boycott must keep the talented man in his place. Now I am bound to be told that this is part of the socialist dream, but I don't see it. It is as different from socialist equality as fascism is from communism. I see it as the human dream of security perverted by the fears of the middle class hiving off from the threats of communism, the coloured races and the bland terror of infinite space; trying to give their customs a universal validity flouted by life, time and the multiplicity of planets. They huddle to reassure themselves that their habits are beyond question, and difference and unconformity question them. It is a dream, too, of the middle class wanting to compensate for the daily routine of competition: life is cruel, business forces you to shoddy tricks, but in our dream let us relax and be jolly good fellows. The New Zealander enacts his dream in certain social functions—the few drinks with the boys, the Masonic meeting, the smoke concert, the stag party. The fake solidarity and bonhomie, the boozy brotherliness and slobbery back-slapping are part of the dream: each man knows he has in some way sinned against society: this is his devotion, he is proving that at heart he's a decent chap. The more money he has the more likely he is to be vulgar, just to show that he really is no better than anyone else. In the army some officers used to pride themselves on taking off their pips and drinking with the other ranks. Christmas Eve is the occasion of a ritual. Everyone is out to show how nice he can be when he is drunk: don't they say a chap's real nature comes out when he's drunk? It is a festival of holy conformity, of sameness and glozing over differences. Thus in certain men's clubs, the Orphans' and Savage Clubs and Buffalo Lodges, religion and politics are taboo: they are unfortunate things that cause differences. You find people in New Zealand who make it a principle never to discuss them, and few can without embarrassment when there is likelihood of difference. When I was at Dunedin Training College the principal temporarily banned debates on sex, religion and politics: he said he had a duty to the students' parents to see that they left the college without any disturbance to the beliefs they entered with.

The goal of the dream seems to be, like a Dickens happy ending, a kind of inertia. Think of the week-end torpor of the suburbs. Where is everyone? Well, we know they are at football, at the races, on the beaches, or in back gardens. Yet these activities are half-hearted. The farmer brooding against a gate, having his Sunday afternoon snooze on the front verandah, the soldier or airman on fatigues downing tools as soon as the corporal has gone, the mechanic having a smoke while the foreman is away, are expressing a common reluctance to spend labour to a purpose not evident. Paradoxically the farmer's wife with her continuous day of hard work can't enjoy a sit-down when she gets one; she has to pick up some knitting or darning: work has become a drug to her as lassitude is a drug for most New Zealanders. Why? Why this desire to 'pass time'? Time passes you. If you want to fill in time you must be waiting for something and sometimes I wonder if it isn't death the New Zealander waits for. But being human we are afraid of death. At least it shows a craving for narcosis, a dissatisfaction with life, with one's own resources, to want to pass time as if it was a football, or the buck that gets passed in government offices. If death is too decisive there's sleep: how many servicemen off duty put in hours on their bunks? Somebody may again impute this laziness to socialist pampering: 'Now when I was a lad. ... ' I can hear the platitudes Professor Algie thinks up from the comfort of his seat on the night express. But the local inertia is not a fear of work, it is an idea that each of us should do no more work than the next man, and in doubt it's better to do a little less than a little more. This idea is capitalist. Dr Lauwerys of Unesco in 1946 warned us we'd never get success from socialist legislation so long as every man's private ambition was to be a little rentier—to make enough money to employ somone else to do his share in work that would profit him. The ambition is a coveting of other men's riches without the will to work for them, a willingness to get the same by a short cut like the black market or an art union: the mentality of the running-board of the middle class; and there is no bigger Tory than a spiv. But even the New Zealander who is turning over money fast is only passing time. The New Zealander's ideal state is half-consciousness; his ideal activity is reunion, physically expressed in the old boys' reunion or the football dinner, spiritually it is immersion in an inert blubbery Oversoul like Mr Holcroft's collective mind.

VII

But that is the dream, and the dream never comes off. The New Zealander does not always blame God or nature or human nature: he generally imputes the evil to '*some* chaps'. Men are in two classes, the 'white jokers' and the 'bastards'. When it's all boiled down there aren't many in the world you can trust. The untrustworthy are the people one doesn't have direct contact with—the watersiders, for example, seen through the polemic of Mr Holland's radio turns and the daily press—or foreigners: a foreign tongue sets a New Zealander's nerves on edge, he feels the speaker is deliberately taunting his incomprehension. Even people who speak English with an accent are watched, like yanks and 'pongos'. The New Zealander lost among strangers is as trusting as a provincial asking his way in a big city, yet of people he doesn't see or speak to, or of minorities, he is as suspicious as anyone in the world. Wilfrid Meynell mentions a New Zealand major of World War I who told him that British statesmen of the nineteenth century were far too trusting when it came to dealing with foreigners. (Wilfrid Meynell, *Who Goes There*, London, 1916). At the fall of France an aunt of mine said, 'It only goes to show you can't trust foreigners.' So there's no one satisfies a New Zealander but a New Zealander. The New Zealand way of life is unquestionable and what is not like it is 'mad'. Europe is backward and uncivilized in his eyes, they haven't the same comforts and their art and architecture is of course 'antique' and 'educational' but it's out-of-date. On a 3ZB radio quiz one man, asked his opinion on the Greek treatment of women, said, 'Well, that was in the olden days. The Greeks weren't civilized.' Asia is worse than Europe. There are only two countries in the world we may emulate—the U.S. and Britain, and perhaps the 'white' Dominions. The attitude is not only provincial, it is bourgeois. It is the arrogance of the American labelling other peoples 'gooks' and 'wops': the New Zealand soldier had his 'Wogs' and 'Ites' and 'Teds', at home there are the 'Chinks' and 'Ikes' and 'Dallies' and even the 'Horis'. It is the smallness of mind of the man brought up to believe his own customs infallible and people who don't observe them worthless.

But middle class attitudes don't play so hard on the worker as they do on farmers and small tradesmen and clerks and civil servants. The worker has questioned the assumption that each man is his own economic responsibility, though he will hold no brief for the 'cadger'; but he has no other measurement of success than material comfort. Now I'm not pleading 'spiritual needs': I accept the right of men to material goods. What is wrong is the closing of mind to everything not tangible or immediate. The worker's object for his son is to see he gets a good job: what doesn't lead to it is a waste of effort. (So he often doesn't approve of higher education for his daughters.) To have a trade or a training for a profession is the aim of 'schooling': a humanist concept of the bringing out of innate abilities is beyond him, so is a socialist concept of developing one's capacities with the aim of serving society or any concept of converting matter and energy for the benefit of his grandchildren. The world is the world: his world is Ashburton or Waimihia, he wants to set his boy right in the system he knows: he has no wish either to change the system or to make his boy bigger than the place Waimihia will allow him. Life is a race: education (as the editor of this journal said) is an obstacle race; the modest aim is to be in the running, and the decent thing is to slow down the pace.

The competition is not so fierce that all energy should minister to it: if you're in the running you're in the good company of the majority, the thing is not to be left behind. The worker does not resent the businessman's devotion to his bank-balance, only that he should perform it without decent moderation.

So the New Zealander's idea of social reality is the way things are. 'Times' change, but that is a matter of fashions of clothing, architecture and popular music. Any talk of changing the status quo meets with resistance. The government can do it by quiet legislation without anyone noticing the implications of a new law, because the government is part of the status quo and bigger than anyone who may object. It is when an individual talks of change the New Zealander resents and resists the discomfort of being forced to think up reasons for defending the existing order. Any man who thinks or reads beyond the immediate requirements of getting a good job is a fool—'wet', 'gormless', 'dilberry', etc. Baiting him is the good sport of the enterprising wag: in New Zealand (but not so much overseas) little minds in the army used to whet themselves on men who read books with big words, to the entertainment of the hut. A method (used even among training college students) is to pick up another man's book, to read aloud a sentence without attempt at comprehension as if to demonstrate that the words meant nothing but were the mutually flattering cult-lingo of a class of intellectuals pretending to be better than the ordinary chap. It is common for some people to accuse people who go to symphonic concerts of not understanding the music and going out of snobbery. They have some ground for their idea because the idea has produced the habit: an aunt of mine went to the Old Vic plays in 1948, to see the film stars, but confessed the plays were 'awfully dry'—she didn't know what they were about, but that was only to be expected because they were 'educational'. For good-humoured baiting recall the attacks on anti-conscription speakers in Nelson in 1949: most spectators would describe this as a 'bit of fun'.

VIII

Now the New Zealand child is not noticeably different from children of other countries—he tends to be impulsive, rough, afraid to be seen crying or in need of affection, and among his mates he prides himself on defying authority. Yet if we honestly compare our childhood and maturity we know we have lost something—life was full and rich, we never asked if it had a purpose, that was self-evident, we were confident and happy and there was always something to look forward to, and our homes were the centres of our world; in maturity we are bored, doubtful, dissatisfied and afraid. For between his boyhood and maturity the New Zealander asserts his manhood by losing it. He becomes a coward with a ready sneer, an ugly little man with a routine bar-side guffaw. The change occurs in adolescence. The road forks here, so that the ordinary chap goes one way, the future intellectual another. Adolescence involves a widening of prospect of future experience. For the New Zealand adolescent the emphasis is on the possibilities of forbidden sensual enjoyment. He begins to hang about street corners in small gangs, watching the world. They do little these gangs, except drink milk shakes, swear profusely, whistle at girls, chaff one another and engage in the unnatural fiction that every man's target, secret or acknowledged, is the vulva. It causes a strained and furtive attitude of mind; out of fear of being thought 'soft' or 'wet' the youth reads double meanings into the most harmless of quips on radio and film, keeps a store of dirty yarns, most of them without wit or fun. He is impatient to be a man, to be manly, he lives in fear of being called a 'drip': he affects to be callous and blasé when at heart he is afraid and innocent, and alone with a girl may be clumsily tender. But he will jump to scorn any attitude that is not callous.

The sensitive and intelligent youth takes another way. Adolescence presents him with more distant possibilities. He becomes 'dreamy' and idealistic. If he goes to university his philosophy is widened. For a while at least he proceeds by widening his knowledge and developing himself in ways denied in his home town (in drama, debate and talk), where his former classmate proceeds by narrowing his aims and denying the many inchoate sensibilities and doubts and enthusiasms of adolescence. This lad prides himself on being 'hard as nails'. He takes to smoking and enjoys a surreptitious drink. His first 'piss-up' is a landmark in his life: he relishes the sensation of following an impulse without check, the sense of expansion and dissolution, his next-morning wonder at the foolish things he did, his eager response to the attention he has drawn to himself in the chaff of his mates: he has begun to discover himself. But the student discovers himself by alienating himself. He is unlikely to go back to his former classmates who are mechanics, apprentices, clerks and counter-jumpers in his home town. He will probably pass his exams, marry and settle in a comfortable suburb, forget his student pranks and vegetate as a political conservative whose counter to every argument is, 'That's all very well, but. . . . ' He will have retired, for life, from thinking. But a few students don't retire, they keep their romantic dreams of self-fulfilment, their hopes of creative writing, their interest in ideas. They are destined to grow into an artificial and alienated class living a threadbare life not so different from that of the English colony in an outpost of empire. They have grown to fear the philistinism of businessmen and clerks and 'retired' professional men, the narrow range of interests of the worker, and the vigour with which they all will sneer at what interests intellectuals. Because they are few they become a kind of cult with no devotion but to a sense of their emancipation. What they do not realize is the number of attitudes they have carried over from the community they feel emancipated from.

1. There is their interest in the people they know rather than ideas. They tend to gossip about one another, each to assert himself by criticizing an absent member in front of others.

2. The desire to have all the answers. If he can disparage another man's ideas, the intellectual can think his philosophy is superior—but he seldom has any. He cultivates a scepticism inconsistent and eclectic—criticizing different systems from inconsistent angles. In this he is just as determined as the man in the bar to sneer off uncomfortable or challenging ideas. He loves to discover a disreputable motive that will explain and explain away another man's ideas: if he can say, 'Of course Thackeray never cut his mother's apron-strings', he implies that Thackeray's novels aren't worth reading. He is always looking for an excuse not to read what he feels he should have if he is to be any authority. His intellectual coterie is a closed shop and he resents intruders: he is grateful that the gate-crashers from the college lit. clubs fawn on him, but he never acknowledges them. Anna Kavan noticed the exclusiveness: 'What happens when a stranger enters what's called intellectual circles? Do the sturdy Colonial intellectuals care if Einstein or the Cham of Tartary is in their midst? Brother, they do not care, they do not wish to hear from you, and unless you can speak louder than they can you're as good as dumb. . . . ' Every reader will smile and say, 'Evidently she was annoyed that no one would listen to her.' But that proves my point: we love to look for a hidden motive that will dismiss challenge. Or someone will say he knew Anna Kavan and she was an unusual woman. But that is like the argument of the man who tells you, when you are discussing the Labour Party, that he lives next door to Walter Nash and sometimes he doesn't even come home for his dinner and you can't tell him anything about Labour.

3. The idea of education as obstacle race occurs in the idea that wisdom can be attained by a reading-list. Too often the intellectual says, 'Oh, but have you read Lenau?'—or Camus, or Jean Genet. Too often an intellectual discussion becomes a sparring-match fought with book-titles. The intellectual is as snobbish in his attitude to books and writers as other New Zealanders are to many things, notably to returned soldiers—whether they had been 'coconut bombers' in the Pacific or had been 'really overseas' to Africa, whether a man was Second Echelon or Thirteenth Reinforcement, etc.

4. The desire to be an authority in all fields. The intellectual wants talking knowledge of art, architecture, education, politics, religion, literature, psychology, sociology, anthropology and philosophy. His philosophy is an old rag-bag of tags from Marx, Jung, Freud, Frazer, Toynbee, Frank Lloyd Wright and possibly Mr Holcroft. It is of course impossible to be

an expert in all these subjects: one might hold some fundamental principles which could be applied to them. The New Zealand intellectual seldom has these, yet he likes to have the last word. His judgments are often shallow, ill-informed and traceable to the text of a hastily-read Penguin. Is the popularity among New Zealand intellectuals of *Time* and *The New Yorker* a result of their shallow clever pontifical attitude which flatters the vanity of their readers? The most objectionable part of the intellectual's attitude is the readiness to cheat, take short cuts to knowledge (in the same way as the frustrated money-hunter takes to the black market), the interest in knowledge not for its discipline or its application, but as a weapon to impress other intellectuals or a means to the private satisfaction of knowing better.

5. The enjoyment of being different. Since the community holds that being different is snobbery, being different becomes snobbery. The intellectual feels socially superior just because he discriminates and disagrees. His cultivated sighs and languishments at vulgarity and commerce are the luxury of one who is grateful that they exist because they are the condition of his superiority. He may pretend to be an exile in a hostile country: he knows it is better to stay home as a big frog in a little pool than go abroad and be humble.

6. Often his clique meets at a beer party. Book-titles apart, his party is not so different from the Saturday night boozeroo in the Sydenham side-street with the keg in the kitchen-sink. Harry the poet is just as liable to swing on the lampshade, irrigate the piano or urinate in the hydrangeas as Tom the welder.

7. The only habit the intellectual has which the common man has not is scepticism, but scepticism is a dangerous and destructive habit of thought and it leads, for example, to the contemporary impotence of American intellectuals. A generation of sceptic intellectuals opens the way for the burning of the books. *La trahison des clercs* is suicide.

There is nothing new in this. I have said nothing that any intellectual I have mentioned these complaints to in private has not agreed with. It is time they were brought into the open. Again, I want to make clear that I am not siding with the philistines of city newspapers, stock and station agencies, and Parliament House. An English friend tells me that all these things are true of London literary cliques. This weakens my claim that the attitudes are home-grown, which is, I admit, a tenuous claim. There is this difference, however, that in London honest men can, and usually do, avoid or escape from the society of the impostors. In New Zealand many an honest man has been soured, emasculated or turned showman because he cannot get away from the poky little minds that milch and destroy him. And the New Zealand hypocrisies are cruder and more patent.

IX

Of course this is to concentrate on the worst and forget the virtues. These intellectuals and writers have in the last twenty-five years created something that wasn't there before, the beginnings of an articulate national culture. I am not blind to the achievement. What I want to say is that if we continue to alienate ourselves from the people we live amongst we will etiolate our art. It is a matter of balance, and no one can lay down a programme. If we capitulate too easily to the narrowness and the puritanism we can't write honestly. If we flatter ourselves we are above it, we may be just as dishonest. If we do nothing but fight it, we put ourselves in a position just as narrow as that of our opponents.

The intellectual usually assumes that the worst enemy is puritanism: disinfect the snuffy tin-roof-chapel conscience, he says, and our way of life will flower. But this is questionable. The puritanism of Littledene is not all debit. With the concern for our neighbours' morals goes a concern for their welfare. The gossips are at least interested in other people, they help them in sickness, help with one another's ploughing and shearing and harvesting. But when the puritan shell is cast there is nothing to replace it except perhaps a dimly expectant hedonism inspired by radio-serials and films. And the intellectual has nothing to offer either except a tepid and equally prim hedonism which he calls 'the good life'— conscientious and enlightened self-indulgence. When puritanism goes the New Zealander is left with that ugly 'reality': he begins to look after number one and connives at his neighbour's devotion each to his own pleasure and security. Already in the North Island there are attitudes emerging which haven't yet shown in Littledene—shallow and sneering hedonism, the disavowal of responsibility to and for one's neighbour, less restraint in antipathies to minorities like Maoris, Catholics and especially Jews, priority given to the pursuit of money and pleasure— generally a slicker and more hard-boiled attitude. It is possible for a South Islander in Auckland to feel uprooted in the indifference and hostility of the people.

Puritanism runs in a spiral: first its religious context is lost and with it the justification of the restrictions on enjoyment of the senses, it hardens into habit: second, a younger generation rebels and seeks what was forbidden, the thrill of the chase is spiked with a sense of guilt. What they hunt is symbolized in the sex act: but since the pleasure, if isolated, is momentary and the more it's sought the less it can be found, they are tracking down a mirage, and they end in and out of the lupins with this girl and the next one, and have to remind themselves that they did get what they were looking for. When they marry, the men and women of this generation transmit their dissatisfaction to their children, or the children sense it and grow up with a cynical, street-corner dog-like attitude to sex: everyone is after it but there's nothing in it. A new austere puritanism grows which is a contempt for love, a sour spit, a denial of life itself: the puritanism of Graham Greene and George Orwell (e.g. Pinkie in *Brighton Rock*, Scobie in *The Heart of the Matter*, and the official attitude to love in *1984*). We in New Zealand are somewhere early in the second stage. Intellectuals who talk of getting rid of the nonconformist conscience should take care that they are not allying themselves with Hollywood, the ZB stations, the gutter press and the American-style comics that our children and jockeys read, in ushering in a period of decadence. The breakdown of puritanism is the dissolution of one of the cementing elements of our society: when every man co-operates only so far as he has to earn money and in his leisure pursues his sensual pleasure, society is due to break down. Because we are then, in working hours, a community of convenience; in leisure we are, in Coventry Patmore's image, like the sheep's carcass that looked alive from a distance but only because it was a mass of maggots busy battening on the corpse. The process would probably have to take its course if it were to be left to itself. But it is likely to be interrupted by the political upheavals occurring all over the world. If, for example, the American generals and financiers succeed in their plans for a third war New Zealand is due to suffer as it has never before suffered, and out of that bitter experience will come the themes of later poets. By then, puritanism as we know it will be a thing of history and all I have said about the New Zealand character will no longer be true.

X

Anna Kavan explained our ways as due to dependence: we hadn't, she said, cut the umbilical cord, we were still obsessed with the mother country. But, tropes apart, do any of us think of England as a mother? It is true that we are culturally and economically dependent. But that very dependence has given us until recently a disproportionate independence, the independence we used to pride ourselves on as a national characteristic, and especially in international conduct. We have always said 'we' in a war as if we were a strong nation: we have always shouted loud from behind someone else's coat-tails, as when Mr Doidge branded China aggressor. And now that Britain is weak Mr Holland has, by his speech of January 23, 1951, chosen the United States as our protector. If we were independent we would be far more humble in international affairs. But dependence is not at the root of our behaviour. The reason for our odd ways is something deeper, something creeping up on the whole western world. We haven't any sense of purpose. We don't know what it's all about, and we are frightened to find out. Other nations have lost their sense of purpose; we, a colony, never found one—we had been living on their capital. And caught between the mountains and the sea, never far from the silence of the bush and the stars, we are in the bland frightening witness of the infinite, and we haven't created a social convention strong enough to reassure us. We live, as Anna Kavan said, 'like reluctant campers, too far from home'. And, as Mr Fairburn said, we treat our land like campers: cheer up, mate, we're not here for long, make the most of it while you can, it'll all be the same in a hundred years; the land is not for farming but mining and if in the end we ruin it, well, we'll be under the sod before that happens. So we sneer at our own countryside: we think it effeminate to admire it, we pride ourselves often on not knowing the names of hills and rivers. We only venture into the wilds when we have a utilitarian purpose—pigshooting, deer-stalking, or tramping and even then we aim to cover a certain mileage in a certain time, and seldom pause to look. A bus-load left Greymouth one Sunday to go to Lake Brunner. At Mitchells everyone got out. On one hand there was the lake—true, its shores were flax-swamp, but no one looked at it. A few climbed with that sense of concession to duty, to look at some falls. But most went into the bar where someone turned on 3ZR's request programme, the chaps drank and nurses danced in pairs on the polished floor. But the hostility is not in the landscape: our countryside is as admirable and lovable as any in the world. It is we who are hostile, because we haven't made up our minds whether we have accepted it, whether we mean to stay, why we are here anyway, or what life is all about. Though, this is not quite true: rather, we know we are staying, we can't get away and would be afraid to now if we had the chance, but we still haven't faced the question of whether we accept it or not. We haven't made friends with the land. We use it as a convenience, an expedient: no farmer that I know draws breath with a change of light on the foothills, sieves the earth through friendly fingers. If he did he wouldn't let it run wild with gorse and blackberries, then cruelly put a match to them regardless of soil erosion. His ambition is to retire to a seaside or suburban house like anyone else's where his wife can buy cakes instead of baking them, and he can grow a patch of beans instead of a paddock of wheat. His attitude is not so different from that of the publican who takes a country pub with the hope of making big money in three years, then retiring and buying a racehorse. We are afraid to relax and settle, and we are afraid to look into the future: do we plan to get the most out of the land for ourselves, or to develop it for our grandchildren? We won't face immediate questions let alone ultimate.

So we huddle together under our threadbare conventions but the cold blows through. We try to iron out our inarticulate doubts in a self-evident self-propelling system of habits. Variety and innovation, except where they feed an illusion of progress which is a substitute for purpose, frighten us because they raise the ultimate questions. When we lose faith in the conventions we behave by, we grope and despair: our writers become obsessed with exposing the rot and the hollow. They concentrate, we concentrate, as Mr Woods said in *Landfall* (March 1949), on the seamy side; we are haunted by the bitterness of disillusion: life is a hoax, a dirty trick played by an unknown power. But our disillusion is phoney and shallow: how can we lose faith in life when we haven't let ourselves live? Such a writer aims at exposure, muck-raking: but the muck is only muck to little puritan minds—away from Littledene it is a handful of dust. And anyway New Zealanders will not listen because they want to cover up: it's cold outside. In our talk and our habits we put off the ultimate questions. Walk into a Saturday-afternoon bar and hear the noise: do you get the impression of *stalling*? The tobacco-smoke is dense with small-talk: a huddle of urgent men proofing the void with the saga of Highland Prince, greasing the unknown with a bookie's pencil. We were faced with the brave challenge of ordering our society to the end of security and happiness and justice: we hoped Labour socialism would do it, but we stopped half-way with second thoughts because there were too many questions implicit: perhaps the old coat would make do. We funked, and we are still funking in the light of history and in the light of eternity; here we are, in mid-ocean, adrift and alone, confused and talking loud, wondering where to go next. In the meantime perhaps, we hope to sleep it off. But our next cue comes from a people we have to learn not to despise. The people of Asia, especially China, will decide the destinies of our grandsons and after them the Africans. They have the vigour, where is ours? It is a coloured man's world we are moving into and a communist one, and if we are to have any estimable place in it, we will have, in our own phrase, to jack up our ideas. And that means waking up, accepting our responsibilities and using the initiative and confidence that lies buried within us, and learning to live with a purpose. If I have said little about the virtues and strengths of New Zealanders, their loyalty, their strength, their unwillingness to promise more than they know they can do, their belief in action in the face of challenge (once they recognize the challenge), their humility before material things and physical laws, their practicality, their modesty, their kindness to neighbours, the thousands of lettuces that cross back fences daily in the summer, their alertness and freshness which show up best overseas— most of these virtues, in fact, show up when they are in minorities abroad, so that as that woman said, everyone likes them—it is not because those qualities aren't there. It is because as a New Zealander I find it difficult to praise anyone to his face without embarrassment, and because it is bad for New Zealanders to read praise: it lulls us when we need to be made alert. New Zealanders have far more virtues than intellectuals give them credit for and if artists can tap those virtues their work will take strength and, if they have as well the confidence of their intuitions, fertility.

XI

As I see it that is the only solution to the so-often-talked-about plight of the New Zealand artist. There are two facts we can't escape: first, that we are a cultural colony of Europe, and second, that the culture of the west is dying. A paragraph Alice Meynell wrote in 1891 is so apt that I need not apologize for the length of the quotation:

The difficulty of dealing—in the course of any critical duty—with decivilized man lies in this: when you accuse him of vulgarity ... he defends himself against the charge of barbarism. Especially from new soil—transatlantic, colonial—he faces you, bronzed, with a half-conviction of savagery, partly persuaded of his own youthfulness of race. He writes, and recites, poems about ranches and canyons; they are designed to betray the recklessness of his nature and to reveal the good that lurks in the lawless ways of a young society. He is there to explain himself, voluble, with a glossary for his own artless slang. But his colonialism is only provincialism very articulate. The new air does but make old decadences seem more stale; the young soil does but set into fresh conditions the ready-made, the uncostly, the refuse feeling of a race decivilizing. American fancy played long this pattering part of youth. The New Englander hastened to assure you with so self-denying a face he did not wear war-paint and feathers, that it became doubly difficult to communicate to him that you had suspected him of nothing wilder than a second-hand dress coat. . . . Even now English voices, with violent commonplace, are constantly calling upon America to begin—to begin, for the world is expectant. Whereas there is no beginning for her, but instead a continuity which only a constant care can guide into sustained refinement and can save from decivilization. ('Decivilized', *Merry England*, October 1891. Reprinted in *Essays* (1914).)

But refinement and armchair cultivation won't help us, and Mrs Meynell doesn't mention what happens when the parent culture becomes decadent or vulgar. For a truer historical precedent is not the New England school or the American regional novelists of the nineteenth century, but Latin writers in Carthage and Gaul and Spain in the latter days of the Roman Empire. It would be inevitable that such writers would look to the classics for their models, that they would be alienated from their neighbours and exiled from their cultural centre, and that their work would yet have a colonial ring. I cannot pursue this analogy since I have little knowledge of these writers, but I believe the increasing social dissolution made them look backwards and away, and that is why they are forgotten today.

The solution for us is to look to the here and now, and, in spite of Mrs Meynell, to concentrate on the very things she might have called provincial and vulgar, and develop them to the point where they mean something to people outside New Zealand, to make a meaning out of the drives and behaviour of common people. 'A writer must want to think—think through and with his people. If *they* will not think, how can he use them?' Sean O'Faolain said of the Irish (*The Month*, December 1949). But our people have tongues, glands, nerves and minds and souls: they cannot help thinking and feeling, however torpidly. Our job is to penetrate the torpor and out of meaninglessness make a pattern that means something. I hope no one thinks I suggest a rush to the proletariat— the self-conscious patronizing discovery of the worker of some documentary writers of the thirties, talking down to him and writing him up, slumming on the wharves and in factories and shearing-sheds. *Rapportage* in New Zealand is dull twice over because the New Zealander keeps his motives out of his talk. I mean living not only among but as one of the people and feeling your way into their problems, their hopes, their gripes and their gropings, without like them trying to sleep them off. For us who are trained in a sophisticated self-conscious tradition of art it is very difficult because the audience we would like to reach will never read us even if we were to start back with folk-tales, and because the problems that obsess us are problems Littledene has hardly heard of. But there is no other way if we hope to create anything that is not like so much else in New Zealand a makeshift but something our grandsons will thank us for. Some sense of isolation is inevitable, some detachment and discrimination, but that is the occupational hazard of every artist and especially of the novelist who must always be, so long as there are conflicts within his society, something of a spy in enemy territory. The thing to avoid is developing one's isolation because that way lies desiccation, etiolation, clique-writing that will get yellow in manuscript and deserve to. Emigration is no solution, even for the novelist or dramatist to whom ideas are more important than sense-impressions. There is stimulation at first, a sense of expansion—but in England the artist's loneliness that we have known longer is beginning to be felt, and publishing, because of rearmament and American stockpiling of paper, is getting costly and difficult, and liberties of thought are slipping away too. But after the stimulation you will dry up: you can neither feel completely at home in your adopted country, not enough to write deeply of it, nor can you write of your own country except through a mist of nostalgia and unappeased resentments. We New Zealanders have far less in common with the English middle classes than we may think* and at best they will patronize

---

* The English intellectual for example, thinks with detached disciplined reasoning. His education has involved a strict mental discipline that is not in favour with New Zealand educational pundits—either the writers of the late periodical *Education* or the 'correct use of the full-stop' inspectors. But we approach problems by a subtle adjustment of moral and emotional reactions, either puritan or snobbish, either moral favour and moral disapproval, cheer and sneer, clapping and booing; or humility and superciliousness, crawling and snubbing. But since I can only draw on my own mental habits for example I'd better shut up.

us and emasculate us. We could no more lose our national habits if we were to try, than we could, if we wanted to, disguise our kiwi twang. Our accent stands out a mile and the time will come when so does the accent of our literature, but not before we have a social system that makes possible the meaningful liberation of the talents and energies of the common people. Until then there is hard work to be done, there are quiet mortifications to be suffered, humiliations and misunderstandings to be put up with, and yet one will meet a lot of cheerfulness to ease the effort.

Since I first wrote this last June, the Police Offences Amendment Bill has become law, and there are fantastically terrifying bills in preparation— the Coroners' Bill, and the Official Secrets Bill. So we can expect worse discomforts—smear campaigns, imprisonment, continual impounding of one's writing equipment, closing of printing-presses. For these reasons it is our job to take a lead in awakening New Zealanders from their fretful sleep.

London, January 1952

Colonial 'County'

At first it is refreshing to read a local novel free of attitudes common in our writers—there is no sentimentality, no posing, neither puritanism nor revolt against it; only a hard mind playing without pity or accusation on our society. But the author's unwillingness to question the assumptions of his characters prevents the novel from rising above competent mediocrity. His assumptions are essentially those of Minhinnick, *The Weekly News*, L. K. Munro, *The New Zealand Herald* and *Observer* and the society notes of *The New Zealand Mirror*. Paganism and the social values of the stock and station agencies make a repulsive combination.

Julien Ware is the son of a rabbiter on an estate on the flanks of a range in eastern Nelson. The Torrens, the section on which he lives, has been abandoned to the rabbits, and the owner John Cecil lives fat on the green acres of the Sherbourne. Julien as a boy conceives a burning ambition to own the Torrens and make it fertile. That is the theme, Julien's ambition and how it is modified as he matures; the ambitious individual will battling with society.

It is a world from which most of us are excluded, a world of landowners, wool-cheques and mortgages, snobbery and marriage for money, Plunket balls and Hunt Club balls—colonial 'County'. Land is not fertility to the Cecils, it is profit, it is above all property, and the prestige and good living that go with it. To save the Sherbourne, Stella Cecil will sell her body, and her father will ask her to do it.

Julien dreams of the Torrens made fertile. But property lures him too. The boy without property or prospects determines to fight his way into the owner class using their methods, adopting their customs. Underlining the theme is the incredible story of Bracegirdle the coalminer who forced his way, in Edwardian England, into a brilliant wealthy law practice, to whom the slump brings the Sherbourne and other estates.

This essay was first published in *Landfall*, March 1953, as a review of Guthrie Wilson's *Julien Ware* (Robert Hale).

But Mr Wilson is not even true to his assumptions. He connives at Julien's ruthlessness, but he has to invoke a series of timely windfalls for Julien to achieve his ends—his father sends him unexpectedly to Nelson College where he learns the manners of gentlemen, he wins a scholarship only because his rival withdraws out of friendship, Bracegirdle offers him a partnership, Bracegirdle dies and leaves him his immense property, including the Cecils' land. The author has avoided the powerful satirical possibilities of his theme.

By this time Julien is less single-minded. He has matured because 'infantry war, life's supreme teacher, the multiform Dr Arnold' has made a man of him. It was in *Brave Company*, this worship of war: only two things mattered, love and war, and the greater of these was war. The unsentimental Mr Wilson is getting close to the sentimentality of the R.S.A. reunion. There are soldiers who still hanker for the war years, though they cursed every minute of them. It is the only time when they lived in comradeship with a zest born of danger, when they were tough, cunning, death-daring animals. Now, pedalling in from the suburbs to hire out their minds and muscles, when can society offer them such fulness of living? Mr Wilson's voice has a familiar ring: Anzac Day, the R.S.A., Come on lad, it's your turn now. . . .

Except that Mr Wilson is too honest to deal in the humbug of Anzac Day speeches; he values honesty so much that he seems to imply that Julien is excused by his complete honesty with himself. Self-deception is unforgivable. 'We like to be judged harshly,' says John Cecil. 'We're not weak, we aren't filled with tender feminine understanding of others.' Mr Wilson is impatient of Amyas Craig, ex-M.P., mayor, president of the Chamber of Commerce, editor of the local paper, tireless warmer of boardroom chairs, because he believes the humbug he talks. But the Cecils are made secure by the Craigs: it is the Craigs who concoct the daily doses of soporific for the landless two millions who never get a look-in in this novel.

Julien's relations with women are handled fully and in more masculine fashion than by any New Zealander before Mr Wilson. There is his passion for Stella Cecil, his protective love for Beth Craig—one restless and destructive, the other too placid for him to believe in—eros and agape if you like, but more than that. For Stella he feels what he felt for her class—hatred, envy, coveting, so that when he marries her he wears her like a trophy, the spoilt arrogant little lady who used to turn up her nose from the back of her pony at the rabbit's blood on his pants. Love to him is a disgusting emotion. He kills their child without even knowing that she is going to have it. How could be love Beth, good though she is? Her father lives off investments and his newspaper, but the Craigs own no land, they excite no envy in him. Even at the end, though he has promised Beth she shall be his second wife, he recognizes that he prefers Stella.

What then is Mr Wilson's conclusion? That a man's will, however fierce, will be diverted by his mature sexual desires (wantings he calls them). That the will alters the world, and the world the will, to produce something different from what either intended. But it is not the end that interests Mr Wilson, only the effort. 'Whether one built or destroyed, it was only the striving that gave satisfaction.' Purpose doesn't matter, only activity. And Julien's dream of the Torrens never comes off; wells are bored, irrigation channels dug, and he dies in Italy. He has willed the land back to Stella, to the Cecils whom it never should have left. And although Stella will take the hint and make the Torrens green, she will never do it as he would have done it. Some future Julien Ware might attempt it. 'Let him plan from nothing also.' Only in the striving is the reward; but behind it all is a sneer, is Bracegirdle's slaty, cynical eye, tired after the effort of forcing himself up, knowing that at the heart of everything is nothing. His judgment on the human situation is 'tiny arrogant man, strutting under the rays of the sinking sun and imagining the long shadow he cast to be his stature'. All that courage, and a mortar can spatter it over Italian snows. Amyas Craig believed in his humbug, but (at heart) Mr Wilson doesn't believe in his. Is this the heart of it all? —of Minhinnick, the National Party platform, the Anzac Day speeches, the society notes of the *Mirror*?—self-contempt under a sinking sun, the self-contempt of an insecure feudal class rapidly becoming demoralised, the self-contempt that justifies war, emergency regulations, the ditching of all this Christian kid-glove stuff?

How much is the war responsible for Mr Wilson's stripped masculine style? There is nothing tender, sensuous or nervous in his style, none of the animation of each moment that we have learned to expect from Mr Sargeson and our short-story writers. The landscape might as easily be Australia or South Africa: in fact one English reviewer finished the book under the impression that it was Australian. The people are not distinctively New Zealand; there is no re-creation, even in the background, of a life recognisably New Zealand. Mr Wilson eyes experience as he describes his women, as John Cecil might appraise land or horseflesh. No irrelevant detail, only what is essential to the plot. It is an advantage in characterisation. As in *Brave Company* the characters are effortlessly distinct, if undeveloped; no bother about mannerisms, no studious descriptions, yet you can recognize them as soon as they speak. Julien's father and Stella are most successful, Beth doesn't quite come alive, Bracegirdle is unconvincing. For Julien Mr Wilson relies on repetition rather than development and he soon becomes a bore.

This novel has a beginning, a middle, an end; it is satisfyingly told; the theme is engrossing; some of it is deeply moving. It is worth the attention of everyone who follows novels by New Zealanders, because Mr Wilson can become increasingly important as a novelist. One is anxious to know if in his next novel he can widen his social range, ask himself more questions, humanise his outlook, and take time off to observe or share in the common life about him.

John Guthrie

In 1935 *The Little Country* did what no New Zealand novel has done since, ranged satirically about our society. With verve, good humour and the cheek of a journalist it took us into a newspaper office, courts, borough council and dairy farmers' meetings, even a tangi. Mr Guthrie is good on meetings. But the breadth was out of proportion to the depth. Characterisation was superficial and the plot was unrelated to characters. For example, the young man who runs away from home thinking he has killed his father is essentially unchanged by the experience. Mr Guthrie set out to 'show our faults as well as our fun'; he complained that we hadn't produced any works of art, we were a lot of sobersides, too bent on making money; we didn't know enough of Life, Laughter, Romance. It was a criticism of the group he knew best, suburban and small-town professional and business people. By his long apologetic preface Mr Guthrie made it clear that we weren't to take the criticism too seriously; he was really only pulling our legs; he finally summed us up as 'Non angeli, sed Angli'.

So They Began (1938) was a mildly iconoclastic account of pioneering in New Plymouth; with pioneers just as delightfully irrational and impulsively childish as—come, let's face it—ourselves. In this novel the verve turns to glibness ('The sea was the colour of pearl, very still and softly radiant, as if God had just been walking on the waters.'). The fun turns into scouting for gags like in a vaudeville script. It is worth while quoting:

'What do you mean by kissing that girl of mine?' he demanded.
'Did she complain?' asked Amory.
'That's just the trouble. She didn't.'
'If there's anything of that sort to be done round here,' said the

This essay was first published in *Landfall*, September 1954, as a review of John Guthrie's *Paradise Bay* and *The Seekers* (Werner Laurie).

Englishman, 'I'll do it. You're older than I am, but I'm afraid I shall have to black your eyes for you.'

'You can't,' said Amory. 'I have to see the Governor to-night.'

'I can't help that. What else can I do?'

'Black her's instead.'

'By George, that's an idea . . . I'd never thought of that.'

This involves a very cheap attitude to humanity; the men-only poses of the New Plymouth bourgeoisie must be anathema to a humanist, and a great novelist must be a humanist. Sometimes Mr Guthrie is plain hypocritical: an agnostic with a great respect for the conscientious Christian, he has Richard deterred from murder or mayhem by a vision of Christ; soon after he gets his revenge inadvertently and breaks loudly into singing, 'Yes, Jesus loves me!' Or consider the tongue-in-cheek smirk behind this account of gold-fever:

'Pick, pick, pick! What did God think about it all? "Gnaw, mouse," laughed God, "till you reach the larder."

And when he got there the cupboard was bare . . .

Lord, if it was . . . ! What if God was a great cat playing with the little mouse . . . run . . . so far . . . ah, back . . . caught . . . run . . . so far . . . He always finished you off in the end! Dear God, let me only find the gold first, and I'll give up drinking and lying and running with women. Please, Pussy, let me just find the cheese.'

The author's verve has become irresponsibility; he is like a comedian who imagines that he can increase the sympathy of his audience by playing tricks on them. Richard believes he has been forced to eat the flesh of his sweetheart's brother. 'Tears came into his eyes. He saw himself alone, unloved, outcast, the victim of a tragic fate.' And so on for a long paragraph. 'The fact is, in his own particular way, he was enjoying himself immensely.' It is the author who is enjoying himself, sniggering like a boy who has broken wind in church. The cheapness is inhuman; it is one thing to make fun of artificial conventions, it is another to play tricks with permanent and fundamental human sympathies. When a dwarf falls down a mine shaft and is hoisted up unconscious the author is less concerned with his condition than the odd impropriety of Richard's comment, 'The poor little basket's broken!' Only, of course, he isn't dead. An Evelyn Waugh would have Richard really eating human flesh, the young man a murderer, the dwarf dead. Mr Guthrie is too kindly-natured to be a satirist, too cheap to be a humanist. The boy who broke wind in church ends up by taking round the collection plate.

Since these two novels Mr Guthrie has lived in England and his later writing has been affected by his war service and his expatriation. *The Man in our Lives* (Nelson, 1946) is a trivial, episodic sentimental memoir of a father, a lesser *Life with Father*. It might have had some value had the memories been set in their real country: transferred to England they are meaningless. The father is a blustering minor tyrant, effectively managed by an indulgent wife and family. In this book Mr Guthrie begins to repeat himself; it is usually a fault of a first novel to state the obvious; it is also the risk of long expatriation, at least if you work within terms of realism. ' "Look at her," father said, turning round. "She's miles away." He meant mentally. "She's dreaming." ' Just in case you didn't get it the first time.

In his three post-war novels with English setting Mr Guthrie is a much chastened writer; he doesn't clown, he is witty. And there are some things a man has to take seriously, damn it all; the sexual relations of hero and heroine, for example. England is in difficult straits; leisure has quite disappeared; we've got to hold firm to every scrap of tradition and culture and religion that we've got. More of the characters are serious; the heroes are pallid, ill-defined and have a habit of thinking in quotation marks all sorts of occasional comments on London and the world that would have been better made, if at all, by the author himself. At least these three novels are economical.

In *Journey by Twilight* (1949) the theme is, according to the dust-jacket, that no man is an island. Any Guthrie reader will know that when the hero goes to his office after strangling his wife because he thought she had kissed her father too passionately, he only thinks he has strangled her, and she pops up in a later chapter. He does poison himself but there is no sense of tragedy. There is some social comment: a small Edwardian gentleman of a publisher about to sell out to a parvenu, power-hungry mogul, backs out because the mogul finances Mosley's Unity Party. *Is This What I Wanted?* (1950) is a serious attempt, within the limits of the outlook of a salaried sleeper on the fringes of London, to cope with the problem of the threat of war. Hammer, editor of a national daily, afraid that the Labour Government will go too far, has a great inspiration to bring the classes together with the mateyness he knew in a prisoner-of-war camp. Every night at Hammersmith members of his inexclusive club drink and listen to Victorian music-hall compered by a prominent rightwing trade union leader. The impending war is unpopular; coastal artillery is trained on the Welsh mining valleys; war comes, the miners strike and are shelled. Cabinet forbids publication of the news of the strike; Hammer defies the order but his second-in-command Leighton countermands his instructions; all is saved, the miners return to work, and England goes to war—very philosophically and without hope of winning, with everyone sitting round as if at a picnic, on Hampstead Heath, waiting for the end. It is an admission of spiritual bankruptcy. Leighton, who loses interest in women the moment he seduces them, is meant to be a symbol of twentieth century man and presumably war is his judgment. There is some social analysis in this novel, but Mr Guthrie's political insight reflects that of *The Times*. For example, it isn't typical of communists to have a chip on the shoulder, they don't work singly like the one in this book, they would only be amused by the Victorian music-hall, let alone want to break it up, getting the razors out. In *Journey by Twilight* the fascist-communist clash is presumably based on the 1949 Sunday night street-fights in Hackney, between Mosleyites and anti-fascist ex-servicemen. Neither the ex-servicemen nor communists would try to silence a fascist speaker by mobbing his platform, trampling a little girl to death and shrugging it off as inevitable. A social analyst has no right to take his characters at second hand.

A chapter of *Merry-Go-Round* (1950) was written every time the 'most adorable of playfellows' to whom it is dedicated refused a certain request. It bears little sign of the passion. It is a slight farce about an organization like the British Council; its best humour is unconscious—a League for the Propagation of Basic English to which twelve non-English-speaking nations belong; a Czech prison governor who is so worried by a letter to *The Times* about two English prisoners that he transfers them to Moscow, just like that.

When Marghanita Laski called *Paradise Bay* 'a potential New Zealand —at least—classic', she showed how little she knew of writing in New Zealand. If, as Mr Alan Mulgan claims, there is Delight in this novel, delight must be a very pallid state. It is no more than a pleasant tale of New Plymouth centennial celebrations and jiggery-pokery on the stock-market, with an ambitious youth at the centre. Somehow it does not convey the 'feel' of New Zealand; the outlook is from London and New Plymouth comes through as a far-off colony. Mr Guthrie is again betrayed by the attitudes of the small-town businessman. It is right to make fun of the shock of the town's best citizenry when the newly-found descendant of the town's founder turns out to be illegitimate and Maori; but the author has no right to laugh up his sleeve as if the Maori woman was something comical in herself. And the author develops a soft spot for Bertie Dryden, the only outstanding character in the book; what if he was a swindler? he knew a thing or two, old Bertie and it was only those Aucklanders he diddled. Richenda may appear as if she's going to have a baby, but this is John Guthrie, it'll only be a disease. The author seems to stand in awe of the ruthless ambition of Colin Dryden set on medical school and where else but Harley Street, as if this was something sacred: the small-town businessman always does respect the successful. The minor characters are walking quirks: you could invent thousands of characters this way: think of a mannerism give it a proper name and put it through its paces. Like the lady in *So They Began* whose only conversation was about her eggs, like Lady Laurel of *Merry-Go-Round* who is always saying 'Halloo!', like Mr and Mrs Truscott who will argue every time they come on, over the pronunciation of a word; she will say that he's deep and he's the whitest man she ever knew. Uncle Henry is not a character so much as a vaudeville joke: ordered a long voyage as a rest cure and unable to afford it, he buys a season ticket and plies all day to and from Devonport, writing letters about his travels. One pities Richenda the heroine (staying with her author husband in a Park Lane hotel) who had to wait for what must be all of fifteen years before he would treat her 'as if . . . as if [she] were a bad woman'.

Almost all of Mr Guthrie's books begin with apologetic notes. *The Seekers* acknowledges Elsdon Best and pays tribute to the Maoris as a race. On the first page we learn that they sweated in terror at nights because they believed devils walked abroad. This is a strange and rather grandiose little epic, a minor *Green Dolphin Country*, and I found it wordy, repetitive and boring. Mr Guthrie states and restates the obvious till it irritates; one has the feeling that he forced this novel, that his inspiration ran dry and he was always trying to pick up the threads; on p.229 Marian makes four separate statements that imply that her husband and her baby are her only interests. This is Mr Guthrie's only humourless book. The characterization is now almost completely derivative; a good Maori chief who wants to stop intertribal war but dare not; a wily tohunga; maid Marian pure and vivacious and practical too, the ideal pioneer's bride; Wayne, tall, muscular, purposeful but so devoid of definition that one supplies it in the image of Errol Flynn or Alan Ladd; a servile office tyrant straight from Dickens; a dastardly father who changes from a man opposed to his daughter's marriage into a grotesque from Victorian melodrama who immures her with a discarded mistress in a derelict Mayfair house where a sinister doctor is slowly poisoning her . . . But lo! Prince Charming arrives in a carriage and whisks her off to New Zealand. There she finds time often to swim far out to sea 'like a boy', to get up before her husband and spend a few hours painting bush scenes, to play Beethoven, convert the good chief to Christianity, cook, clean and sew for husband and baby. The Maoris attack; Marian puts on her best ball dress to inspire the men; the pakehas must win—but no, Mr Guthrie breaks the rules and they are burnt, except the baby. (Presumably the film company will adjust this.) Whatever interest Mr Guthrie has in this theme that was in *So They Began*, the white child brought up by Maoris, he gives it no significance.

Mr Guthrie is a born story-teller without profundity. If he had stayed home he might have become a very entertaining novelist or journalist. Since he writes now as if continually clearing his way through a fog, one wonders if the sophistications and pressures of London have left his mind so punch-drunk that he no longer knows what values he can expect his readers to share, or what he believes at all. He gives the impression of struggling to convince himself that he believes the Edwardian assumptions about the British heritage and destiny, on which no doubt he was reared. Perhaps that is why he strains so hard to define sentiments that turn out after all to be trite. If *The Seekers* was not written simply to attract a film offer, one suspects that it was written to answer a question the author himself could not take seriously, something like this: What mystic force impelled these white adventurers to desert the comforts of the mother country, to seek new lands and carve new fortunes out of these strange, wild, hostile, beautiful islands, to build anew without hope of reward in their time? Where lies the secret of our greatness? If so, it seems that the answer has convinced Mr Guthrie no more than the question.

The Little Country and *Paradise Bay* will always have a modest place in New Zealand writing. The rest of Mr Guthrie's work vanishes in the yearly output of English novels.

A Self-Exacting Writer

Maurice Duggan's *Immanuel's Land*, a handsomely produced volume, is a collection of ten short stories and a travel diary. It is an event in New Zealand writing because—apart from the Oxford anthology—it is only the third volume of New Zealand stories to appear in the fifties. In the forties there were eight, as well as Frank Sargeson's anthology.

Some of the writers of the forties produced one volume and no more; and we could have done with more, in particular, from A. P. Gaskell and John Reece Cole, whose clean, confident prose added something distinct to our understanding of life in this country.

Mr Duggan's course has been different. In 1945 Mr Sargeson called it 'an unusual line of development for a New Zealander'. Mr Duggan seemed to be trying to get at some core of experience, something at the heart of our sensations for which words are scarcely adequate: and perhaps this is why his writing could become florid and wordy.

Now his prose is more disciplined. It is hard, calculated and precise—it shows him to be the most painstaking writer of short stories this country has had. He has turned over every experience in his mind, till he has found for it the only words that satisfy him. For example, we often hear someone in mock hysteria use a certain tone of voice—in this case a teacher speaking to a pupil—'*Get on!*' But how would we indicate the tone itself in writing? Mr Duggan calls it 'whinnying in frenzy': and we know just what it sounds like. Again: 'Miss Mackintosh walked past, and with a look of bitter satisfaction cut him dead'. It is true, and right, and touches a memory in all of us. But I don't think his prose is so assured, for all its carefulness, as that of Mr Gaskell or Mr Cole.

Mr Duggan merits serious critical attention; but if he is to be given it, it must be in a different spirit from, say, the effusive praise of James Bertram in the *Listener*, who called his writing 'clean, firm and sinewy in

This essay appeared in *Here and Now*, September 1957, as a review of Maurice Duggan's *Immanuel's Land* (The Pilgrim Press). Originally written for radio.

the notation of the most elusive nuances', or the log-rolling tone of Maurice Shadbolt in the *Evening Post*.

I think 'Voyage' has been overpraised: it is a diary of travel to England, Italy and Spain, and it is detailed, observant and sometimes witty, but it is shot through with metaphysical comments that strike me as half-baked and pretentious. The unsigned telegram he gets, 'Do not let yourself be imposed on by reality'—what does it mean? Or, 'Man is altogether an Evil'? There is the odd and profitless speculation on the consequences to the earth if a boy takes a globe apart and puts it together again with India touching America; the rather precious pose behind the comments, the prose that seems to owe something to Cyril Connolly and the back pages of the *New Statesman*, to those mannered contributors Edward Hyams, G. W. Stonier and V. S. Pritchett. Some of the constructions are hardly English: 'if she had ever given him a moment of curiosity, her eye withered now the gift.' 'Shall fervour, shall it save us?' 'The woman behind me prods me ungently awake.' In fact some of the manner has become mannerism: verbs that call attention to themselves come to be repeated—buses and trains *bore*, sunlight and car-lights *rake* what is in their path. It is a pity that some of the writing is so self-conscious because in his early story 'Six Place Names and a Girl' there is some beautiful writing, about the hero and Pelly, a Maori girl.

The stories themselves are better. There are a number of stories of an Irish Catholic family, the Lenihans, and one of them, about the children being told that the new maid is now their stepmother, is poignant. There are two stories of life in a Catholic boys' boarding school, and one of the best is of a journey through Northland. Mr Duggan is a detached writer. It is as if, like one of his characters, he is seeing life through binoculars, seeing a vision from which 'silence has taken all but the charm', and the sounds are as remote and muted as shouts from a distant playing-field; or, like another of his characters, watching a woman crying from behind the window of a passing train and never knowing why; or, like another, searching anonymous love-letters in the hope of an explanation. He is apart from his situations, and not involved in them except when there is no solution and he can look down, pity and understand. It is an injustice that a boy is expelled when his teacher has baited him to the point of revenge, but nothing can be done about it, the boy has to go. There is unresolved tension, too, in the situation of old Brother Ignatius, tired of trying to quell the sin in the boys, yet the boys will go on sinning and Brother Ignatius will continue to fret. The Lenihans farewelling their son don't feel as much as they pretend, but that is the way of things and nothing will change. The magistrate doesn't understand why the youth shooting goats fired at another youth, nor do their parents, but you can't expect them to, and yet the youth isn't to blame.

In Mr Duggan's stories things don't change or develop. Something is revealed, perhaps, or someone is disillusioned, but things stay the same. His vision is static, held still by adjectives and a painter's interest in colour and patterns of colour. Sometimes he intensifies beyond plausibility—what seems to be a hot, treeless desert turns out after all to have been a little flat between scrub country north of Whangarei. The tired static vision avoids dramatic incidents. It gives a certain lack of perspective and direction to the collection: they don't seem to add up to a recreation of New Zealand: they remain a collection of experiences, only slightly connected. I feel that the author, like one of his characters, is afraid of being involved. After all, a writer cannot hope always to *possess* experience, sometimes the experience possesses him, and he sees things more clearly as a result, and gains a deeper assurance. Reality does impose itself, though not impose on you, whether you try to steer clear of it or not; and you can't ask: 'Am I real?' You have to accept yourself as real before you can look at reality.

I have been forced by the default of some other reviewers to spend too much time on the weaknesses. But for all these Mr Duggan is an important and dedicated writer who will continue and strengthen. His view of some aspects of life in this country is worth sharing, not only because of his patient and detailed observation, but also because life in New Zealand has changed a good deal since Mr Gaskell and Mr Cole were writing.

Attitudes to the Maori
in Some Pakeha Fiction

In this essay I hope to analyse the attitudes towards the Maori shown
by some Pakeha writers of fiction who have chosen to write about Maoris
or Maori-Pakeha relations.[1] I should like to make these qualifications,
however. This essay is no attempt at a complete historical survey of
Pakeha fiction dealing with Maoris. A complete survey would mean reading
at least a hundred books in six libraries from Auckland to Dunedin; I
venture to doubt if it would reveal more than repetitions and variations of
the attitudes shown in the novels and stories I have read. Further, one
should recall that a full history of Pakeha attitudes to the Maori has already
been patently expressed in the post-European history of New Zealand,
in Land Court proceedings, in statutes and in political acts of peace and
war, in the thousands of day-to-day actions of officials, policemen, clergymen, journalists, teachers, landladies, employers and store-keepers; and
that this study is subsidiary to that. All that it amounts to is a survey of
attitudes to the Maori as expressed in more easily available novels and
stories by some (mainly male) Pakehas of some intelligence and sensitivity.
I think that, with some slight variation, these attitudes are representative
of common contemporary attitudes, conscious and unconscious.

It seems necessary to begin with some survey of Maori attempts at
adaptation to European occupation before the period in which these
novels and stories were written. This sketch is, of course, a compilation
from the research of historical writers and may contain errors of interpretation (though I hope not of fact) for which I am responsible.

We should recall that in pre-European times the Maori were an
industrious people, that their main energies went to producing food
and clothing and shelter with primitive implements, that their tribal
fighting was confined to the season between planting and harvesting. It

---

This essay was first published in the *Journal of the Polynesian Society*, September
1958.

was after the Pakeha's introduction of the musket that fighting became so fierce, so destructive and depopulating. Hongi's murderous campaign killed tens of thousands. In the north, the Ngapuhi were exposed to rum, disease and traffic in women, from escaped convicts and deserted seamen. Throughout the North Island, the missionaries were destroying old beliefs, and the new religion was quickly accepted by the tribes ravaged by the wars of Hongi and Te Rauparaha. The Maori at first welcomed the Pakeha, and recognised that they could learn much from him: they were very adaptable and soon began to make progress. By the mid-century, a very high proportion of Maoris could read and write. They grew wheat, potatoes, maize and kumara for the Pakeha market in Australia and New Zealand; they ground the wheat in their mills and bought and manned schooners to deliver it.

But this prosperity was interrupted by a sudden fall in prices, which they could not understand. Then, when the Pakeha population came to equal that of the Maori, when the Maori could see that, in spite of the Treaty of Waitangi, their land was steadily being bought and that the Government was encouraging the sale of land from individuals who, by tribal tradition, had no right to sell it, Maoris sought to forget their tribal differences and to oppose the further sale of land. So there was the King Movement and then the bitter wars and the confiscations of land that followed. Yet it was not the defeated tribes who were first adversely affected and whose population first began to decrease. Ironically, as Mr Sorrenson has shown,[2] it was the friendly tribes, from whom the Native Land Courts were busy prising their lands. The Courts would establish the title of those Maoris who were willing to sell. Storekeepers would ply Maoris with goods on credit, especially liquor, and run them into debt, and then claim their land in payment. Since the Courts met in towns away from the tribal lands and since they sat for months but did not announce when cases would come before them, those Maoris who were opposed to sale of land and wanted to establish their title to it, were forced to spend months in town with unsatisfactory shelter, poor food, accumulating debts. As well they had to pay Court and survey expenses and the expenses of a Pakeha lawyer. When the bills came in they had to sell the land to pay them. Either way they lost. Maoris said the white man's peace was more devastating than his wars.

The consequence was a disruption of the old Maori social organisation. Those, like the Taranaki Maoris living at Parihaka under Te Whiti, who tried to preserve their old social forms and at the same time adapt themselves effectively to the new Pakeha order, were successful and maintained their self-respect and rate of population till their settlement was destroyed by the Pakeha government. Any attempt at social integration was impossible without land, and Government and settler were hungry for land. Except for those areas which had been least subjected to pressure for land sales, the Maori people were defeated, their leaders dead or dispirited, their lands gone, and their old traditions broken: besides this, they no longer had much confidence in the Pakeha, in his laws or his religion. This distrust was old: writing of the period before the outbreak of the wars, Keith Sinclair has said: 'The European, as the Maoris saw him, was as unpleasant a figure as the settlers' stereotype Maori: he was greedy, arrogant, lacking in courtesy, selfish—in a word, "individualistic". He treated Maori women as prostitutes, and being without natural decency, deserted his half-caste children.'[3] If in the fifties the Maoris were so suspicious of the Pakeha, they were even more so in the seventies and eighties.

The Maori lost confidence in the future. This is the period in which the Maori population declined (42,113 in 1896), and the race was thought to be dying; when the Maori tried to make adjustment in the form of part-religious, part-nationalistic cults, beginning with the Hauhau movement and ending with Ratana, which tried to incorporate old Maori traditions with European innovations as a means of survival; when Maori prophets arose; when the Maori got the reputation among the Pakeha for indolence, improvidence, shiftlessness and unreliability. He was inactive because there was no hope for his people; the Pakeha found him unreliable because the Maori didn't trust him; he was improvident because there was no future for him. The old people smoked their pipes, brooded and asked, *E taea te aha?* What is the use? Many Maoris worked under contract, clearing forests, draining swamps, cutting flax, surveying, building roads, fencing; when they worked for the Pakeha, they worked mostly at unskilled jobs.

In 1906, Dr Pomare, Maori Health Officer, wrote: "There is no alternative but to become a Pakeha . . . There is no hope for the Maori but in ultimate absorption by the Pakeha."[4]

It was in this period that Alfred A. Grace's stories and Baucke's sketches were written. Pakeha attitudes to the Maori throughout this time were either hostile or patronising. According to Dr Sinclair: 'They called these brown folk, whom they regarded as dirty, degraded, lazy or immoral, "blacks" or "niggers". They despised them: but in many parts of the country they also feared them.'[5] Allen Curnow has drawn my attention to the ambivalent attitude much earlier than this in Alfred Domett the poet, who found it poetically appropriate to see the Maori as the noble savage:

> A fine old sturdy stalwart stubborn chief
> Was Tangi-Moana the "Wailing Sea":
> Both brave and wise in his degree . . .
> Did he not look, aye, every inch a chief?
> Did not each glance and gesture stamp him then,
> Self-heralded a God-made King of men?

But as a practical politician speaking in the New Zealand Assembly in 1860 his attitude was very different. When he was invited by T. F.

Forsaith, member for the city of Auckland, to envisage the deathbed of Reretawhangawhanga, father of Wiremu Kingi, and to imagine the dying father's last instructions to his son, Domett was reported: 'he had gone in imagination with him into the hut, in spite of the many disagreeable little occupants it probably contained, and had pictured to himself, emerging from the gloom in the corner, the red eyeballs and blue face of the old—ruffian he would not say, but of the venerable marauding cannibal and freebooter.' Domett imagined his 'ferocious features' illumined by 'the last gleams of baffled cupidity', and presented in opposition to Forsaith's touching description of a dying father, a picture of a vigorous man in full health, with 'jawbones probably yet aching with the mastication of title-deeds in the shape of the limbs of former owners.'[6]

At worst, the Pakeha attitude was that he had every right to occupy the land of uncivilised heathens and the sooner they died out the better. At best, it was one of indulgence, as in two of Blanche Baughan's stories (1912)[7]: being kind to them, showing yourself as cunning as they are, and then giving them some tobacco. Naughty, lovable children, but you could manage them if you understood them.

Grace's stories, *Tales of a Dying Race* (1901), do make some effort to understand. Grace had had a lot of experience of Maoris and he had quite a respect for them. His attitude is a little like that of a Pakeha-Maori, who, as he calls it, 'speaks the lingo'. He takes it for granted that they are rogues, but he prefers to write of their way of living rather than of conventional and self-righteous Pakeha life for which he had little sympathy. 'The heathen in his blindness,' he said,[8] '[is] blessed with an ideality of which the cultivated, artificial, unnatural *pakeha* knows nothing.' So he tells two stories in which white men 'take to the blanket' and marry Maori girls, when their Pakeha fiancees have jilted them because of their (till now, innocent) acquaintance with the Maori girls.[9] Grace was the son of a missionary and he has a dislike for missionaries, for the tohunga of either Maori or Pakeha religion. He admires the Maori's freedom from puritanical conventions and he likes to offend conventional Pakeha tastes with stories of Maori warfare and cannibalism. One of his *Maoriland Stories* (1895) is of a Maori girl spurned by a white lover, who agrees to marry a Maori suitor if he will go to Auckland and bring back the head of her old lover's new Pakeha wife—and he does.[10]

'Te Wiria's Potatoes' is told in Grace's usual clumsy fashion of short episodes, like scenes in a play.[11] The people are the Ngati-ata, a small *hapu* on the coast. Te Wiria is Villiers, a Pakeha who has built his house on an old *pa* and farms the land around it, and who maintains an attitude of benevolence towards the Ngati-ata. Their chief Tohitapu offers him the manpower to dig his crop of potatoes, but in the night the fifty sacks disappear. When Villiers goes to Tohi to complain, all the chief does is reproach his men, and he resumes his meal of pork and baked potatoes. Grace makes no generalisations: he only says that these people helped themselves to Villiers's potatoes, and that if they were unrepentant, Villiers was a romantic old fool to expect them to feel grateful to him. It is ironic that while Villiers, who has dispossessed the Ngati-ata, feels that they are downtrodden, and that they are his *protégés*, Tohitapu their chief calls him *his* Pakeha, as if he is his *protégé*. But while Grace thinks Villiers's original attitude to the Maoris sentimental, he does not conclude that the Ngati-ata should be treated harshly. He prefers Villiers's attitude to that of a prim maiden aunt in another story who is scared out of bed and back to England by an early-morning visit from a toothless, half-blind, half-dressed woman a hundred years old.[12]

William Baucke was a successful farmer in the King Country and like Grace, he had a natural sympathy for the Maori and many Maoris respected him. His book *Where the White Man Treads Across the Pathway of the Maori* (1905) is a selection of articles contributed to the *New Zealand Herald* and the *Auckland Weekly News*. He is more earnest than Grace, less tolerant. We haven't treated the Maori well, he argues, and we've got to elevate him whether he likes it or not, and that is 'the weight of the white man's burden'. The trouble with you Maoris, he says, is that you are lazy, you imitate the vices of the Pakeha, and you keep inter-marrying within your own tribes. What you have to do is marry women of other tribes, forget your tribal jealousies and your distrust of the Pakeha, and learn to imitate the Pakeha virtues while avoiding the vices.

One of his sketches, 'A Quaint Friendship',[13] tells of a meeting with an old Maori woman first on a train and later at her whare in the King Country. There he meets also the old woman's grandson who is rude to both of them. This particular sketch is, as Miss Sturm has pointed out to me, comparable with Goldie's paintings of the same time and attempts to show the changes happening to the race: changes symbolised by the gulf between the generations—the old grandmother living on her memories, condemning the modern generation as drunkards, gamblers and lechers, and her demoralised, ill-mannered grandson. She is of Ngati-Maniapoto; her husband had been killed in the wars in the Waikato and she had strong reason to hate the Pakeha. And though she despises the ways of her grandson, she loves him because for her he represents the future of the race. Baucke, admiring the grandmother and despising her grandson, represents the sensitive conscience of the Pakeha, appalled at the results of his own work, and he is anxious that this continual reproach should be removed.

But in fact the regeneration came, as it had to come, from the Maori themselves, and partly by a means that Baucke condemned as useless, higher education, by the efforts of the group of ex-students of Te Aute College who formed the Young Maori Party. The Ngati-Porou of the East Coast, who had been less affected by the Pakeha occupation and had retained most of their land, turned to sheep-farming, and later also dairy farming; a thing which, according to Grace and Baucke, was impossible for a 'warrior race'. Sir James Carroll, a part-Maori, urged the people not to forget their *Maoritanga*. There were signs of the beginning of a new hope and consciousness of identity, a determination not to be absorbed or assimilated. Since then, the Maori economic position has improved and Maoris are now taking up skilled and professional jobs more than formerly. The population in June, 1958, was estimated at 148,248, over three times what it has been in 1896.[14] Of the Maori population at the end of 1955, 59 per cent were under 21 (as against 38 per cent Pakeha).[15] The birthrate in 1957 was 46 per 1,000 (as against 24 per 1,000 Pakeha) and the natural increase of the Maori population 3.6 per cent (as against 1.5 per cent Pakeha). Even so, the average Maori has fourteen to sixteen years' less expectation of life than the average Pakeha; and infant mortality in the five years 1953–57 was 67 per 1,000 births (compared with 20 per 1,000 Pakeha births).[16]

Further, according to the 1951 census, the proportion of Maoris among the lower income-groups was higher than that of Pakeha; and about one-eighth of Maori houses were of a standard most Pakeha would despise—huts, whares and baches.[17]

None of the serious writers of the period between Grace and the depression wrote of the Maori as he was living at the time. In the collection *New Zealand Short Stories* (1930), in spite of the editor's handsome mention of 'the delightful Maori race', his assurance that 'many stories' in the book are about Maoris and his hope that in time Pakeha absorption of the Maori would give New Zealanders both 'a slight golden tinge' and 'a love of high poetic imagery' to offset their oppressive practicality, there are in fact only five stories of Maoris, and only one of them of contemporary Maoris, and that one is hostile.[18]

There were the 'Maori romances', like F. O. V. Acheson's novel *Plume of the Arawas* (1930), like two of Grace's *Maoriland Stories*[19] and his *Atareta, Belle of the Kainga*, like H. B. Vogel's novel *The Maori Maid* (1896), and like two of Robin Hyde's stories.[20] These often concerned the tragic love of two Maoris, or the tragedy of a half-caste girl. It is strange that Pakeha writers felt that they could best confer a noble dignity on the Maori when he could be made a tragic figure, as Jessie Weston had done with her half-caste heroine Mary in *Ko Méri* (1890), daughter of a British general and a Maori chief's daughter, whose tragedy was to return to her people from genteel London society and share 'the primitive, soulless existence of a barbarian race'.[21] Often too the subject is the love of a white man for a Maori maiden, sometimes a 'princess'—it is often she who dies—but hardly ever of a white woman for a Maori man. That would be getting too close to the bone, because these stories tended to move from real possibilities into an idyllic world of the imagination.[22] G. B. Lancaster's

'The Story of Wi'[23] is a story of a Maori baby most improbably abandoned by its tribe because its mother had died of disease, just as improbably bought by a white man who raises the boy and, determined to train him to serve his people, trains him so hard that he whips him and draws blood. However, just as improbably, the boy is grateful and is training to be a parson, until he makes the mistake of falling in love with a white girl. He is smartly put in his place and rebels against the white man's culture and religion, and says he will sit in the sun and drink brandy instead. It is not a good story: its people act like puppets and it is worked out like the solution to a problem in algebra. But it is a rare demonstration of a discrepancy in the Pakeha attitude to the Maori.

There had been novels and romances of the Maori wars, in which the Maoris were either ferocious and treacherous, or, later, were sentimentalised melancholy and noble savages and brave warriors.

There were also James Cowan's *Tales of the Maori Coast* (1930) and *Tales of the Maori Bush* (1934), all of them yarns rather than stories, and not of great merit. Like Satchell's *The Greenstone Door* (1914), they represent the Maori with dignity; but like that novel they are an attempt to record, before it is too late, the old Maori life before the Pakeha and after his coming till the end of the Maori wars. Some are comic, pathetic, romantic; they emphasise the Maori as a warrior and perpetuate the idea of the noble savage, now no longer with us, a pious memory.

Those who did write of contemporary Maoris were hardly serious writers and their attitude is a dilution of the sardonic humour Grace saw in the situation of the Maori adapting himself to Pakeha ways. Grace began this tradition (which still exists in occasional pub-yarns) with his *Hone Tiki Dialogues* (1910). In these twelve sketches, which first appeared in journals so diverse as the intellectual *Triad* and the popular *Free Lance*, a mythical character in a dented bowler hat philosophises shrewdly and ineptly on Pakeha customs. Sometimes we are meant to wonder at his shrewdness, especially when he remarks on Pakeha women and parsons, but on these subjects Hone Tiki is voicing Grace's own opinions. On the whole, Hone is presented as a clown, and it is notable that Messrs. Gordon & Gotch designed the book for sale on railway stations as light travelling entertainment. These sketches imply, in Joan Gries's words, 'the hopelessness of the Maori's efforts to adapt himself to the European way of life'.[24] It is a rationalisation of Pakeha superiority to laugh at any Maori attempts at adaptation; and there were many.

Pat Lawlor's collection of over a hundred *Maori Tales* (1927), only some of which he wrote himself, is a feeble modern imitation of a jest-book like the *100 Merry Tales* of the 16th century. It is a collection of paragraphs partly culled from the light Sydney monthly *Aussie*, rather like those that readers used to write about Aboriginals in the Sydney *Bulletin*, stories about cunning, simple old Hori, his speech full of 'prurrys' and 'py korrys'. In an introduction to the collection, Dick Harris writes of 'that Maori mentality so delightfully compounded of guile and simplicity'. The text of one of the illustrated jokes is enough:[25]

> Look here, Hori! That horse I bought from you dropped dead when I was driving him yesterday.
> Py corry! That funny, he never do any trick like that when I have him.

Letters from Private Henare Tikitanu was written during the First World War, by V. C. Fussell, Vicar of Waiuku,[26] and the profits of the first edition went to the Blind Soldiers' Fund. It was followed by *Corporal Tikitanu, V.C.* (1918). Private Tikitanu, described on the back cover as 'a fine stamp of Waikato Maori youth' and by the *New Zealand Herald* reviewer as 'a typical Maori soldier', is half-literate, simple-minded to the point of stupidity, and writes home in mongrel English. He is shrewd to the point of cunning, but his heart is in the right place, full of what the author calls 'the latent courage and devotion of his countrymen'. It may be that this book was intended to counter Pakeha hostility at the opposition of Waikato Maoris to enlisting in the white men's war, especially when outstanding claims had not been settled; a hostility that may have pained a vicar who liked Maoris, though he saw them in part in his own image. Here are some of Henare Tikitanu's observations:[27]

> My korry, te British Empire te big place all right. I tink half te world belong to us.
> One Sherman bloke he wery frighten when I grab him. He shake all over an' say 'Please no you eat me mister.'
> I tell him: 'Py cripes, I eat you all right when I find te cook. Te Maori like te poaka.'
> When I catch te ole Sherman Kaiser I bring him home in the cage for you to see him. Some feller say more better we drown him over here, but I want you see what he like first.

So the attitude is as to our pet natives: as if to say, how lucky we are to have a native people who are such simple, lovable children but good fighters when there's a war on, and not always as stupid as you might think either.

Of course, such a view implies that if the native doesn't co-operate, he must be taught a sharp lesson. And that is the attitude of that patchy exponent of the brotherhood of man, the Australian Henry Lawson, in his story 'A Daughter of Maoriland' first published in 1897.[28] Lawson taught for about eight months in 1897 at a native school at Mangamaunu near Kaikoura. The South Island Maori were notoriously dispossessed and depressed rural outcasts in South Island society. The village itself had also suffered earlier from Te Rauparaha's invasion. Lawson's early disillusion is rather like that of those occasional South Island training college students of about fifteen years ago who, never having seen a Maori except on the street, thought it would be exciting to apply for a North Island Maori school and resigned the service within six months.

Lawson's story is of an altruistic teacher who has an ambition to be a writer and hopes to write romantically about a Maori girl pupil. For this reason he helps her when she poses as an ill-treated child and takes her into his home. She deceives him, steals the food, organises her relations against him till he loses patience and fires shots at them and they take to the heels of their horses. It turns out that her relations had plotted the whole strategy, so that they could live cheaply off the teacher. After that he had no more trouble. He gave up his 'universal brotherhood' approach and they respected him. This story is sub-titled 'A Sketch of Poor-Class Maoris'. The Maoris of the village are described as 'lower classes'. The girl is called a 'savage' and likened to a cow, a dog, and a pig; she brings 'a native smell' into the house; she is 'fat, and lazy, and dirty'. This is the only story I have read in which the adjective Maori is used as an epithet of contempt, as it is in these passages:[29]

> (August has stayed overnight to look after a sick sister. She is to return to the teacher's at lunch-time.)
> [She] had not touched a dish-cloth or broom. She had slept, as she always did, like a pig, all night, while her sister lay in agony; in the morning she ate everything there was to eat in the house (which, it seemed, was the Maori way of showing sympathy in sickness and trouble), after which she brooded by the fire till the children, running out of school, announced the teacher's lunch hour.
> Her 'romance' was briefly as follows: she went, per off-hand Maori arrangement, as 'house-keeper' in the hut of a labourer at a neighbouring sawmill. She stayed three months, for a wonder; at the expiration of which time she put on her hat and explained that she was tired of stopping there, and was going home. He said, 'All right, Sarah, wait a while and I'll take you home.' At the door of her aunt's house he said, 'Well, good-bye, Sarah,' and she said, in her brooding way, 'Good-bye, Jim.' And that was all.

The hostility of these passages is consistent throughout the story. It is difficult to get behind the malice to sort out what most likely did happen: one more than suspects that the facts have been distorted by editorial comment.[30] But what one notices especially is the unconsciously arrogant assumption that the scale of values of a white man from a colony of European culture in the 1890's (itself no model of enlightenment in its policy towards its indigenous people) is the standard by which the conduct of another people of a different culture and history is to be judged; themselves the victims of aggression and trickery from members of another colony of European culture. Evidently, to Lawson, the brotherhood of man is a closed shop.

No doubt Lawson's attitude represented the prejudice of a number of Pakehas of his time (and of a minority today), but they were not the sort of people who wrote fiction (and today are unlikely to write anything more than an occasional letter to a newspaper).

There were other attempts to reinforce current unsympathetic Pakeha attitudes. Two play on the popular fallacy that a man of mixed parentage is a vicious man because he inherits the worst qualities of both races.[31] In one of them,[32] the villain, just about to present a false grievance to his people, is arrested by a stereotype Irish policeman for robbery, deserting his wife, and other crimes. The writer of this story makes the remarkable statement that 'the older generation of Maoris knew but two conditions, of mind—the phlegmatic calm such as succeeded a big feast, and the wild ecstatic excitement which took charge of them when they danced the haka'.

Fundamentally, all these attitudes have one thing in common, a feeling of guilt about, and a distaste for, the contemporary Maori. The novels of the Maori wars that show him as fierce and treacherous or fierce and brave try to justify his present condition: either he deserved his defeat or he lost in fair fight. The romances look away from the present to a noble past, interpreted according to contemporary European literary attitudes, seeing him as a heroic but pathetic victim inevitably sacrificed to Progress. Pat Lawlor and his contributors and Fussell tame him into a comic figure, look for the 'good' in him and seem to imply that his present condition is how he likes to live: when you look for the good in anyone, you don't think much of him. Lawson tells you, quite firmly, with no nonsense, that he has to be kept in his present condition. In more subtle ways some of these attitudes persist in the modern stories of Maoris.

There were also attempts to exploit the mystery of tapu and makutu: often unbelievable ghost stories written only to play on a reader's sense of awe. Such is Dennis McEldowney's story 'By the Lake' (1947).[33] In this story a boy who enters an old burial-cave disappears and a new skull appears on the ledge: a shepherd had previously disappeared and they found only his boots. Now it is true that some of the old-time Pakeha had a great respect for Maori beliefs, and it is true that breaking a tapu can, or at least until recently could, so oppress a Maori with guilt that he becomes sick and dies. But tapu would not so affect these Pakeha of Canterbury, to whom the Maoris are only a memory, as it is made out to do in this ghost story. And if tapu kills, the body is there waiting for tangi and burial; it does not just disappear, so that a new skull appears in a cave. Again, when the old shepherd was spirited away his boots were left behind, but what happened to his clothes? I suppose this story does represent some sort of awe at the past and at a culture not understood, just as the early 19th century felt strange emotions in contemplating ruined medieval abbeys. But there are rational ways of understanding a strange culture.

Just as incredible is the story of Constance Player-Green, 'The Bird of Rameka',[34] in which a Maori woman, spurned years before by an English lover, kidnaps his daughter. A tohunga, as wily and evil as tohunga usually are in such writers, inspires a magpie with his own malicious spirit so that when he dies the magpie is the girl's constant guardian and keeps her mad. She becomes sane again as soon as the bird is throttled. In the same collection of stories Arnold Cork's 'Te Atua'[35] tells of a man who, believing himself possessed by the spirit of an ancestor, walks in his sleep with a hurricane-lamp, scares his chief to death and his fellow-villagers to evacuation until a Pakeha surveyor shoots him in self-defence. In an obscure way I suppose these stories represent the conflict of European and Maori cultures: two of them dabble with mystery but celebrate the triumph of a materialistic culture, and in Mr McEldowney's story European culture suffers a small depredation.

A more credible story is Phillip Wilson's 'Whare Fever' (1947), in which a Pakeha gum-digging in Northland with a Maori partner comes up against a mystery he respects though he cannot understand it. The young Maori becomes inexplicably ill and the cause seems to be guilt at violating some tapu; the illness disappears when the Pakeha suggests that they should move south.

The temptation of modern writers is to find in the Maori the virtues that are missing in the Pakeha and to use him as a criticism of Pakeha society. It is interesting that though there is something of this in Grace, it first appeared seriously in Katherine Mansfield, in that part of her Journal written in 1908 when she was sent on a caravan tour from Napier to Rotorua before she left again for England. The attitude, in spite of her 'visions of long dead Maoris, of forgotten battles and vanished feuds', is a real recognition of an unappreciated quality that the romances had conjured away as an old nobility remaining from a simpler and heroic society. Katherine Mansfield writes:

> There is one fellow ... who speaks English. Black curls clustering round his head band, rest, almost languor in his black eyes: a slouching walk, and yet there slumbers in his face passionate unrest and strength.

And again:

> Here, too, I meet Prodgers. It is splendid to see once again real English people. I am so sick and tired of the third-rate article. Give me the Maori *and* the tourist, but nothing between.

At this place where the Maoris talked English as well as Maori and dressed in Pakeha fashion she 'found nothing of interest', it 'proved utterly disappointing after Umuroa, which was fascinating in the extreme'.[36]

And in her story, 'How Pearl Button was Kidnapped' (1910),[37]

Pearl Button, a little girl who lives in a suburb of 'houses of boxes' in a row, from which men go daily to offices, is led away by some Maori women who shower her with affection and make her feel shy and happier than she has ever been. They eventually persuade her to paddle in the warm (and symbolic) sea which had frightened her. But her journey to Utopia is interrupted when 'little men in blue coats' come blowing whistles to take her back to the box-like houses. It is interesting that in this story the Maoris are not called Maoris, and they speak good English: so that the reader approaches them with no preconceived attitudes.

And the contrast between Maori courtesy and Pakeha 'civilisation' is expressed in Mr Sargeson's story, 'White Man's Burden' (1936).[38]

We should remember that the Maori's tradition is one of communal living and co-operation: he is thrown into a competitive Pakeha world with an economic system foreign to his traditions, in which the emphasis is on the individual acquisition of money and property. The adjustment is difficult for him, and it is not for us to lecture him. The most we can do is understand and help where help is needed *and desired*. But even there, we have to remember that we are dealing with people who have their own thoughts and sentiments. Understanding the Maori mind can be just as fruitless as refusal to understand: ask ourselves, none of us would feel easy if we were being observed and questioned by someone humourlessly determined to understand us. There are dangers in the Pakeha writer, with his different traditions, trying to see a Maori from the Maori point of view. He is apt to create a puppet figure of his own, covering his own frustrated aspirations in a brown skin, like a hermit crab.

Mr Sargeson in his short novel, *I Saw in My Dream* (1949), uses the Maori as a symbol of the uncorrupted simple life as opposed to the more callous, selfish and inhibited life of the Pakeha. Roderick Finlayson in his stories of Maori life of about twenty or thirty years ago (when the population was less than two-thirds of what it is now) announces his purpose in the preface to *Brown Man's Burden* (1938): notice that is not Baucke's 'white man's burden', it is the brown man who is carrying the burden.

It may be asked why I have written almost solely of the Maori people in these stories of New Zealand life . . . Only among that remnant of the Maori race does one find such unconventional humanity so immoderately generous, so quietly courteous with such a cheerful neglect—often to the point of squalor—of material surroundings, and such a fine disdain for those banes of the European world—time and money. For, in spite of the destruction of Maori culture by the European, and the gradual invasion of Maori life by modern materialism, the Maori still retains much of the poetic life of his forefathers. By 'poetic,' one doesn't mean a sentimental enthusing about flowers and moonlight, but rather a life dependent on the forces and powers of Nature—a life governed by poetic justice (which in the end is God's justice) rather than by convention and mere formal justice, which can be no more than man's substitute.

Now this poetic quality is wanting among the European inhabitants, who lack a true right to the land they live in, having, as yet, no deep love of its familiar and unprofitable aspects, nor intimate understanding of its nature as the Maori had, but only a kind of curious patronage of its 'scenery' like any other alien tourist. The machine age and modern education have at once removed the means and killed the desire for identity with the soil, which is the pride and birthright of the native.

For my part, I prefer to write of those, left almost landless by the European, who are still more truly of the land than we who have dispossessed them. Others have written romantically of the old-time Maori culture. These stories deal chiefly with the annihilation of that culture by our scientific barbarism, and the something, pathetic or humorous, that yet remains.

Mr Finlayson is turning his back on Pakeha society because it is cold and callous and convention-ridden, nagged by the clock and obsessed with money and property. And his Maoris embody the antithesis of all these evils, and little else. They are pathetic and humorous, and their lives are 'dependent on the forces and powers of Nature', which means that they are governed by impulse and instinct and are frequently the victims of their own passions. Their passions are simple: love, hate, jealousy, revenge; and because they are simple, Mr Finlayson can only solve their problems by simple expedients. In the twelve stories in *Brown Man's Burden*, two stories end with suicide, there are two murders, one death by makutu and a sudden fatal motor accident, and one story ends with an old man getting his revenge by setting fire to his brother's whare. Mr Finlayson finds pathetic humour in Maori Christianity, when Wi gets the gospel[39]; when Henare, the man of good religion who does not believe in divorce, re-marries twice, on both occasions when the earlier marriage breaks up, and so becomes a trigamist.[40] He is sceptical and amused at Maori efforts to forget old tribal jealousies. He finds such virtue in the carefree life of the village that he appears to be pleased when the slump forces Peta out of his Government clerical job in the city and makes him come home to work at flax-cutting.[41] In another story a Pakeha is made a little more human by a brief acquaintance with the Maori.[42]

Mr Finlayson does not often try to enter the minds of his Maori characters, and when he does he is not convincing: their thoughts seem to be too trite and simple. He is at his best when he is observing and describing, especially scenes that involve a crowd, as in 'The Totara Tree',[43] or in 'Sweet Beulah Land', where a hapu is celebrating the sale of some land to the Government on the Government's terms, celebrating but knowing that it has been tricked,[44] or as in 'The Everlasting Miracle', when a young prophet announces that he will walk the waters, and some swear that he did.[45]

In 'The Totara Tree' a Power Board inspector wants to cut down a totara which is the birth-tree of an old woman Taranga. She climbs the tree and refuses to move.[46] Below her old Uncle Tuna and Panapa, who is presumably of middle age, and younger Taikehu watch with other villagers: the younger ones get excited, dance a haka and inadvertently set fire to the scrub. When they rescue Taranga from the fire they find she has been dead for some time. The villagers bury her under the tree, so that in the end the Power Board has to leave it standing and carry the power lines clear of it.

'The Totara Tree' is successful because Mr Finlayson is describing without comment, and because he catches the tensions within this Maori community, tensions caused by different ways of adjustment to the European occupation. Uncle Tuna is of the oldest generation, as is Taranga herself; he fully believes in tapu; he is angry at the younger generation because of their mad excitement and he tells them that they have been corrupted by Pakeha ways. The younger ones do not pay much heed to Uncle Tuna now; they are caught between two worlds and they express the conflict in humour. Panapa at first sides with the more powerful: the Pakeha's 10,000 volts will make Taranga spring out of the tree; the police will drag her down. But all the same he'll laugh to see her claws on the policeman. The children too rejoice to anticipate the fun. They caress the inspector's car, symbol of his power. The soldiers will come with machine-guns and go r-r-r but Taranga will just swallow the bullets. She is a witch all right, but all the same they don't believe that old witch stuff. But when the inspector threatens them the Maoris become serious. Taikehu, who is Taranga's grandson, has no awe for Taranga but he respects the tapu of her birth-tree.

They express their communal excitement in a haka, but it is a half-humorous one. Later the haka becomes mad and excited and Uncle Tuna, knowing that this haka is a mockery of an old tradition, watches the fire they have started and sneers at this senseless generation of Maoris working their own destruction. Panapa's last comment concedes to the winner of the struggle; the Pakeha may have had 10,000 volts and a police force, but Taranga had cost them thousands *and* thousands of pounds. He is making his judgement in Pakeha terms.

It is Mr Finlayson's natural sympathy for the Maori that gives his stories their virtue; so long as he is sympathetically observing, he is at his best. But we should realise that 'The Totara Tree' is not only concerned with the conflict between Maori values and Pakeha values: it is also a declaration against what we usually call progress. Mr Finlayson does not only want the Auckland Electric Power Board to respect Taranga's tree; he does not want any power-lines at all. He does not ask whether the Maori objection is to offending tapu or to electricity. Yet Te Whiti laid on electricity eighty years ago at Parihaka, and right now I doubt if the people of the East Coast would object to power-lines.

In an essay published two years after *Brown Man's Burden*, *Our Life in this Land* (1940), Mr Finlayson laments the disappearance of the virtues of the pioneering period of New Zealand, what he calls 'free and natural qualities, strength of character, and healthy manhood'. Following the poet D'Arcy Cresswell, he sees science as sorcery and he deplores centralisation of government, the development of telegraph and railways, and all planning of society. So far as he offers any remedy, it is to return to a simple small-holders' agriculture under provincial governments, with horses and no tractors, growing what we need and exporting nothing. It is a romantic anarchism and Mr Finlayson may have outgrown it; but these ideas were in his mind when he wrote 'The Totara Tree'.

And, I think, that would be, from the point of view of the Maori people, the weakness of his attitude: that when he praises their 'cheerful neglect of material surroundings' he is making squalor seem charming. He is persuading us that that one-eighth of Maori houses, the huts and baches and whares, are all right; they like to live like that; good housing would spoil them.[47] He does not like them coming to the city. He is amused at their efforts to help themselves, and the more they try to adjust themselves to the fact of the Pakeha culture, the less he likes it. There is something in common between his attitude and Grace's. It is fair to insist, however, that his point is that there are values more important than material well-being.

Mr Finlayson has written with more recognition of the complexity of the problem in later stories in *Sweet Beulah Land* (1942), showing the degradation of Maoris in city slums or working for market gardeners near the Manukau, and in a recent story 'A Little Gift for Harry' (1952), in which a near-Pakeha's threat to disrupt a Maori community is foiled. In his short novel *Tidal Creek* (1948), he turns mainly to Pakeha characters, as he does again in *The Schooner Came to Atia* (1953), a novel of a Pacific island, presumably in the Cook group. Recently he has written some very good Primary School Bulletins which to my mind are the best historical fiction dealing with Maoris that I have read.

In 'The Totara Tree' it is not always clear whether the characters are speaking in English or translated Maori: one would expect Uncle Tuna to use his own language. In other modern stories the Maoris speak in their own English. This is a difficult thing for a writer to reproduce, unless he has a good ear. It is too easy to slip into a preconceived illiterate English, full of 'py korrys' and 'e hoa'. And the Maori use of English is changing all the time.

Maori English has always presented a problem to the Pakeha writer, though it is increasingly less likely to. Baucke solved the problem by having his character in 'A Quaint Friendship'[48] speak Maori and translating it into a sort of imitation Biblical English, which is nevertheless dignified and stands out against the stale poetry with which his own pretentious journalese is sprigged. Grace's Hone Tiki, Fussell's Henare Tikitanu and Lawlor's Horis all speak an illiterate English, which no doubt had some of its origin in actuality but had the unfortunate effect of reinforcing the impression that they were half-wits. Dick Harris in a preface to Lawlor's *Maori Tales* makes an apology that only half meets the objection:

> Accurately to reproduce the phonetics of unlettered Hori endeavouring to express himself in English would be of no value save, perhaps, to the philologist, and would be a confusion to the many. How incomprehensible to the general reader such conscientious rendering would be is indicated by that distinguished authority on all matters pertaining to the Maori, Mr Elsdon Best. Mr Best, asked to give, as nearly as our alphabet will permit, the actual sounds that would be uttered by Hori in making such a simple statement as: 'I killed a sheep last night if you want to have it', gives this as his phonetic rendering: 'Ai kiri hipi rahe naiti e whiu ana hawhe'.[49]

I will quote one successful attempt to record a more modern Maori English. It is by Magdalene Giles in a story which appeared in a Canterbury students' publication in 1947.[50] A fourteen-year-old Maori girl is talking about school:

> Then one of the girls *scream!* Rick's after her, cause he finish his fight. He run slow, long, slow steps, cause he's *very* big—he's six feet two now, and he's only sixteen yet. There he's running after this girl, I know he won't stop, *never* stop, till he caught her, give her a real good hiding. So I sing out to Edna and Fanny and Annie Riwhi, we go after him. We soon catch him, manhandle him good oh, then we let him go, tell him that's what he get when he bully the girls. He *clear* off home up the hill.

A. P. Gaskell is also successful in reproducing Maori idiom in 'The Picture in the Paper',[51] though one should realise that Sammy, the Maori who is speaking in this case, is also unintelligent:

> Then one day it rain pretty hard. Plenty more rain next day too, so the flood in the river, eh? Muddy too and the water pretty swift. After school young Tuki he take his horse over the ford. All the kids say, 'Don't you go over that ford Tuki'. And he say: 'Too right I go over the ford'. They tell him to go over the swingbridge and leave his horse behind for tomorrow. So me and Miss in school doing sums and all the kids run in and yell, 'Tuki gone over the ford'.

This is a story of a Maori who, pleased that his picture was in the paper when he rescued the teacher from a flooded river, is just as pleased when his picture is in *Truth* after he has converted a car and smashed it. It is not much more than a more subtle picture of the comic ill-adapted Maori, and it would seem to be, for the writer, mainly an exercise in using Maori English.

Mr Gaskell has, however, written one of the best stories to do with Maoris, 'School Picnic' (1947).[52] It gains strength because the writer makes no attempt to see things from the point of view of the Maori characters, but sees things completely through the mind of a Pakeha schoolteacher, though it is plain that his sympathies are not with her. In this story Miss Brown, a teacher relieving at a sole-charge King Country school, reluctantly gives up a Saturday to attend a school picnic organised by the parents. She is the first to arrive. She is disgusted with the food, the old women, the parents and the children. It comes on to rain and they are all crowded in the school-house singing and doing action songs. At last she can stand it no longer and accepting a coat they offer her, heads off in the rain along the four-mile bike-track to the stationmaster's where she boards.

The contrast between the outlook of Miss Brown and that of the Maoris could not be sharper, and the irony of the story is that it is the Maoris who are more civilised than she. She is, as Miss Sturm calls her, a 'sophisticated but uncivilised city bitch'. She is concerned with her clothes and her appearance; her ideal is Joan Crawford looking wizard over a cocktail; no tactic is too dirty for her when she wants George (back in town) and Vonnie threatens to cut her out. She is contemptuous of the elderly, and she cannot talk to the old women. She judges the Maoris by her own mean standards: if the men are laughing, she suspects that they are telling dirty yarns. She isn't interested in babies, though she is prepared to have one to make George marry. She won't object if the whole Maori race perishes; and she'd feel much safer if they acted like the comic Maori of the illustrated papers. Selfish and sophisticated pleasure is her ambition: pictures, launch-trips and bathing, cocktails, boyfriends, all as symbols of what she calls the civilised life. Her values have been created by Hollywood, *Vogue* magazine, popular songs and the advertisements.

At first reading, she makes you angry; but at second, she comes through as a comic figure. The irony of the story is that the Maoris are enjoying themselves and she isn't, that it is she who retreats, biking off through the rain to get away from what she calls a pack of bloody savages. It is the Maori scale of values that emerges as the stronger.

Mr Te Hau explained to me that in any situation a Maori is confronted with two codes of values, two courses of action, Maori and Pakeha; and that which one he chooses depends on the time, the place and the circumstances. Mr. Gaskell seems to understand this, because the two codes are there: the men organising the races and going out into the bushes for some beer, the women insisting on providing Miss Brown's dinner but, instead of the traditional Maori food, giving her a pie in place of her own dainty lunch. You can see the double code in the words of Terari, the first of the parents to arrive. He opens with a welcoming remark that could be applicable to Maori or Pakeha company:

'Hello, Miss Brown ... You the first one here? Look nobody else here. You pretty keen on these picnic, eh?'

'You said ten o'clock, and look at it, nearly eleven.' Her eyes focussed, hardened.

So Terari switches to her point of view:

'Crikey, that late? By golly I ring the bell. Wake them up. Those lazy Maori must sleep in, eh? You can't trust those Maori. Always late.'

Of course, he may be pulling her leg, but he is anticipating all her objections, too. Terari has made such a gracious concession: what *could* Miss Brown say to that?

But then he's back to the Maori point of view.

'You didn't light the fire?'

It may be that he thought that was a woman's job; or it may be that he simply looked on her as one of the working party at the picnic.

'I certainly didn't light the fire.'

And, always resourceful, adaptable, not to be perturbed by mishaps like this, Terari says, 'Nemind'.

And you can see the two codes operating in the climax of the story, when Terari is posturing an action song in front of her and she slaps his face. Both the audience and Terari are speechless. Had it been a Maori who had insulted him, Terari might have taken offence, but here they solve the tension in laughter, and Terari clowns his way out of it. A lot of Maori jocularity comes from having to live in two worlds at once. And as Douglas Stewart says in his story,[53] 'understanding is easier than anger'. They were turning on a picnic for the kids, and bad feeling would have spoilt the day.

But again, the Maoris in this story, for all the accurate observation of detail, are stereotypes: they represent hospitality, generosity, unhurriedness, enjoyment of life, and a communal spirit. They are not so simple as Mr Finlayson's Maoris, but they are still simple. Within the limits of the story, however, you could hardly ask for a complex picture of the Maori. And I don't think it fair to ask, as Miss Sturm did, are they always as happy as this, on the days when there are no picnics? have they no anxieties and problems?—because this story is concerned with the picnic, not with days when there are no picnics, and mainly with Miss Brown the teacher, not with the Maoris.

Douglas Stewart's 'The Whare' goes deeper and recognises a complexity in the minds of his Maoris. This is the only Maori story in his collection, *A Girl with Red Hair*, published in Sydney in 1944. It concerns a young man trudging the roads in the depression of the thirties, who drifts into a Maori settlement near the Kaipara Harbour. He is offered permanent hospitality with an old couple who live in a flea-infested whare, who talk vaguely of him perhaps marrying a Maori girl, of working together on contract cutting rushes, of some day pouring boiling water on the fleas. He becomes panicky at the prospect of endlessly living with people whose thoughts he cannot share, and slips away in the night, leaving a note of apology. His story is of Maoris who have not had much contact with the Pakeha; like Mr Finlayson, he can still refer to them as natives.[54] He doesn't romanticise or sentimentalise over the Maori way of life: he acknowledges the fleas, which Mr Finlayson would have thought unimportant. He neither approves nor disapproves of the man who has been college-educated returning to his village. He is aware that another generation might break the tradition of unquestioning hospitality. He is honestly enough rooted in Pakeha prejudice, when he notices that the old man's features were almost European, to say that he had 'the stamp of aristocracy' in his features. He is dismally conscious of the lack of common ground on which he and his hosts can meet; and there is among the three of them only the 'primitive human sympathy', 'that deep mindless sympathy', the 'dark tide of physical sympathy' touched with a vague sadness, while the rain drums on the iron roof.

It obviously isn't the fleas that drive him away, or the possibility of falling in love with a Maori girl. It is the fear of being trapped by their hospitality, of becoming a Pakeha Maori living with them but not belonging. It is this that puts him in a state of 'queer urgency, almost panic'. It would be for him a retreat from his own culture to have to sit and rely on that physical sympathy and not understand the complexity of their thoughts, as they would not understand his. And so he sneaks off in the night, feeling guilty.

This is a sensitive story because it touches a sensitive point of race relations; only it asks no questions, it goes no further. And again it is the Pakeha who is retreating. Was he justified, or was the challenge too much for him of having to attempt to bridge a gulf, to understand another conception of life, to adjust himself to another culture and outlook? I don't know. But it is worth thinking about. We couldn't expect him to give up his own culture completely. But there are many Pakehas who expect the Maori to do that.

In contrast to Mr. Stewart's story there is James Forsyth's 'The Roofs of Dargaville' (1947)[54a], that expresses the ignorant fear of the well-suited Pakeha: a commercial traveller in Dargaville is lured to visit the bach of some young Maoris who then try to overpower him and rob him. I don't believe that this story reflects any knowledge of Maoris: it is more likely what the writer thought would happen if he did dare to associate with Maoris.

A very recent development has been stories which treat not of Maori villages but of brief chance meetings with Maoris by writers who, because they distrust sentimental preconceptions of the Maoris, simply observe and record with a sympathetic detachment, not cold, but not warm either, nor very informed. O. E. Middleton's 'Discrepancies' (1951)[55] observes the discrepancies caused by the double set of values mentioned by Mr Te Hau, and his 'A Day by Itself' (1952)[56] seems to carry a faint regret that the two Maoris he meets are engrossed in an old motor-bike and lack his own preference for an unhurried, unmechanical life. In 'It Happens Here' (1951), however, he is warm with anger at finding a hotel bar that refuses to serve Maoris.[57] Maurice Duggan's 'Chapter' (1955)[58] observes with detached accuracy the conduct and attitudes of some Maori youths off to a dance somewhere in Northland, singing sentimental Hawaiian songs, enjoying themselves drunkenly and mindlessly. The advantage of this approach is that it avoids the presentation of ready-made types. There is the novel of Sylvia Ashton-Warner, *Spinster* (1958), and a few stories,[59] expressing a teacher's bewildered admiration for the hectic energy of her Maori and part-Maori schoolchildren, their directness of feeling and their involvement with one another.

Increasingly, as more young Maoris move to or grow up in the cities, as more young North Island Maoris move to the South Island as tradesmen, apprentices, and other workers, one must expect to find that younger writers write of Maori characters not as members of a Maori community, as Mr Finlayson, Mr Gaskell and Mr Stewart have done, but as individuals they have known or worked with.

Sometimes such characters as they appear in some recent stories seem little more than brown Pakehas with easier consciences and friendlier faces; a sort of young Pakeha man's ideal of the decent joker. Certainly there is little appreciation that their background is very different, and none at all of tribal affiliation: these writers not only do not know, but do not think it matters, whether their characters are Ngapuhi or Ngati-Porou. At times the writers are regretful that the Maori character does not share a Pakeha character's concern for something, that the image they have seen is in fact an imperfect reflection. Thus Brian Fox in 'Talk to Them' (1957)[60] writes as a trade unionist who, though he likes Maoris, is concerned at Maori labourers who provide scab labour during industrial disputes: he solves the problem by inventing one union-conscious Maori worker who, though he has been sacked from his work for assaulting a unionist who had been baiting some young Maoris fresh from the country, goes to the Community Centre and talks all night to them and wins their support for the 'go-slow' on the job from which he has been sacked. Mr Fox, like the vicar of Waiuku before him, has solved a problem by creating a Maori after his own desire.* A more convincing story by a Pakeha who calls

---

* I do not suggest that there are not, or cannot be, Maori workers as loyal to union principles as other workers. My objection is that it is unlikely that a man sacked from his job will show so much interest in militating for better conditions on that job.

himself 'Ngawha'[61] is of a worker who is pained to hear his young Maori friend echo his foreman in expressions of anti-Semitism and resolves to tell him that he himself is a Jew from East London. Maurice Shadbolt's Mick in 'The Funniest Thing' (1957) cannot awaken any response in his fellow scrub-cutter Rangi to his garrulous speculations on life, death and the extent of the universe. In David Anderson's story 'The Stuff of Life' (1958) the Pakeha corporal is disappointed that the Maori lance-corporal will not help him in trying to prevent a cruel mob-attack by other soldiers on a soldier who is imbecile and doesn't wash: the implication seems to be that Pukaki the lance-corporal (who is little more than the stereotype of a cheerful, loyal fellow with an outsize penis) understands, as the corporal does not, that life involves cruelty.

The stories that I think are most successful in their treatment of Maori characters are two by Magdalene Giles and one by Maurice Shadbolt. In 'School' (1947)[62] Miss Giles gives a warm and realistic account of life among the pupils of a Maori school; it is amusing, and in a human way. In 'Old Sam' (1947)[63] she creates a sympathetic and dignified old man living away from his hapu with his daughter; though he has refused to return home, where there is no peace for him, his sons are coming to take him, but he dies on the morning they arrive. Both these stories are imbued with experience and understanding of Maoris, and a spontaneous sympathy otherwise only found in Grace and Mr Finlayson.

In Maurice Shadbolt's 'End of Season' (1956), a young Maori footballer, who works on his father's farm, who has two close Pakeha friends (but apparently, apart from his girl-friend, no close Maori friends of his own age), is killed at football. There is the tangi and burial and the story is concerned with the effect of Sammy Kahu's death on those who loved him. What I think is distinctive in this story's treatment of a Maori is the successful blending of an appreciation of Sammy as an individual and not a stereotype, with some knowledge and understanding of a different culture. It is, I suppose, not a spectacular achievement, and as an ideal for the Pakeha writer, it is a modest one. Yet that is probably, as yet, all the Pakeha writer can fairly do, observe with sympathy, be accurate in his observations, try to understand and be honest in his conclusions. As Miss Sturm puts it, if he uses Maoris as symbols, they must be true and significant symbols. But I think he is on dangerous ground if he uses them as symbols at all.

For an expression of an authentic Maori outlook we must look to Maori writers. The quarterly *Te Ao Hou* has recently published a number of such stories, and this opens the possibility of Maoris being attracted to fiction as a form of expression.

One of these stories, 'For All the Saints' by J. C. Sturm (1955), is written in English and is a sympathetic character-study in the European tradition, of a hospital cook who is a bit odd and is finally committed. Of two that won prizes in 1956, one by Hirone Wikiriwhi is written first in Maori and is a warm account in the traditional style, with references to traditions and old poetry, of the royal visit to Waitangi, Turangawaewae and Rotorua.[64] The other by Mason Durie is in English and is a moral tale warning Maori students against loafing when there's swot to be done.[65] By European standards it is a tract rather than a story, but we must remember that a Maori writer at the present time probably feels that he must serve and help his people with his pen and that the standards we apply to the short story might seem to him to be dilettante and unfruitful. It is perhaps indicative of the current attitudes of older educated Maoris that prizes should have been awarded to moralistic stories. Another prize-winner, in 1957, by S. M. Mead[66] tries to deal with the problem of young Maoris who come to the city and take to crime: instead of arresting a lad running from a burglary, a constable, too good to be probable, lets him off, helps to put him on the right path and for that occasion fulfils the role of *kaumatua*.

Far more promising (by European literary standards) are those stories that express the Maori attitudes to life which have escaped the Pakeha writer. They are written in English. In two autobiographical stories, Rora Paki reminisces on experiences which would be unfamiliar to the Pakeha[67]: being brought up by two grandparents, two aunts and an uncle; the atmosphere of loving comradeship in a hapu; children feeling free to wander from home to home since all the old women were grannies one way or another; a girl marrying a cousin not because either of them wanted to but because the parents of both wanted it, and settling down, nevertheless, to a happy married life; trying to keep the house big enough for a family that increased almost every year. Four stories by Rowley Habib are moving and evocative, written in the European tradition of the short story: of a young boy's hope that when he is as old as his brother he too will be as attractive to the girls;[68] of a fatal accident at a sawmill;[69] of citified relations who are prepared to sell their dead brother's farm over the heads of his children;[70] and one of the burial of a boy's father.[71] The stories are not only very good in their own right; they express experiences whose full meaning is otherwise inaccessible to the Pakeha. One cannot imagine in a Pakeha community the bereft boy finding comfort away from his mother:

> Then Willy Hagg began to shovel the earth back into the grave and as the first lot hit the coffin, it echoed hollowly and loudly, and their mother lurched forward with a small cry, her eyes wide and frightening. The two women held her and she almost fell. And Pane spoke to her sharply.
> At the sight of his mother Kurram felt a sudden horrible shock run through him. And in desperate bewilderment he turned about looking

for somewhere to go. Then he felt someone quite close beside him and
he looked up. His cousin Paul stood over him and he said to the boy,
'Never mind Cur you hold on to me.'
He put his arms around the boy and the boy put his face against
his cousin's shirt and began to cry. Paul stood for a while letting the
bôy cry then he began to squeeze his shoulders and say,
'Never mind, Cur. It's all over now. Don't cry now.'

Again there is, running through this passage, a sense of belonging:

By the apple trees a group of women were busying themselves with
their shawls. Two of them were lifting their babies onto their backs,
and they bounced them around a little to settle them more comfortably
in the blankets. Down by the Hepis' fence the priest was talking with
old Doc and Tita. He was gesturing slowly with his hands and now
and then he would look off across the paddock at the sun. Every one
was talking about the beautiful day, everything except the burial.

A Pakeha writer describing the same situation might have been arrested
by aspects of the scene unfamiliar to him and have sought a metaphor
for the women with the babies in their shawls, an image that would make
them memorable and fix them, like a tourist's camera, for all time, and in
such a way that no deeper meaning could be penetrated.

At the present time a Maori writer is more likely to prefer English as
his medium, yet he is likely to come up against the problem of reaching
an audience: conscious of speaking *for* his people, he may find that he is
speaking *to* only a few of them. This is a problem that the Maori writer
will have to deal with himself.

At the same time, if Pakehas want to appreciate the authentic expression
of Maori values, they must make an effort of understanding in relation to
Maori culture, so that the Maori writer can write for a Pakeha audience
as well as a Maori audience without having to adopt a different set of
values. And when this effort has been made, and the Maori writer is sure
of a wide and sympathetic audience, then we may expect some writing
that may well have qualities that Pakeha writing lacks.

Notes

1. As a pakeha I felt it necessary to seek the opinions of three Maoris on the stories
   from which this study took its start, i.e. those reprinted in Davin, D.M.
   (ed.), *New Zealand Short Stories*, Oxford, London 1953.
   To these three people, Miss J.C. Sturm, Mr Matiu te Hau and Mr Hirone
   Wikiriwhi I acknowledge my indebtedness.
2. Sorrenson, M.P.K., 'Land Purchase Methods and their Effect on Maor
   Population, 1865–1901', *Journal of Polynesian Society*, 65, 1956, pp. 188–99.

3. Sinclair, Keith, *A History of New Zealand*, Penguin, Harmondsworth 1959, p. 114.
4. *Appendix to the Journals of the House of Representatives* 1906: H-31, p. 67.
5. See note 3.
6. Curnow, Allen (ed.), *A Penguin Book of New Zealand Verse*, 1960, p. 72. The passages quoted are from Alfred Domett's *Ranolf and Amohia. A South-Sea Day-Dream*, Smith, Elder & Co., London 1872, pp. 88, 94; and *New Zealand Parliamentary Debates* 1860, p. 213.
7. Baughan, B.E., 'Pipi on the Prowl', 'A Grandmother Speaks', *Brown Bread From a Colonial Oven*, Whitcombe & Tombs, London 1912.
8. Grace, Alfred A., *Tales of a Dying Race*, Chatto & Windus, London 1901, p. 90.
9. Grace 1901: 'Told in the Puia', 'Why Castlelard Took to the Blanket'.
10. Grace, Alfred A., 'Hira', *Maoriland Stories*, Alfred B. Betts, Nelson 1895.
11. Grace 1901: 'Te Wiria's Potatoes', reprinted in Davin 1953.
12. Grace 1901: 'Pirihira'.
13. B[aucke], W[illiam], *Where the White Man Treads Across the Pathway of the Maori*, Wilson & Horton, Auckland 1905, reissued 1928. 'A Quaint Friendship' was reprinted in Davin 1953.
14. *Monthly Abstract of Statistics*, 30 September 1958, p. 13.
15. *New Zealand Official Yearbook* 1957.
16. The 1957 figures are from the *New Zealand Official Yearbook* 1958.
17. *New Zealand Population Census* 1951, VIII, pp. 63, 65. The statistics show 3.36% Maoris earning £700 or more in a year, against 18.6% pakeha; 12.06% Maoris living in huts, whares and baches, against 2.08% pakeha.
18. Gillespie, O.N. (ed.), *New Zealand Short Stories*, J.M. Dent, London 1930. There are 32 stories in all. The hostile one is by Maori Mac.
19. Grace 1895: 'The Chief's Daughter', 'Reta the Urukehu'.
20. Hyde, Robin (Iris Wilkinson), 'A Ceiling of Amber', in Gillespie 1930; 'The Little Bridge' in Allen, C.R. (ed.), *Tales by New Zealanders*, British Authors' Press, London 1938.
21. Weston, Jessie, *Ko Meri: or a Cycle of Cathay*, Eden, Remington & Co., London 1890, p. 365.
22. It is probable that there were in fact no liaisons between Maori men and white women well-bred enough to qualify as models for fiction. Grace's Hone Tiki thought so and had his explanation: the pakeha woman did not attract the Maori man since she was thin, ugly, too talkative and unsubmissive, whereas the pakeha man preferred the Maori woman because she was plump, quiet, kind and submissive.
23. Lancaster, G.B., 'The Story of Wi' in Allen 1938.
24. Gries, Joan, *An Outline of Prose Fiction in New Zealand* (2 vols. unpubl. doctoral thesis, University of Auckland, 1953), vol. 2, p. 237.
25. Lawlor, Pat (ed.), *Maori Tales. A Collection of Over One Hundred Stories*, New Century Press Ltd, Sydney 1926, p. 121.
26. Fussell, J.C., *Letters from Private Henare Tikitanu* (2nd ed.), Worthington & Co., Auckland 1917.
27. *ibid.*, pp. 11, 26, 28.
28. Lawson, Henry, 'A Daughter of Maoriland' in *The Antipodean*, 3, 1897. Reprinted in *Over the Sliprails*, Angus & Robertson, Sydney 1900, and included in *The Prose Works of Henry Lawson*, Angus & Robertson, Sydney 1948.
29. Lawson 1948: pp. 283-4, 285.
30. I have considered the facts behind this story more fully in *Henry Lawson Among Maoris*, A.N.U. Press 1968.
31. Maori Mac, 'Harry Kingi's Broken Vow' in Gillespie 1930; and von Keisenberg, 'Within Sight of Kapiti' in Allen 1938.

32. 'Harry Kingi's Broken Vow'.
33. McEldowney, Dennis, 'By the Lake', *Book*, 9. Reprinted in Davin 1953.
34. In Allen 1938.
35. In Allen 1938.
36. The four preceding quotations are in order from *The Journal of Katherine Mansfield*, (ed. J. Middleton Murry), Constable, London 1954, pp. 24, 30, 29, 29.
37. Mansfield, Katherine, *Something Childish and Other Stories*, Constable, London 1924.
38. Sargeson, Frank, *Conversations with My Uncle*, The Unicorn Press, Auckland 1936.
39. Finlayson, Roderick, 'Wi Gets the Gospel', *Brown Man's Burden*, The Unicorn Press, Auckland 1938.
40. 'A Man of Good Religion', *ibid*.
41. 'On Top of the Hill', *ibid*.
42. 'Standards of Living', *ibid*.
43. *ibid*.
44. Finlayson, Roderick, *Sweet Beulah Land*, The Griffin Press, Auckland 1942.
45. Finlayson, Roderick, *Tidal Creek*, Angus & Robertson, Sydney 1948.
46. Mr te Hau tells me that the story recalls a real incident in the King Country when an old woman who allowed a mining company to lay a loco-track through her land claimed a higher royalty than she was given and lay for three days across the tracks to prevent the loco passing.
47. At the time of which Mr Finlayson was writing, the proportion of Maori dwellings of one or two rooms was over a half, and if one adds temporary dwellings the proportion was 67% (*New Zealand Population Census*, 1926, XIV; 8–9). The corresponding figures for pakeha dwellings were 9.1% and 13.5% (*ibid*. XIII: 4).
48. William Baucke 1905.
49. Pat Lawlor 1926, p. 9.
50. Giles, Magdalene, 'School', *Canterbury Lambs* 2, 1947.
51. Gaskell, A.P., 'The Picture in the Paper', *New Zealand New Writing*, 1. Reprinted in Gaskell, *The Big Game and Other Stories*, the Caxton Press, Christchurch 1947.
52. Reprinted in Davin 1953.
53. Stewart, Douglas, 'The Whare', *A Girl with Red Hair and Other Stories*, Angus & Robertson, Sydney 1944. Reprinted in Davin 1953.
54. The word was in official use in New Zealand until 1947.
54a. In *Book*, 9.
55. In *Landfall*, 5.
56. *In Landfall*, 6. Reprinted in Middleton, O.E., *Short Stories*, The Handcraft Press, Wellington 1953.
57. In *Landfall*, 5.
58. In *Landfall*, 9. Reprinted in Duggan, Maurice, *Immanuel's Land*, The Pilgrim Press, Auckland 1956.
59. 'Agonies', *Here and Now*, 47, 1955; 'The Least Thing', *Here and Now*, 49, 1956; 'Floor', *Here and Now*, 51, 1956.
60. In *Fernfire*, 1, 1957.
61. 'Morning Lift', *Fernfire*, 1, 1957.
62. In *Canterbury Lambs*, 2.
63. *ibid*.
64. Wikiriwhi, Hirone Te M., 'He Korero Hararei' ('A Holiday Story'), *Te Ao Hou*, 4, nos. 2–3, 1956.
65. Durie, Mason, 'I Failed the Test of Life', *Te Ao Hou*, 4, no. 2, 1956.
66. Mead, S.M., 'Constable McFarland', *Te Ao Hou*, 5, no. 2, 1957.

67. Paki, Rora, 'Ka Pu Te Ruha Ka Hao Te Rangatahi' ('The Old Net is Cast Aside, A New Net Goes Afishing'), *Te Ao Hou*, 4, No. 3, 1956 – the story is in English; 'A Home is Made', *Te Ao Hou*, 5, no. 3, 1957.
68. 'Love in the Mill', *Te Ao Hou*, 5, no. 3, 1957.
69. 'Death in the Mill', *Te Ao Hou*, 4, no. 3, 1956.
70. 'The Visitors', *Te Ao Hou*, 5, no. 4, 1957.
71. 'The Burial', *Te Ao Hou*, 5, no. 2, 1957.

O.E. Middleton's Stories

Mr Middleton has developed a great deal since his more modest and sketchy *Short Stories* of 1953. His aim in his new collection is still modest, but the five stories, one of which is quite long, are both deeper and more extensive in their range than the earlier stories.

The common subject of the five stories is awe in the face of unexpected, often tragic, experience. Billy is surprised at his own temerity in giving the Maori skeleton a decent burial and is not altogether clear why he does it; another boy is awed when Mr Larsen accidentally shoots his favourite pig-dog; Donald Skinner is overtaken by the events of his childhood and adolescence and runs away from their consequences; the corporal is impressed by the Prof's devotion to his brother and shocked by his suicide; Tony feels a religious reverence when he is involved in the common mysteries of fatherhood and bereavement. It is the mystery of living that concerns Mr Middleton and each of his protagonists comes out of his experience with a discovery, a freshly-learned lesson that owes nothing to what he has been told by others, and everything to his own attempt to digest the experience. Tony, after the birth and death of his first child, is not, and can never be, the same man that he was at the beginning of the story.

Mr Middleton's theme involves a limitation of range; it means that he has to confine his characters to states of mind that are, in no derogatory sense, naive: there are two boys, one adolescent, a corporal confronted with a philosophy of life he doesn't quite comprehend, and a young married man going through experiences for the first time in his life, finding his bearings without the help of a chart. The stories are told either in the first person, or in the third but seen through the mind of the main character. The advantage of this simplicity and subjectivity is that each experience, however familiar it may be in life and literature, comes through freshly,

---

This essay was first published in *Mate* 4, February 1960, as a review of O.E. Middleton's *The Stone and Other Stories* (The Pilgrim Press).

without preconceptions or sophistication. Mr Middleton writes with humility towards his subject matter, even to the experience of the discomfort of a long bus-ride after neglecting to relieve oneself, or the pride of a father in making his first cot. The stories are honest, free from pose or sentimentality. The story of Mr Larsen and his dog might have been sentimental if its real subject wasn't the effect of the experience on the boy who tells the story. The story of the married man might easily have become sentimental or melodramatic, touching as it does the most ordinary and the most meaningful experiences of life—love, parenthood, birth and death, and yet Mr Middleton walks sure-footed through it all, with a naivety and honesty that belong quite naturally to him.

Most of the stories are set in the country; even the married man, though he is a city worker and can discuss Dr Grantly Dick Read with his wife, is a simple, unsophisticated fellow. One finds it hard to imagine Mr Middleton writing of sophisticated urban life or of complicated people, yet his sureness of essentials might enable him to do so.

Of the five stories, the title-piece and 'A Married Man' are the most engrossing. In neither 'First Adventure' nor 'A Bit of Bad Luck' does the experience affect the reader as much as it affects the protagonist. Even in 'The Stone' I have one quibble: Miro's appearance in Auckland, on the arm of an American serviceman, so shortly after her departure from home because of illness is not satisfactorily explained — was the illness pregnancy? If it wasn't, did she return home before she went to Auckland? What did she tell her father? One can make guesses and fill the gap, but I feel that some hint of an explanation could have been offered. The most serious lapse is a more obvious one, in 'The Corporal's Story'. Mr Middleton no doubt understands the mentality of this intellectual soldier, loyal to his conscientious-objector brother and living apart from his fellow-soldiers. Yet one cannot accept (and one doubts if the author accepts) the Prof's objection to the padre taking the name of Jove in vain. In what way do the Prof's actions reflect any devotion to Zeus? Nor can one accept his plunge into the crater like Empedocles — the imitation is not only too consciously literary (and foreign to Mr Middleton's kind of writing), but its literary model, Arnold's Empedocles, is himself, in his fatal plunge, a little comic and unconvincing. There is one discrepancy: Arnold's Empedocles, so far as he believed in Zeus at all, was no admirer of his 'subtle, contriving head'. Yet this lapse of Mr Middleton's is so obvious that rather than irritating one, it puts one in a good mood; it does not destroy the authenticity of the rest of the story.

Mr Middleton's style is the flexible vernacular of the Frank Sargeson tradition, and a great deal of thought has gone into it. The language acts as a faithful medium of transmission of the experience and the mind of each protagonist. At no stage does it come between the reader and the experience. Neither is the background over-played. The stories belong to

New Zealand, mainly the King Country and inland Taranaki, but the author's concern is with *living* in New Zealand, an indivisible experience to him, and the background is taken for granted.

Mr Middleton is engrossed in his subject, and his stories engross the reader rather than move him dramatically. Mr Middleton's special quality is his natural sympathy for ordinary, uncomplicated people, for common desires and simple experiences. His whole achievement is neither brilliant nor spectacular, but is satisfying, healthy and honest. It is over two years since these stories were finished and one looks forward to what, one presumes, has been written since.

The book is attractively produced by The Pilgrim Press and illustrated by Dennis Turner.

A Mixed Performance

After all the éclat it is necessary to pass a cool eye over Mr Shadbolt's achievement, to see it not as some sudden exotic, blooming for a summer on London book-stands, but as work that has some relationship to New Zealand and is to be measured in the light of the New Zealand writing that London has not heard of.

The title alone stakes a grand claim; from that and from the setting of the stories one would expect some picture of New Zealand life: two of the eleven stories are set in the North Island backblocks, one at a Hokianga harbourside settlement, one in a North Island small town, one in a King Country mining town, three in Wellington or Auckland. There are three others set in London and Prague. Yet the total impression is one of disappointing confusion. The performance is so uneven that it is necessary to consider the stories separately.

The best stories are the first four (all of them set in the country) and of these the best is 'The Strangers', which poses a contrast between the ambitions of a young Maori and a pakeha farmer. I have said elsewhere that Mr Shadbolt is rare among New Zealand writers in that he does not use Maori characters as symbols or make them stereotypes: in this story Tui comes close to being a stereotype and there is something symbolic about him, yet there is a legitimate purpose in this. The theme of Maori-pakeha relations occurs in several stories: it is there, rather nebulously, in 'A Woman's Story', where the girl's close relationship with Ruia is part of her identification with her Northland environment, and it recurs, melodramatically, in 'The Waters of the Moon', where the liaison between the middle-aged teacher and her adolescent pupil is the source of her peace and identification with Northland. Yet, even in the best stories in the collection, there is a certain arbitrariness of theme and a lack of direction. The theme of 'The Woman's Story'—the rejection of 'Home'—is no longer

This essay was first published in *Comment*, Autumn 1960, as a review of Maurice Shadbolt's *The New Zealanders* (Gollancz and Whitcombe & Tombs 1959).

a real one, and it only gets any force in this story from the fabrication of a very unusual factor—that the girl's mother, who resented Northland, brought the girl up to think that she would eventually settle in England. The main advantage of the theme here is that it provides a thread on which to hang a good deal of interesting local background and history. Mr Shadbolt has tried to supply the story with a clearer direction than it has by inflating the ending, turning the girl's acceptance of her homeland into a 'moment of revelation' which almost knocks her over, though in fact she had realised six pages earlier she was a New Zealander.

'Love Story' too is impressive and moving, and its ending is free from false dramatics; if it does not go deep or tell us anything new about delinquency, it is a picture of small-town adolescent life and adolescent injustice: but again the conditions from which the injustice springs are arbitrary and untypical—Paul's mother with her continual catechism about her love for him, and the character of Gloria's mother is improvised rather than convincing. In 'After the Depression' the point is the hopeless dedication of the militant unionist and the privations it causes his wife and child, but in this case the choice of technique—observing him from a rigid distance, like a film without score or commentary—prevents one from getting to know the man's mind.

In 'The Paua Gatherers' and 'Knock on Yesterday's Door' Mr Shadbolt moves to city life among young drifters, and the theme is their search for themselves and some kind of sexual arrangement which will disturb neither their vanity nor their right to infidelity. These stories of vain, wise-cracking, frightened men and level-headed women are inflated as if their self-made dilemmas were important. A more perceptive writer might have made one care whether Ann kept sleeping with Tim or went off with Ted, or might have made one understand what Val saw in Roger. The technique of 'Knock on Yesterday's Door'—moments of the present in slow motion sandwiched between long lapses into flashback—is quite ably handled.

In 'Play the Fife Lowly' the contrast now is between sensible women and empty-headed men, ex-college boys who know what they want and where they are going. There is some ambiguity in this story: if Tom, the homosexual desecrator of the college ikons, is meant to be preferable, he is nevertheless objectionable in the way he makes use of his Maori friends (they were Islanders in the *Landfall* version of the story) to further his own vindictive ends. Nor is it likely, in spite of Tom's bossiness, that the Maoris would have stayed so long at the party, singing and dancing, when they were made so unwelcome. The ending too is unnecessarily ambiguous: when Helen and Sylvia reach a moment of understanding, does it mean only that they have rejected their ex-college boy-friends, or more? If the point is worth making, it is worth making unambiguously.

The remaining New Zealand story 'The Waters of the Moon' is an unashamed exploitation of the exotic. Mr Shadbolt appropriates the name of Te Waiotemarama and confers it on Opononi or Omapere. He introduces not only the middle-aged teacher in love with her pupil, but also a lesbian nymphomaniac from Auckland, a sick retired journalist almost in love with the teacher, a mad old man who sits on the verandah of his house (where Hobson, Wakefield and Samuel Marsden had called) looking through a telescope for steamers that never come. What direction this story has comes from the question, posed by Cheryl and wondered about by Mr Fail: how is Isobel so calm and happy and what does she do for sex? It is essentially a vulgar question, and the ending when it brings the answer is overdone: the answer kills Mr Fail.

The other stories are set in Europe. 'Maria' is about a young smart-alec who thinks he has all the answers but is really afraid. 'Thank You Goodbye' is a slight and sentimental sketch of the parting of a Czech girl and a British visitor who had been to bed with her. The slickness of this piece depends on the gimmick by which their relationship is neatly expressed by the few phrases of English that the waiter knows. Mr Shadbolt's main interest in the story would seem to be its setting in a Communist city— which is described very superficially as a brief visitor might see it—and the foreign English of the Czech girl.

By far the worst story is 'River, Girl and Onion', which is embarrassing. Fabrication has become fanciful, spun out of emptiness. In this story, written in what is probably meant to be a style of witty irony, we are invited to connive in arch attitudes to sexual and political behaviour more factitious than real. None of the characters is real: each embodies a pose and each has been improvised from an invention that owes little to observation.

All this adds up to an unsureness of direction and purpose, reflected in the changes in stance and style, in ambiguous or worked-up endings, in the uncertainty whether to be flippant or serious in 'River, Girl and Onion', in the fact that in 'Love Story' the author, while he knows the motives of all other characters, only speculates on those of Mr Jackson, in his determination to believe that there are only two valid intellectual responses to the modern world, either the certainties of Communism or the uncertainties of smart bohemianism.

But if the author is unsure of himself, he is sure of everything else. He has that sort of confidence by which a feature journalist overrides subtleties and complexities in his topic. With as little diffidence as he introduces dialogue in Czech, Russian and Spanish, he can refer to Maori as 'a language almost forgotten', and write of '1350, the year of the great Polynesian migration.' He even writes with assurance about life in pre-revolutionary Russia. Too frequently he feels obliged to process the experience for the reader, to get between the reader and the experience with his own confident interpretation.

Mr Shadbolt does not dare to doubt his own preconceptions, and some of them are immature: Grafton beatniks are more vital people than undergraduates; the university is a sterile morgue of learning where lecturers pretend that Marx never existed; feeling is better than thinking: creation better than criticism; bohemianism is as valid as Communism. Such attitudes act as a barrier to the exploration of his characters: he has them all weighed up before he starts; they are idealised or dismissed in terms of his ready prejudices. There are few discoveries in his stories: the ending of 'Maria' does no more than reinforce what one knew from the beginning, that the hero's cleverness was inadequate. Where Mr Shadbolt should go deeper he usually adds; instead of revealing or exploring further depths of his characters, he adds details of biography or other incidentals, even to Mrs Benjamin's opinion of Franco, or the potted dossiers ('Joe, who wrote morbid sketches about rapes and suicides until the day he took a job in an advertising agency and then slashed his wrists seriously enough to be taken to a mental hospital;') which incidentally have the effect of implying a New Zealand urban life more complex and sophisticated than in fact it is.

The style itself, especially in the earlier stories, calls for some objection. Far from faithfully transmitting the experience, it acts as a screen. There are such fruity passages as 'leafy curtains of evergreen', 'fathomless landscapes of the heart'; such women's magazine stuff as 'her face twisting against him', 'tears stung her eyes', 'her teeth flashing'; such reverberant periphrases as 'one hand had fisted tightly around sand'. He has a fondness for verbs too dramatic to be exact: thunder slams, stars pepper the sky, air rasps a running girl's throat and feet hammer behind her, a hand gashes the mist on a carriage window, fire blooms blue-grey smoke. It is as if the writer has believed those manuals of advertising copy-writing that tell you that verbs are the most vivid and meaningful words in the language. Even more irritating is the trick of using intransitive verbs transitively and in unusual contexts—'the wind purred the dry grasses', 'feet scribbling the water', 'water glistens pale bodies'. Some of the verbs are repeated in so many ways that their vagueness of meaning becomes apparent: a fantail flickers, the glare of a match flickers Ann's face, light flickers the sea, lightning flickers the windows, a crowd flickers the light from headlamps; Ruia's head is snapped back as she dances, Ann snaps on the radio, the wind snaps a wind-breaker, a lock snaps shut, Mr Fail's body snaps into motion; feet and bicycle wheels alike husk over dry grass; a lawnmower chatters, a typist chatters the keys, Ann chatters dishes through soapy water, a sea-breeze chatters the pines; a breeze whispers curtains, Val's limbs whisper. One could go on. There is something essentially journalistic in this, an attempt to impress. But, far from being more vivid, the effect is misty. Mr Shadbolt is lacking in what is surely an indispensable quality in a writer, a feeling for the language. And the attitude to the reader is not one of equality, but rather condescending.

All these devices show that Mr Shadbolt is a self-conscious writer, with an audience closely in mind. That the audience is sometimes the English is indicated by his confident explanatory asides on Auckland ('that squat impassive city sprawled casually over a green South Pacific isthmus'), the West Coast ('a lawless part of the country'), on Hauhauism, and the 'great Polynesian migration.' But in the cosmopolitan stories he seems to have a New Zealand audience in mind. One cannot avoid the suspicion that Mr Shadbolt wanted to impress the English that he was not one of them, but of a sturdy independent race that had long cut itself free; and at the same time wanted to impress the locals with his travels, his snippets from foreign phrase-books, his understanding of the big world where things are happening. Nor can one avoid the suspicion that one strong impulse behind these stories is not to pass on some meaningful experiences but to make an impression as a writer.

Mr Shadbolt has a very good ear for dialogue, and is able to imply a great deal about a speaker through his turn of expression. One wishes that he would develop this and speak less in his own person, that he would learn to be humble towards his subject-matter, to forget his confident preconceptions and observe life and people with sympathy, seeing his own prejudices as simply part of the complexity. There is a great deal of good material in these stories which is not used to best effect, and the total impression of the collection is a rather distorted reflection of New Zealand.

M.K. Joseph's War Novel

It is not easy to comment on a colleague's work, or on a novel whose events are so easy to forget as Mr Joseph's; it is, however, an advantage to know that by now, so long after publication, most readers of *Image* will be familiar with the novel.

It does not seem to me that Mr Joseph's main intention was to make a meaningful story out of the lives and relations of a few people. The impulse behind the book is something different.

The novel begins, with the precedent of *Wuthering Heights*, late in the action, in fact, on the point of the climax of the novel, the suicide of Johnny Clarke. The rest is a long flashback of all the events of almost six years before. But, unlike *Wuthering Heights*, the novel stops when it catches up with the climax: the wheel has come full circle, a cycle is over, everything is explained—and this reflects something of Mr Joseph's philosophy. The trouble is that the novel falls apart into two components—the climax, consisting of the Prologue and the last chapter, covering a few winter months and 27 pages, and the flash-back, covering five years of war and eight months of occupation and 234 pages. The climax is dramatically told and interesting, and might have made an impressive short story: the flashback is almost without drama or momentum and is sometimes very tedious. Most of it is only indirectly relevant to Clarke's suicide, and Mr Joseph's purpose is clearly not restricted to explaining that. His subject matter is the day-to-day experience of the common gunner; and the impulse behind the work is, I think, Mr Joseph's desire to recollect and digest his own war experience. The bulk of this book is a war diary.

What fascinates Mr Joseph is what he re-creates admirably, the change in atmosphere and climate of those years in England and Normandy and Germany, from the chaotic muddle of the summer of 1940 through the steady recuperation and preparation for invasion, the cohesion of an

---

This essay was first published in *Image*, August 1960, as a review of M.K. Joseph's *I'll Soldier No More* (Victor Gollancz and Paul's Book Arcade 1958).

artillery unit working with a clear purpose, to the disintegration of the unit during the occupation of Germany, where every man pursues his own pleasures and interests. It is this that is the real theme of the novel and the source of what unity the book might have had.

So it is a pity that Mr Joseph distributes this experience over three characters who are in different camps till they come together in the same unit. The distribution is not only pointless, it prevents him from making the unit the real hero of the novel, and it reduces the flashback at times to a series of log entries of the weather, what they ate, what they said, how they slept, a record of operations and postings and promotions and changes of command; but more important, it prevents the development of what is the main source of interest and momentum in a novel, the relationships between people. It may well be that in an army the men's most important relationships belong to letters and furloughs, and the relationships with their comrades may be limited to what efficiency requires. But a novel on such terms is denied momentum; and it is notable that the most interesting parts of this novel are those parts where relationships are allowed to form: where Clarke visits his wife and her lover, where Gillies falls in love, where Nancy rejects him out of loyalty to her wounded former lover, where Gillies gets involved with black-marketeers, where Clarke finds a frat, and the brief close-ups of liberated civilians in France and Belgium and Germany. It is only in these parts that conflicts and moral decisions are allowed to develop and one is concerned to know how events will work out. The rest is rather a record of suspended animation.

Even the three characters are barely individualised. The writer of the dust-jacket does not make Clarke any more trite than his creator does when he calls him 'the worrier who cracks'. Here and there Mr Joseph makes a perfunctory attempt at interior monologue, but within a few sentences he is back to the detached, third-person, invisible witness's reportage which is the staple style of the novel. It is in its way an admirable style, controlled, evocative, faintly nostalgic and with an undertone of pity. But it is not narrative: there is no impetus from one sentence to the next.

Yet in these three characters, so far as they are developed, Mr Joseph has sought to make a statement about humanity in general. War, as Peter Bonham says, 'does test people. It shakes them loose from their habits, I mean—shows what's inside.' And what is inside these three is meant to be representative of types of attitudes to the eternal. Apparently the contrast is between Clarke and Bonham: Clarke is afraid, conscious of his own inadequacy and incompetence, disheartened by the defection of his wife and the death of his mother; Bonham is more fortunate, but only by the grace of God, in whose will, as he says, is his peace. Bonham passes the test because he has a faith to steer by. Either as a concession to evidence, or drawing on the theological concept of 'natural man', Mr Joseph creates a third man, Harry Gillies the New Zealander, with whom he is less in sympathy than with Clarke or Bonham. Gillies too gets by because, though he has no religious belief, he has pagan self-confidence and courage. It is really a choice of amulets, and poor Clarke has none.

Yet it is Bonham's amulet that proves superior. It is Bonham who intervenes like the grace of God when Gillies has almost landed himself into a court-martial for supplying a black-marketeer. It is Bonham's outlook that dominates the book, and Bonham's trite and pithy comments that underline the author's and point the morals; and it is with the entry of Bonham at page 139 that tedium descends like a North European winter sky. Harry Gillies has a point when he is irritated by Bonham's 'schoolmaster's voice, the pipe, the family photograph by the bedside—yes, and the iron bedstead itself, where Bonham tucks himself comfortably in for eight hours a night, while people with a bit more devil in them are out on the tiles.' In spite of such touches as this, Mr Joseph indulges in special pleading for him, because Gillies comes to recognize Bonham's solidity. In fact Bonham gets by not so much by his amulet as by his unadventurousness, his gentle refusal to offer any resistance to circumstances, his habit of accommodating himself to every new billet by tucking himself into a routine of work, reading, writing a note-book, letters, devotions and early nights. The philosophy of the novel then is not so much a vindication of faith over pagan self-confidence as a vindication of caution as preferable to taking risks. But Clarke only failed because Clarke is Bonham with the wraps off.

Though this philosophy is not integrated with the war diary, it is nevertheless supported by the events. There is further philosophy that is only declared but never demonstrated: it is stated at the end of the Prologue:

> 'For every day renews the perpetual Crucifixion,
> until the end of time.
> And every day the world comes to an end.'

It is the pretentiousness that I object to. The novel does not support the statement. Bonham suffers no more than a few inconveniences and interruptions to his routine, Gillies runs close to thin ice, Clarke worries and shoots himself, but none of them can be said to have been crucified. If the perpetual Crucifixion is the war itself, then something more would have to be shown of the sufferings of the enemy and civilians than is shown. Mr Joseph has let himself be carried away by the attraction of rhetoric.

There are two passages where this is evident, at the end of the Prologue and at the end of Chapter 7. The first is an apostrophe which envisages history moving backwards in order to set the stage for a repeat performance of the war, and it owes its conception to the process by which films can be run backwards. The second is sprung from aerial moving photography and does a quick spaceman's round of the globe touching down or hovering at points of a suffering world, especially where Mass is being said, and culminating in Christmas dawn in Salisbury. Its conception would seem to be derived from a documentary film showing in England in 1949, *Five Days to Sydney*, made for B.O.A.C. or B.E.A., I forget which, consisting of vignettes of life of the common people beneath the air-route and ending with a priest raising the Host at Christmas Midnight Mass in Sydney. What is most to be objected to is that in these passages Mr Joseph steps outside (or above) the novel and so diminishes the importance of the events in it. Traditionally, the novel has restricted itself to human problems resolved entirely according to the decisions of the characters who are involved in them and the consequences of those decisions. Its form precludes the intervention of God or a super-human conspectus of life, or any coasting above it all, seeing things as God might.

There is another occasion where Mr Joseph attempts to reproduce an effect derived from another work of art. His practice is not, like Hopkins's, to admire and do otherwise.

'The rain was falling softly, all over Germany perhaps, on the just and the unjust, on the roof above; on Hardcastle and Barnett; on the sleepy farms untouched by war, and on the shattered towns and cities; on the mortal remains of Hitler and Himmler, and on the white crosses by the Rhine . . .

He floated in and out of the cold black night, disembodied. Darkly it fringed his consciousness.'

(pp. 9–10)

'Softly, insistently, the rain went on, all over Germany.'

(p. 268)

In tone, rhythm, mood and partly in substance these passages echo the ending of Joyce's story *The Dead*:

'A few light taps upon the pane made him turn to the window. It had begun to snow again. He watched sleepily the flakes, silver and dark, falling obliquely against the lamp-light. The time had come for him to set out on his journey westward. Yes, the newspapers were right: snow was general all over Ireland. It was falling on every part of the dark central plain, on the treeless hills, falling softly upon the Bog of Allen and, farther westward, softly falling into the dark mutinous Shannon waves. It was falling, too, upon every part of the lonely churchyard on the hill where Michael Furey lay buried. It lay thickly drifted on the crooked crosses and headstones, on the spears of the little gate, on the barren thorns. His soul swooned slowly as he heard the snow falling faintly through the universe and faintly falling, like the descent of their last end, upon all the living and the dead.'

Mr Joseph handles the style sensitively, and the suggestion of infinite sadness is gently insistent. Yet the purpose of this passage would seem to be only to cover up the lack of inevitability of Clarke's suicide, to create the conditions aesthetically appropriate for such an act. Far from being the logical way out of his dilemma, Clarke's suicide is no more than a gesture in keeping with the weather. One feels that the desire to reconstruct the feel of a German winter and the condition of Germany in 1946 was, at this point, more important to the author than the suicide itself.

In the light of the declaration of the title (which, I think, means no more than that the author is out of the age-group liable for service) Mr Joseph has sifted the experience of six years, faithfully, even lovingly, recorded with an accuracy of detail and a technical knowledge that can only have been transmitted by a clear memory or an actual diary. If he had written a straight war-diary, it would have been an interesting memoir (though perhaps more difficult to publish) and might have had a clearer coherence. But this would have denied him the opportunity to philosophize imaginatively on the testing effect of war. If he had developed this aspect more, he would have had to dispense with some of the diary. And then there is the unsuccessful attempt to see the whole in the light of eternity. The book is a product of mixed intentions. For all that, it is worth reading for the many fine things it contains, and it is written by a man with a feeling for language.

An American Looks
at New Zealand

I

Any intelligent and well-meaning criticism of New Zealand attitudes and behaviour is to be welcomed, and Dr Ausubel took on a formidable job when he thought to storm the fortress of our complacent uneasiness—how formidable is apparent in the unfair newspaper reviews his book has already received.

Dr Ausubel begins by noting a number of contradictions in the behaviour of New Zealand pakehas, for example the casualness of adult relations in contrast to the strictness in rearing children, the history of bold experimentation in social legislation in contrast to the timid conformism of opinion on social questions. By observation, by interviews formal and informal, and by the use of personality tests (they are not described but presumably they were designed for this special purpose) he set out to investigate these paradoxes. It is not possible to give an adequate summary of his findings, but it is particularly desirable that a small island population of predominantly homogeneous ancestry, living in the South Pacific in the twentieth century, should consider them. Even if one has reservations about Dr Ausubel's social philosophy, that the '*real* battle of life' is 'vocational achievement and personal self-fulfilment' (p. 51), the criticisms cannot be ignored.

The national self-image, as Dr. Ausubel sees it, is of a people reserved and modest, easy-going and friendly, practical and adaptable, forthright but courteous. But in fact and in contrast he found us reserved and introverted, hostile to strangers, touchy in our interpersonal relations, contentious on committees, intemperate in the correspondence column, maudlin In Memoriam, prickly under criticism, assertively egalitarian

This essay was first published in the *Journal of the Polynesian Society*, December 1960, as a review of David P. Ausubel's *The Fern and the Tiki* (Angus & Robertson 1960).

in principle but in practice both deferential and secretly resentful towards authority. We are hostile to the intellect; we are lackadaisical in our attitudes towards work, having neither ambition, efficiency, enterprise nor foresight; we reserve our best energy for sport and for home jobs. Our smugness about our place in the world, about our educational system, our standards of public health and our standard of living are not in fact justified, and, further, it covers a sense of insecurity and a sense of international insignificance of which we prefer not to be reminded and which we conspire to ignore.

Now all of this is true, but much of it has been said before. I find it hard to believe that Dr Ausubel, whose coverage of New Zealand habits was so wide, should have been unaware of an essay by R. M. Chapman and another by myself,[1] both of which describe and criticise the behaviour and assumptions of the New Zealand pakeha. He might have found too, that, less explicitly, some of his criticisms have been anticipated in New Zealand verse and fiction for the past 30 years. If he had consulted this literature he might have been able to use the introspective insights of the native social critic to reinforce the insights special to a trained psychologist from a different and more complex society. He might have been able to detect blind spots in the assumptions of the native critics and advanced the criticism a stage further. He might also have found clues to the discrepancies in national behaviour that could have saved him from some of the more unfortunate errors into which he is led by his assumption that he is first in the field.

It is of course a criticism of pakeha New Zealanders that they could not respond to Dr Ausubel's comments and questions without a mixture of defensiveness and aggressiveness, often anti-American; but it is unfortunate that their response should generate in a trained psychologist the occasional tone of rancour that spoils Dr Ausubel's criticisms. It has led him too into unnecessary self-justification and advocacy of the superiority of American behaviour and into a tendency to repeat himself: for example there are four occasions on which he mentions, not without resentment, that many New Zealanders think of most American schools as blackboard jungles.

In many places his interpretations are hasty and wrong, and it is here that he has laid himself open to the unfair strategies of journalist-reviewers who have simply lifted sentences from their context with little more comment than an exclamation mark. For example it is not generally true that pakeha New Zealanders think that American culture and public taste are inferior; it is not unexceptionally true that they are always careful to list their degrees and qualifications (p. 10)—as, to score a cheap point, Dr Ausubel himself does on his title-page; or that a student at a New Zealand university has to be over-polite in disagreeing with his professor if he wants to obtain his degree (p. 20); or that he has to 'knock timidly on his professor's door' and 'wait quietly, cap in hand' and 'act the part of humility and deference once admitted' (p. 113). Few New Zealand students wear caps and if they did, where else could they carry them but in their hands? Do American students keep theirs on? If Dr Ausubel is figuratively describing a mental, rather than a physical, attitude, then I can only say it is not my experience with students. It seems that Dr Ausubel's partisan spirit has disabled him from distinguishing between servility and good manners. One might reasonably suspect from his remarks on this point that there *is* a difference between an American university student's attitude to his teacher and that of a New Zealand student, but Dr Ausubel has not defined that difference. It would have helped his case if he had.

Again, Dr Ausubel shows confusion on the question of the state and status of New Zealand universities, a confusion which is all the more surprising when one recalls that he was in New Zealand at the time of considerable public debate on the question. It is true, as he says, that university teachers devote more time to teaching than to research, but it is not true that this reflects their 'inclination' and 'conception of university role' (p. 65). The fact is directly due to understaffing, and university teachers are very much aware that they should be free to give more time to research.

There are examples of reporting so inaccurate as to be misleading. Commenting on press reports of guest speeches to meetings of professional societies, he says: 'Suggestions and hypotheses are misreported as assertions and conclusions; and "possibly" and "sometimes" are changed to "definitely" and "always".' If in the second clause Dr Ausubel had added the phrase 'by implication', I would have agreed wholeheartedly; but the suggestion is that the press reports of such meetings are not only misleading but cynically doctored; and Dr Ausubel has, not by implication but by assertion, been guilty of the very fault of which he accuses the press. In his discussion of secondary school discipline he treats 'strap' and 'cane' as equivalent. His definition of a bodgie on p. 131 is arbitrary and so is his classification of 'four main types of rebellious teen-agers' on pp. 133–4. He is infected himself with some of the Mazengarb Committee hysteria when he says that Hamilton, Whanganui and Whakatane are 'currently plagued by bodgieism and larrikinism' (p. 131). There may or may not be an increase in juvenile crime in these towns: from a social scientist one expects language both dispassionate and precise.

Dr Ausubel traces many of our peculiarities to the authoritarian discipline of the secondary schools, which, he says, strikes pupils as arbitrary, tyrannical and unrelated to the standards of conduct they know they can expect to live by when they leave school, and so fails completely to develop self-discipline, creating an unwholesome adolescent hostility towards adults and the public attitudes they profess but do not observe. He lays so much stress on it that he imputes to it these consequences: 'unsigned letters to the press; discourtesy towards those authority figures who currently lack specific power to punish such behaviour; participation in immoderate and personally abusive public debate; extreme contentiousness and unnecessary bickering about trivia in various public and quasi-public bodies; lack of graciousness in personal and professional relationships; resentful and punitive attitudes towards youth; antagonistic attitudes towards foreigners; competitive automobile driving; brash and swaggering drinking habits and a fondness for rowdy, drunken parties; and anti-intellectualism and indiscriminate egalitarianism' (p. 114). The list is so extensive that he feels it necessary to correct himself in a footnote explaining that these traits of behaviour (which I in no way question) may be caused by a number of factors.

The single explanation to which his partisan spirit has led him will not suffice, even to explain the current increase in adolescent hostility to adult institutions and traditions. In every case of delinquency some enquiry into the individual's relations with his parents, attitudes to learning, scholastic and sporting achievements and social status among his peers is more than a little relevant to establishing a cause. Further Dr Ausubel shows no understanding of the fact that the strict school discipline has to be seen in a historical context of a sudden increase (since 1945, when the school leaving age was raised to 15) in secondary school populations, so that, as Phoebe Meikle has recently said, the secondary schools have had only a short experience in dealing with pupils of all ranges of ability, and of a concurrent desperate shortage of teachers, with a consequence of over-size classes.[2]

By implication at least, Dr Ausubel claims that his case rests on his 'particular background and training, as a psychologist especially concerned with problems of education, the development of personality, and social relationships' (p. vii). One would reasonably infer a claim to objectivity based on the research methods appropriate to a sociological investigation. But, as they are presented, Dr Ausubel's judgements are subjective and impressionistic. This is not to assert that they are not supported with instances or that he has not observed extensively and, where his own predilections are not involved, objectively. It means that it is impossible to offer such comprehensive interpretations as Dr Ausubel does without a bold reliance on intuition. I do not object to this, provided that the work is openly presented as such, and provided that the observer recognises than an outsider's intuitions are less reliable than those of the native critic, that his special advantage is not intuition but non-involvement, and that intuition is most unreliable to an observer who spends only a year in the field and covers so wide a field in that year.

One illustration will serve. On p. 75, in a context of a defence of the conduct of American servicemen in New Zealand during the war, Dr Ausubel writes:

' ... I have seen groups of New Zealand sportsmen, not bodgies, assembled in a certain North Island town for a sports meeting, behave very loutishly in public, i.e. push people off the footpaths, torment

Chinese merchants, ridicule old Maori women, shout obscene remarks at strangers, and make advances to and fondle women passers-by in the street. Yet most spectators were thoroughly amused and thought this was quite normal behaviour for the occasion.'

I want to subject this statement to some scrutiny. As one who has commented before on the willingness with which pakeha New Zealanders violate the morality they profess, I can accept that every *attitude* represented by the behaviour Dr Ausubel describes is true. Yet I find it hard to envisage the scene without providing details whose absence (to my mind) seriously affects the reliability of the description. My first reaction was to want to know *what* town? *what* sport? what *particular* sports meeting? Did the 'sportsmen' physically shove people off the footpath or did they just stand there so that they had to walk on the road? How did they 'torment' the Chinese merchants, physically, verbally or by facial or vocal mockery?—and for how long? Was each merchant tormented by *one* sportsman or more than one, and if so, how many? On further reflection I found what I think might be the clue: that it was not the players themselves who indulged in this behaviour, but their supporters, perhaps a whole train-load of them from another town, come to barrack at an inter-provincial rugby match, holding a Saturday-morning demonstration behind their mascot; in carnival spirit (and probably away from home) their saturnalia took the form of aggressive and mock-serious persecution of strangers and people of minority cultures—which they themselves (and local spectators conniving) would see as no more than good-humoured baiting. If my reconstruction is right, it is an alarming symptom of our psychic health (more alarming than the recent Hastings affair) that a semi-institutionalised holiday from our professed moral code should release so much contempt for human decency and dignity; and we need to be told so. But I am not sure that I haven't filled out the picture too much. And my questions have still not been answered. Few New Zealand readers will have given Dr Ausubel's statement the scrutiny I have given it, in order to extract the valuable criticism that underlies it. If Dr Ausubel had been here longer he wouldn't have confused sportsmen with supporters. If he had provided important details and removed the criticism from its partisan context, he might have had the effect he so clearly desires—to shock pakeha New Zealanders out of their complacency into critical self-scrutiny. It is a recurring fault of this book that its author spoils his own case.

I began by thinking that these objections were minor; that it was more important to consider Dr Ausubel's main criticisms and to count his misjudgements as marginal, but now I think that they are consequent on his method. He has been too quick off the press. A year was long enough to observe the paradoxes in the behaviour of the pakeha New Zealander and to describe his real image as distinct from his self-image; but the time that passed between field-work and publication was not long enough for Dr Ausubel to do more than organise his material and process it into a number of general findings partly based on improvised intuition. What is missing is the more profound mental effort that would have followed up his intuitions and tested them against further data from the field. Dr Ausubel needed to stay longer in New Zealand if his criticisms were to have that kind of percipience and aptness that is incontrovertible. If, after testing his guesses against further evidence, he had explored them further, or revised them, or both, he might have found deeper explanations than he provides. As he leaves us, the paradoxes—which are undeniable—are not satisfactorily explained. In the last analysis the most valuable part of this section of the book is the list of discrepancies, and its value for the sociologist is that it points general directions where some careful and objective research might be done. In fact, it is arguable that future visiting research psychologists and sociologists will find more formidable material in New Zealand pakehas than in the compatriots whom they more frequently come to study.

II

By far the best section of the book is the two chapters on race relations. Here Dr Ausubel has been more fortunate in his informants, both Maoris with their traditional courtesy, and pakehas, since there are few subjects on which a New Zealand pakeha is so willing to pronounce, often without knowledge, as what he probably calls 'the Maori problem'. Dr. Ausubel conducted extended and informal interviews with 'hundreds of Maoris and pakehas in all walks of life and in a large variety of North Island districts' (p. 152). He does not claim that his findings are representative (pp. 152, 171) or that he can determine the proportions of some of the expressed pakeha attitudes to the Maori. Nevertheless, he has presented a wide (and probably complete) range of such attitudes, and most New Zealand readers will have met some of them in their own experience. I can confirm, from experience canvassing several hundred houses and flats in Parnell with the recent petition against the exclusion of Maoris from selection for the South African tour of a national rugby team, that most of these attitudes are current, and that a common pakeha attitude is one of confused patronising goodwill that is fundamentally hostile to attempts by Maoris to order their own affairs. Besides this, Dr Ausubel presents, what is unusual in discussions of race relations in New Zealand, a range of Maori attitudes to the pakeha and Maori reactions to pakeha prejudice. For a brief popular survey of current pakeha attitudes to the Maori and current Maori attitudes to the pakeha, these 67 pages are both valuable and unique.

Dr Ausubel admits that the racial situation is, in relation to that of some other countries, reasonably good (pp. 155–6, 211); he complains, however, that the situation is not nearly so good as most pakehas like to believe, and that the worst feature is 'the national self-delusion which blocks recognition of the existence of a problem' (p. 156). He was surprised at the frequency of frankly anti-Maori sentiments; he soon could define the outline of a common pakeha stereotype of the Maori as lazy, shiftless, unreliable, improvident, happy-go-lucky, with such occasional concomitants as living off social security and family benefits, being sexually promiscuous and frequently drunk. Behind patronising attitudes he found a deep-seated belief in Maori inferiority, a belief partly reflected in the ignorance of and indifference to the history and traditions of local Maoris, and more seriously reflected in unwillingness to understand current problems the Maori people are facing. Many pakehas are willing to accept Maoris as equals only if they conform to European values and standards, while other pakehas may deride them for attempting to act otherwise than they are expected to. Many pakehas, too, are unable to distinguish between the enforced segregation of a minority and segregation that is desired by them: thus, some pakehas, in the name of an abstract equality will advocate the abolition of the four Maori seats and the Maori schools at the same time as they are complacent about the exclusion of Maoris from the more desirable suburbs. For most pakehas integration means assimilation and they dislike any perpetuation of distinctively Maori values and traditions since it offends their desire for complete conformity. Dr Ausubel is right to point out that a nation that boasts of being a modern welfare state should be ashamed of the standards of health and sanitation that exist in some rural Maori communities. Besides this critical survey of the attitudes of a majority to a minority, Dr Ausubel recognises the existence of a number of pakehas who live and work unselfishly among Maoris, speaking their language, knowing their culture and traditions, and working *with* them for their advancement. Turning to the attitudes of the Maori, Dr Ausubel finds a range of attitudes, from shyness and suspicion through a relatively benign hostility and some surviving bitterness over confiscations to sullenness in reaction to pakeha prejudice. He also discusses the attitudes of Maoris to themselves, attitudes formed in the context of pakeha prejudice: feelings of inferiority and self-contempt, as well as an increasing attitude of pride in being Maori.

Since Dr Ausubel does not generalise too freely, and recognises that Maori attitudes vary from district to district, it is difficult to fault this section of the book. Nevertheless, there are a number of minor criticisms I should like to make. There is a difference in degree between the two expressions Dr Ausubel cites on p. 161: 'Maori physical training' and 'The only good Maori is a dead Maori'. The second I cannot claim to have heard, not in those words anyway; the attitude, as I will show later, I have met, though I suspect it is very infrequent. The first implies a pakeha sense of superiority, but it is (in my experience) said as often in good nature as in contempt. An Auckland Maori student (himself a lecturer, and one who, for various reasons, I cannot suspect of telling me what he thinks I would like to be told) has told me he has had no experience of what Dr Ausubel on p. 179 calls ' "the silent treatment" from pakeha students, and being responded to as if they were simple-minded or incapable of understanding English'. Again, while Dr Ausubel is right to say on p. 159: 'If skin colour had no significance in this country, half-castes would be regarded as half-caste Europeans just as frequently as they are regarded as half-caste Maoris', it nevertheless makes some difference that most half- and quarter-castes prefer to regard themselves as Maoris and associate with Maoris (and, according to Dr Ausubel on p. 182, marry Maoris), and that even eighth-castes frequently boast of their Maori ancestry. If there were any serious social penalty, they would not do so. It would have helped Dr Ausubel's case if he had realised that the extra post-primary and university bursaries he mentions on p. 190 are not 'special privileges' but come from Maori money administered by the Maori Purposes Trust Board. I feel too that Dr Ausubel himself has accepted too readily some of the components of the pakeha stereotype of the Maori on p. 186, especially 'greater incidence of alcoholism, delinquency and premarital sex relations, non- payment of rates; failure to develop their land adequately', which he accepts as 'factually true in part' and extenuates rather too easily in terms of 'acculturational difficulties'. Even to state these half-truths in these terms is to falsify the situations that have led to their currency among pakehas, and to explain them away so loosely is to ignore the real and complex social and economic factors that have produced them: uneconomic land holdings, for example, cannot be fairly attributed, with however much forgiveness, to Maori 'failure'. I would be interested too in the source of the figures on which Dr Ausubel bases his assertion (p. 182, note) that the incidence of Maori-pakeha marriages has been decreasing over the past generation.

This part of the book should be read and considered by every New Zealander who believes or professes to believe that racial equality is one of the fundamental premises of the New Zealand social code. Dr Ausubel makes a prediction that 'as long as New Zealanders persist in deluding themselves that all is well in the sphere of race relations, the only realistic prospect for the future is the emergence of a brown proletariat segregated in the urban slums and living in a state of chronic tension with their white neighbours'. The prediction may strike us as far-fetched but, since we have been warned, we have only ourselves to blame if it should turn out to be true. A similar forecast of the future of race relations in New Zealand, in the light of extrapolations of Maori population trends, has been hinted at in Dr Borrie's statement that in a situation of increasing occupational and residential contiguity between Maori and pakeha, 'the maintenance of cultural and social segregation has explosive possibilities'.[3] The warning has generally been treated lightly in the Round Table discussions at the

Regional Conferences of Young Maori Leaders in the Auckland Province in 1960, where the common opinion has been that the prejudice from which racial tension might develop can be removed by education leading to mutual understanding.[4] It is possible that this view is naive and over-optimistic. It is, in any case, true that a determined effort of patience and understanding, especially on the pakeha side, is needed for the rest of the century, if Dr Ausubel's prediction is to be forfended.

I should like to add a caution of my own. During my canvassing, I ran into an anti-Maori attitude more extreme than I should have thought possible. The speaker was a youth of about 20 who had been in Borstal for some crime against property. He said he would like to see Maoris exterminated, 'just like Hitler tried to do with the Jews'. He added that his hatred was very deep and that it was based on his association with Maori youths in Borstal and that it was commonly shared by other pakeha inmates. It seemed that what he objected to was Maori cliquishness: that his attitude was a reaction to an attitude which was itself probably a reaction to earlier pakeha prejudice. It is possible of course that the antipathy between the two groups reflects a difference in the psychological tensions or pressures that motivated their crimes. Nevertheless, since the racial ratio in Borstal is probably different from that outside, and nearer to what may hold in the cities in the future, I think some research into the aetiology of racial tension in Borstal would be very valuable.

Dr Ausubel's book then contains both a criticism of New Zealand pakeha attitudes, which needs sifting of his own prejudices and hasty conclusions, and a survey of race relations that is valuable and unique. In his Preface he promises another volume on 'Maori national character' and 'the historical forces and current social factors shaping its development, particularly among youth'. It is to be hoped that it is more carefully thought than his section on the pakeha national character, and more in the spirit of his section on race relations. One can be sure that it will at least be more friendly in its approach than his section on pakehas, but it could be harmful and misleading if it is as hasty and reckless.

Notes

1. Chapman, R.M., 'Fiction and the Social Pattern', *Landfall*, March 1953, reprinted in Curnow, Wystan (ed.), *Essays on New Zealand Literature*, Heinemann Educational Books (N.Z.) Ltd, Auckland 1973; and Pearson, Bill, 'Fretful Sleepers', *Landfall*, September 1952, reprinted in this volume.
2. Meikle, Phoebe, 'New Zealand Since the War: School and Nation', *Landfall*, September 1960.
3. Borrie, W.D., 'The Maori Population: A Microcosm of a New World' in Freeman, J.D., and Geddes, W.R. (eds.), *Anthropology in the South Seas*, New Plymouth 1959, p. 261.
4. E.g. Report of the Waikato-Maniapoto Young Maori Leaders' Conference, 20–22 May 1960, Auckland Council of Adult Education, p. 16.

A Parable of Exploitation

Noel Hilliard is the first pakeha novelist to write at length with an intimate and extensive knowledge of Maori life, and at the same time to write without attitudes of patronage or indulgence. The problem for a pakeha writer at present, if he wishes to write of Maoris, is to have some initial understanding of their traditions and their rural upbringing, to write without preconceptions, and to write with a recognition of the rapid changes going on in Maori society.

It is this that Noel Hilliard attempts in his novel *Maori Girl*. He knows the home background of his heroine Netta Samuel in back-blocks Taranaki in the 30's and early 40's. She and her family are credited with as much depth and complexity as any other character of comparable importance in the novel. And he tackles the problem, as it affects one girl, of the current migration of the young to the cities—an inevitable migration, often foolishly called a 'drift'.

In the first eleven chapters of the book Mr Hilliard describes the life of the Samuel family: Netta's schooling, her jobs at home and on the farm, an eeling trip, her father's mortgage and his struggles during the depression, his drinking, and his severity to the children, her thoughts on religion, their first wireless, a visit from Granny, the older children leaving home to find work, the new milking-shed, Netta's sports, rows with neighbours, her extended social life as member of the tennis club, the tennis dance, the pakeha fellow who is after her and the one that she likes who takes her into a paddock and goes straight on to a party with the boys, her shame and her fear of a scandal, her sudden weariness with home and the valley, her departure for Wellington.

That this section is authentic and trustworthy as an account of back-blocks Maori life (at least in the 30's and 40's) I have been assured by about five Maoris who have read it: many of Netta's experiences they could

This essay was first published in the *New Zealand Monthly Review*, September 1961, as a review of Noel Hilliard's *Maori Girl* (William Heinemann 1960).

claim themselves. It is, for a pakeha writer, entirely new ground, and for pakeha readers it will be new to read an account representative of the background of many of the compatriots that, to their own loss, they know so little about. It is in fact the commonest failing in the attitude of people who claim to be sympathetic to Maoris that they will not appreciate that there are differences in the traditions, the outlook and the aspirations of Maoris, and further, that many of these differences are an advantage in that they enable Maoris to cope with the changes that social, economic and policy pressures are forcing on them. Many socialists, like many other pakehas, assume that such differences are inferiorities; and one is likely to be called a racialist if one insists on them.

This introductory section—originally, the author has told me, much longer—is important to the rest of the novel, even if that importance is not as apparent as it might have been, since a good deal of Netta's difficulty in coping with the assaults and temptations of city life can be explained in terms of her life at home, the gulf between her parents and their children (a gulf that is to be expected in any people on whom fairly rapid adaptations are forced), her parents' affection and yet their uncomprehending severity, her quarrels with her brothers and her sisters and yet their affection for one another, the way when they leave home they each go their own way and maintain only casual contact with the family. At heart Netta as an adolescent is very lonely and there is no one in whom she can confide: it is not her parents but her oldest sister Rebecca that she tells of her seduction, but only because Rebecca has recognised the signs, and the advice Rebecca gives her is the sort of worldly-wise advice that she has picked up from her own 'lonely fumbling'. Emotionally, the Samuel family, like many other young Maoris, are orphans.* Though Netta writes home from the city she could never tell her people what has happened to her.

But it is the subsequent and much simpler sequence of events that most pakeha readers will remember: and socialists should be careful not to fall for the temptation to take this as simply an indictment of landladies and restaurateurs who either discriminate against Maori girls or exploit them: the contemplation of such practices, because one condemns them, can give one a very smug conscience. For this section of the book is an accusation against pakeha society itself, the assumptions of which are shared by a great number of those who condemn racial discrimination.

Netta, arriving in Wellington, without friends or relatives, is rooked by her first landlady, finds a job at a private hotel where she can live in, meets up with a boy-friend Eric, who lives by his wits and soon has her selling lottery tickets for him, to whom she gives herself too casually

---

* There is only a small proportion of Maoris over 50, and though they are physically close to the young and tolerate their behaviour, it is doubtful if they understand them.

because she takes the relationship seriously, and who ditches her out of jealousy; though there is some calculation in his jealousy, because he is afraid that if the affair goes on much longer, there might be a baby. What he represents is one side of the face of the pakeha society as it first presents itself to Netta—a very unpleasant face: from the men, exploitation; from the women, disdain. There is hardly a pakeha woman in the novel who doesn't claim an automatic moral superiority to her, and most of the men exploit her in one way or another. There is the boarder at the hotel who, when his wife is away, tries to pull Netta on to his bed, there is the drunk who tries to pick her up in a restaurant, and Eric's is only a more explicit example of a kind of exploitation far commoner than discrimination by employers and landlords. He is ashamed of her at heart and walks ahead of her on the street; the only outings he is prepared to take her to are to the pictures where it is dark. In effect he sees her as something between a mistress and a prostitute, a mistress who doesn't need to be kept, a prostitute who doesn't charge and is for him alone. Fundamentally, in his mirthless puritanism, he is contemptuous of her for giving herself so easily, and it is his neurotic suspicion that she is as free with her body to others that causes him to break off the relationship. What he wants is all fun, no responsibility, only he doesn't enjoy the fun. It is difficult to imagine Eric being nobler with any woman; and yet I suspect that like the other men in the novel he acts towards Netta in a way that he wouldn't to a pakeha girl. Netta has not been trained to cope with such a man.

She makes a fresh start, takes two jobs as waitress, and in the second her employer lets her a room in an apartment-house he owns. She meets her second boy-friend Arthur, a watersider. He treats her decently and he loves her, and she finds the relationship satisfying. But he is like Eric in two ways: he moves in with her in a way that one suspects he wouldn't with a pakeha woman, and he walks out on her when he finds that she is carrying Eric's baby. The day he walks out on her, she is sacked and has to find a new room. Months later he sees her in a hotel lounge in the company of Minnie, a girl who had once been in the dock after a police raid on a ship. He hears that night of a Maori woman taken drunk to the police station, and thinking it might be Netta, he goes to bail her out; but the sergeant will not reveal the woman's identity. It is finally clear that it is not Netta, but the author leaves this slightly uncertain, because the point of Arthur's guilt and dissatisfaction is to pass on to the pakeha reader the guilt and dissatisfaction he should feel at what his society has done to Netta and to the woman in the cell, and any one of dozens of other Maori girls.

Maori Girl is a novel of social protest, and its purpose is to awaken the conscience of pakeha society to the way it corrupts girls like Netta and blames them for it. It is honestly written—the writing is not carefully worked, and is sometimes clumsy, but it is often powerful; the novel is realistic, and Mr Hilliard knows the settings in which Netta moves.

Nevertheless there are some questions I want to raise. The first is to ask whether Netta's case is representative of Maori girls in the cities now. A novelist, of course, isn't obliged to be representative, to produce a fictional social survey, and it would be no criticism of the book if Netta's case was exceptional. Nevertheless, since it is a novel of social protest, it is as well to be clear on this question. Netta arrived in Wellington in 1949; and in that year there would be few Maoris in Wellington, fewer than in Auckland, and fewer than now. Since then there have been changes in urban Maori society. There are far more girls in skilled and professional work and training: nevertheless, they are exceptional, and there are, by the same token, far more girls without skills in the cities. In Auckland at least one will meet plenty of girls tastefully dressed and discriminating and composed in their behaviour; one will meet plenty of wives who are settled and happy. On the other hand, on any Saturday afternoon one can find in any 'cat's bar' in Parnell or Freeman's Bay plenty of drunken women, some of them married, and mainly mixing with other Maoris. There are the girls, too, who sit in the hotel lounges waiting for seamen to buy them drinks and take them to parties. A Presbyterian clergyman working among city Maoris tells me that Netta's case is typical of at least this kind of girl, and of all the Maori women in a city, this kind of girl forms a proportion big enough to be important. And unless they come into contact with a welfare officer or warden or a clergyman, such girls are like abandoned children; without guidance or guardianship, seeking affection and enjoyment, they drift casually from one relationship to another until they sour. Some of them have been in Child Welfare receiving-homes and some sociologists blame their earlier upbringing—an upbringing that throws too much responsibility on children at an early age so that their only moral guidance is from others of their own age or slightly older.

Yet it is as well to realise that, even if she represents a sizeable number of girls, Netta is not representative of most Maori girls in the cities in 1961. She is exceptional in that she has no friends or relatives in the city to give her a start: she is exceptional in that she has no Maori boy-friends, except the three freezing-workers from Moerewa who are passing through. (Her day's outing with them is the most relaxed and pleasant chapter in the novel, like an oasis in an asphalt desert.) She is exceptional in that the only parties she goes to are in Myra's room with pakeha boy-friends—none of those pleasant parties that so frequently upset pakeha neighbours where everyone sings and all the drink is shared and if it cuts early the singing doesn't and there's pork-bones and water-cress to follow. And she is exceptional in that the women she knows are nearly all of a kind—Myra, who has boys to stay the night in her room; Mona with her hangovers; Minnie who specializes in seamen and sometimes asks for money; Hannah, twice separated and alcoholic. Only one, Shirley Whanau, is happily married and proof to the city's corruption. Nor would it be usual in 1961 for a pakeha boy to walk ahead of his girl-friend or for her to stick with him if he did.

Nor does her fate strike us as inevitable. It is rather much of a coincidence that all on the one day Arthur leaves her, she loses her job and her lodgings so that when he reconsiders he knows no way of finding her.

My point in this is not to object but to show that although Mr Hilliard is using realist terms, this is not a realist novel so much as a moral parable, and that his purpose is not to work out Netta's problems so much as to indict pakeha society.

His purpose prevents Netta from becoming a triumphant or a tragic figure. She has sufficient moral and spiritual strength to have come out on top, or a least to have gone down fighting. She has made gestures of protest before, even if they were negative and violent, when she threw a nailhead through the glass door of a boarding-house that wouldn't take Maoris, when she gained her rights by threatening her boss's wife, mock-seriously, with a meat-knife. But the protest she makes at the end is ineffective: drinking in a bar which has a notice to say that 'Native Women' will not be served. It is a feeble protest in that the hotel makes no attempt to enforce its regulations, which had been put up at the request of a welfare officer; but worse, it is irrelevant to her own situation. Netta could have been a more memorable figure than she is. Mr Hilliard has tied himself so closely to the actuality of Wellington of 1949 that he has prevented her from realizing the potential truth of her nature. Nevertheless, one cannot object if he has stuck to an outcome more probable than admirable.

There is some contradiction in the character of Arthur. On the one hand he is seen as a decent working chap, interested in football, races and beer. On the other hand, he acts like an intelligent, left-wing trade unionist, a man who organizes a tenants' petition to their landlord and knows how to meet their objections to signing, a man who calls in the Health Inspector, who is intelligent enough to analyse his own feelings for Netta and know what it is that attracts him to her, and to speculate on the relations existing between the European immigrants who are Netta's fellow-tenants. His intelligence and sensitivity make it hard to accept that he should, at the end, taunt Netta with her colour. If Mr Hilliard's point is that even well-disposed or socialist pakehas often have an unconscious sense of racial superiority, it is a point worth making. But coming out of the blue as it does it is improbable, since Arthur has been genuinely in love with her.

Mr Hilliard has told me that his book was considerably longer and was shortened at his publisher's request; and that as he conceived Arthur and presented him in the longer version of the novel, he could see no inconsistency in Arthur's character. But a reader can only judge a novel from the words that remain when it is published, and Arthur as we have him is not a satisfactory character.

Again, while I have nothing but respect for the author's purpose, I don't think it a good idea to work to a preconceived conclusion. It prevents a writer from making discoveries as he goes. It prevents him from exploring issues that arise in the course of writing, or the implications of his characters' attitudes and the consequences of their acts. For example, the author uncritically accepts the universal dislike of the nosey, self-righteous tenant Arthur calls the Eyes and the Ears of the World, and in never allowing her to appear in a sympathetic light, he shows a Kiwi intolerance of non-conformity, which is basically the same as the prejudice of some pakeha characters against Netta. More fundamentally, certain issues raised by the novel are not examined: how should Arthur (who was casual enough in the way he moved in with Netta and never gave any thought to marrying her till he knew there was a child) have reacted when he found that the baby wasn't his? There is no easy answer; and Arthur's angry rejection of her, though he half-relents, is not the answer. But the author does not follow up his question because he wants to concentrate on Netta, simply as a victim of racial, not sexual exploitation. But since half of the subject-matter of this novel is sexual exploitation it is a pity he didn't explore it more freely.

And again, writing as a socialist, Mr Hilliard prefers to be uncritical of Arthur's friends who gather at the house of Harry Hawkins the unionist. How dull they are and how barren their talk with the nervous compulsion to make cliché jokes to prompt other jokes in rejoinder and laugh nervously as a matter of etiquette, on the assumption that if everyone is laughing the party is a success. And how complacent are their thoughts, how bound to the provision of physical needs and nothing more: I find Harry's definition of the qualities that go to make a good wife smug and unimaginative. In introducing these people the author's point is to introduce Netta to some decent kindly-hearted working-people in contrast to Eric and his cobbers, but because he favours them he has refused to imply any criticism of them. Netta would have found more satisfaction in a Maori party. If the author had no model for their behaviour but that of actuality, the kind of talk and behaviour you would expect from a decent union-minded watersider in 1949, then he had the choice of harnessing his sympathies to his imagination, and creating a better model—one that did not rise too far from reality and yet revealed a depth not apparent in the actual model. I don't mean that he should have made Harry a cardboard figure, voicing progressive slogans and setting an example to his work-mates and to readers. I mean that the author had the choice of either presenting Harry as he is, but with his limitations apparent, or of presenting Harry as he might be in a way that would bring out real strengths that are in Harry but are hidden.

Nevertheless, this last is not a point that seriously affects the novel as a whole. And all of my criticisms are in terms of Mr Hilliard's intention, which I respect and approve. *Maori Girl* impressed me because it is an honest novel and, tackling a difficult subject, it is without any falsities; not only is it new ground for a pakeha writer, but further it makes a pakeha examine his conscience, and helps him to understand his fellow New Zealanders.

Under Pressure to Integrate

The Situation of Maoris in 1962.

The most striking feature of the Maori situation seventeen years after the end of the war is the continued existence, within the welfare state, of rural enclaves of material poverty and, in city and country, spiritual insecurity. It is from these that the current vexed problems derive, determined as they are by acts of history and complicated by European preconceptions of desirable norms of behaviour and the terms of racial co-existence.[1]

Some bald statistics will illustrate my claim. In 1956 the average income for a Maori head of a household was nearly £200 less than for a non-Maori: the position is probably no different today. The money has to go further: in a sample of 24 forestry-town households Jane Ritchie found (in 1956) a median annual income of £85 per head; £41 in one household.[2] The 1956 census showed that 8 in 100 Maori males earned £900+ (17 non-Maoris), that 41 in 100 earned less than £500 (17 non-Maoris). This is not greatly affected by the higher proportion of Maori youths, since there are comparatively few Maoris in low-paid apprenticeships.

In 1939 the Under-Secretary for Native Affairs could say that at least half of the Maori population were inadequately housed, that 'hundreds and hundreds of Maoris are living under appalling conditions'.[3] The 1956 census estimated that 30 per cent of Maoris live in 'grossly over-crowded conditions'. In 1936, a third of Maori dwellings consisted of one or two rooms; in 1956, a seventh. One can still say that hundreds and hundreds of Maoris are living under conditions, which, if not so appalling as twenty-three years ago, would appal most pakehas. 40 out of 100 Maori dwellings in 1956 had neither bath nor shower, 48 no piped water, 50 no hot water, 67 no flush toilet, 80 no refrigerator or washing-machine. (The pakeha figures for the last three are 17, 44 and 41.) One may argue that these

---

This essay was first published in *Landfall*, June 1962 as part of a series by several writers on the subject 'New Zealand Since the War'.

amenities are not ends in themselves; one must agree that it is undesirable that so many of a minority group should be without what so many of the majority group have. Further, most Maori houses are overcrowded: the average Maori house in 1956 had 3.9 rooms and 5.6 people, the average non-Maori house 4.7 rooms and 3.6 people; 50 per cent more occupants and 17 per cent fewer rooms, and the rooms themselves are smaller than in pakeha houses.

It is hardly surprising that most Maori incomes leave little for the maintenance of such houses, let alone (without assistance) the building of new ones. Or that such derelict, overcrowded shacks, with bad sanitation and careless disposal of refuse, should make personal cleanliness difficult and should produce a high incidence of disease and a death-rate much higher in most illnesses than the pakeha. H. G. Turbott's 1935 survey of disease in Waiapu County showed greatly higher death-rates in tuberculosis, respiratory diseases, diarrhoea and enteritis, and typhoid fever: in 1960 medical statisticians could say: 'All the evidence available at the present time points to the fact that no very great improvement has taken place in the comparative health standards of the Maori as opposed to the European during the course of the intervening quarter-century.'[4] Though the crude death-rate of Maoris is slightly lower than for pakehas, when adjustments are made for the different age-structure of the Maori population, the death-rate is roughly twice as high and in the younger age-groups roughly three times as high: and expectation of life for a Maori male almost 12 years less than for a pakeha, and for a female 15 years less. Tuberculosis kills Maori men at 12 times the rate of pakehas, and women 19 times; rheumatic heart disease 5 times; hepatitis 4 times; the Maori death-rate is higher for cancer, measles, hydatids, pneumonia, kidney disease, pregnancy complications, rheumatic fever, as well as for accidents and homicide. The only diseases where Maori mortality is lower are polio and ulcers of the stomach and duodenum. Infant mortality is particularly high. Children under five are particularly susceptible to dysentery, whooping-cough, meningitis, influenza, pneumonia, enteritis and anaemia, and die too frequently from accidents. Forty times as many children die proportionately from heart disease as pakeha children.

Apart from the deaths, the sickness rate of the living is too high. Besides the children's diseases already mentioned, children suffer frequently from scabies and impetigo, and from discharging ears which are neglected (because, I am told, the mothers' grapevine has not yet caught up with the possibility of cure by anti-biotics) and result in the high proportion of Maori children in schools for the deaf: a survey of Murupara in January 1962 showed an eighth of the children as deaf. Anaemia is common in older children; and adults, according to Dr Gollan Maaka, suffer from gum and tooth troubles resulting from starchy foods and lack of oral hygiene, obesity, chest trouble, rheumatism, cancer and tuberculosis. Women, according to Dr Rina Moore, develop heart disease and foot trouble, from poor shoes and overweight.

In spite of these disabilities, as is well known, the population is increasing and especially in the fertile and potentially fertile age-groups. Between 1936 and 1945, it increased by 21.5 per cent; since the war by 71 per cent, from 100,044 to 171,523 (as at last December). The birth-rate (46.41 per 1000) is almost twice as high as for the pakeha (25), and the rate of natural increase (37.57 per 1000 in 1958) is not only more than twice as high as for the pakeha (16.26) but is apparently higher than that of Western Samoa and has been described by a demographer as not only 'amongst the highest in *any* country of the world today'[5] but probably as high as for any people in any period of history. Borrie projects a population of 310,000 within the next twenty years. Of the present population, 57.5 per cent are under 20, and only 3.6 per cent over 60.

It is these facts which, in conjunction with past acts of policy, have determined a number of current vexed questions: the migration to the towns and cities in search of employment, and the consequent increase in contact or contiguity with Europeans; fragmentation of land inheritances; a greater effort on the part of government departments to promote what is called 'integration'; the increase in crime; the uncertain future of the Maori language; changes in patterns of leadership; comparatively poor educational achievement and insecurity of employment; a greater testing of our professions of racial goodwill.

Taken in isolation, the statistics are disturbing; but they have to be placed in a context of change. Maoris themselves are optimistic about the future and are more willingly emerging from their pre-war withdrawal, voluntary in some areas, geographical in others. It must be admitted that sanitation and housing have improved since the war, that the proportion of one or two-room dwellings is much smaller. If the comparative health of the people hasn't greatly improved, their attitude to it has: among the young, especially in the cities, personal hygiene is a matter of self-respect, and in the country there is not the pre-war distrust of pakeha medicines, of district nurses and hospitals. At Kaitaia it was estimated that only about 1 in 20 of the Tai Tokerau peoples would prefer to consult a tohunga for 'Maori sickness'; at Whakatane Dr Maaka thought the few old-time ritualist tohungas among the Tuuhoe and Ngaati-porou were harmless in that they provided psychological satisfactions for patients otherwise incurable.

High infant mortality has been shown to be directly related to poor feeding, swampy housing sites, disrepair of houses, poor sanitation, and shortage of living and sleeping accommodation; and a vigorous housing programme would remove some of these causes. But other causes can be remedied only by Maori parents themselves—ignorance and the system of child-rearing that is forced by large families in small houses. Rural Maori mothers are frequently ignorant of hygiene and diet and the need for a regular routine for babies. Unfamiliar with symptoms of children's illnesses, they do not seek medical attention till it is too late; nor do they have periodical checkups on their own or their children's health. Except in the Hokianga (as a result of G. M. Smith's work) they do not attend pre-natal clinics—if there are any accessible—and often do not seek the services of the Plunket Society after birth. Branches of the Maori Women's Welfare League (formed in 1951) have attempted some education in health and child-rearing, but it is only the converted who belong to the League, and those who do not resent the League's interference. Several of the young leaders' conferences have suggested koreros on health problems at huis; adult education courses in cooking, child care and homecraft; health campaigns organized by the Tribal Committees with the co-opera-tion of the district nurse and the village school. To overcome the shyness of mothers too embarrassed at the condition of their houses to answer the door to the district nurse, it was suggested that Maori girls be enlisted as district nurses and that there be more Maori women doctors.

It should of course be admitted that many Maori mothers are more enlightened than this, but it is true of the majority of mothers of the subsistence farming class and the unskilled working class living in the country or in the single-industry towns of South Auckland. Such mothers are overworked and fatigued. As each new baby arrives, the one just older is consigned to the care of an older sister, and those over four are left to look after themselves. From the time they are confident on their feet, children are kept outside as much as possible, except when called to do jobs, and are forced to become independent of adults at an early age, relying not on their parents but on their siblings and playmates for advice. Mothers at Turangawaewae and Whakatane complained that fathers do not take enough part in child-rearing. Pakeha observers like Ausubel and the Ritchies find both mother's and father's punishment capricious and aggressive—either a 'growling' or a 'hiding'. At several of the young leaders' conferences there was lack of unanimity and some embarrassment at allegations of parental cruelty and neglect. Generally, delegates resented the charge of cruelty, or conceded it but said it was exceptional and usually the effect of alcohol. There was a more general admission of neglect, with the qualification that it was often unconscious neglect. It was said that parents often feel free to go to cards or to parties when the youngest is four, leaving the children alone in the house; that they do not see the need for a steady routine for the children, or plan their lives around the needs of the children. Only at Kaitaia was it said that the common practice of adoption by grandparents or other relatives was damaging to a child's sense of security. At Auckland, Dr Rina Moore strongly urged family planning, but at Kaitaia, even though a recommendation was passed advocating publicity for methods of family planning, the suggestion was clearly an embarrassment to some women delegates. Courses in homecraft and family budgeting were suggested: how to spend less on drink and biscuits and tinned jam and more on meat and fruit and vegetables and children's clothing is a felt need. A Maori friend tells me that this is one of the attractions of the Latter-Day Saints, who provide this and other directions of their members' lives.* It was a Mormon, Dr M. N. Paewai, who inaugurated the Kaikohe scheme by which parents voluntarily submit their expenditure to the supervision of a citizens' committee. The scheme has been hailed by Mr Hunn, the Secretary for Maori Affairs, and copied in several North Island towns: but it has to be run by disinterested people: in Mangakino an enthusiast almost launched one by which the local shopkeepers would have been directing the buying of their customers. On the whole, there is a growing feeling among the younger Maoris—and especially the women—who are more familiar with European child-rearing, that Maori parents should assume more responsibility for their children.

What of housing? Before the Hunn Report, there was frequent complaint at conferences that the Department of Maori Affairs was not only not meeting current demand for houses but that the backlog itself was increasing. Under the 1949–57 administration, Mr Corbett was sympathetic to Maori needs but his Cabinet overruled him: apart from the assistance given by the capitalization of family benefits, Mr Nash's tenure of office was distinguished by its ineffectiveness. In August 1960, Mr Hunn reported 2350 applications for housing loans and 300 for State houses: the Department's target for that year was 620; and Mr Hunn's guess was that, to meet immediate needs, 6000 houses might be needed. Since the Report there has been a greatly increased allocation of money for housing and the Department has been buying group houses and houses put up by State Advances. Several conferences criticised the Department's supervision of building: builders economised by leaving much of the work to apprentices; too often the occupant was confronted with sunk foundations, warping, leaks and windows that wouldn't shut. At Turangawaewae and Whakatane, more freedom of design was recommended. Basically, the 900 square-foot Department house is an economy version of the State house: a roofed box divided into small single-purpose compartments. Most Maoris are so glad to get out of their shacks that they accept it; but it does not meet their needs. It does not lend itself either to large entertaining or to the accommodation of a number of temporary guests; nor can it easily be extended to meet an increasing family. Though the Department has increased its plans by one bedroom and allows applicants to make slight modifications, it continues with its constricting boxes.

Since Peter Fraser, allotting 60 Maori houses to Auckland, insisted that no more than 3 should be built together, it has been departmental

---

* Other attractions, I am told, are the provision of free secondary education, finance for small businesses, and a completely self-contained social life.

policy to disperse them among pakeha houses. Delegates at the Auckland conference generally favoured the policy as promoting better race relations, and as setting Maoris a more desirable standard of housekeeping. Most of the 98 Wellington mothers interviewed by Jane Ritchie preferred dispersal. Nevertheless, Auckland delegates felt that they would like other Maoris to be nearby, either in a block of 4 or 5 houses in a pakeha area, or in several separated Maori houses in the same street, and the Presbyterian Maori Synod has said that those who do not wish to be dispersed should not be forced. The Wairoa conference specifically condemned the action of a group of Tokoroa teachers complaining to the Department of 7 Maori houses together (on the ground that there were 50 children in the one street).

A frequent complaint of rural delegates was of the departmental policy of refusing loans for building in remote areas. The Department has repeatedly replied that it will not lend if the house cannot be resold, and that this is unlikely where there is little prospect of employment. The Department's case seems unanswerable, yet it is often resented as one of the forces driving Maoris into the towns: another is the Town and Country Planning Act which forbids building on sections of less than 5 acres, and forces Maoris to abandon rural land that they own and are rated for, and move to a town where they have to buy a section. The cost of roading required by the Act forced owners of a Rotoiti land block to abandon a scheme of subdivision for eventual, but not immediate, settlement. Modification of the Act was asked for at Whakatane and Kaitaia: 'Pakeha subdivision is for the purpose of sale, Maori subdivision for the settlement of owners.'[6]

It has always been difficult for Maori farmers to obtain credit—except, recently, established farmers on the East Coast; and the Department since 1929 has developed unfarmed land, assuming ownership for a period long enough to recoup part of the outlay and then turning it over to the control of an individual Maori settler on a 42-year lease from its owners, with provision for compensation for improvements. Receipts from the stations temporarily farmed by the Department and repayments from subsequently settled have almost repaid the original outlay. Development has not been fast. The area developed to grass after 30 years was 403,600 acres, and in no post-war year has the area reached half of the 1940 figure of 22,100 acres. The total land remaining in Maori ownership is about four million acres, of which two and a half are considered suitable for farming: of this one million is leased to Europeans, another million is either in departmental control or is being farmed by Maoris. This leaves, according to Mr Hunn's 'guesstimate', about half a million acres to be developed, and might provide, by another guess, for 5,100 farmers. The Hunn Report has proposed a vigorous policy of development of this land, in the national interest, and already development has been put into the hands of the less hampered Lands and Survey Department.

The system, under Maori Affairs control, was not wholly satisfactory in that some settlers, inexperienced, have mismanaged their farms: there has been some incompetent or ineffective supervision of the settler's first efforts; and on the other hand, distrust, apathy and hostility from settlers towards the mortgagee Department which still retained some control over the land it had turned over to them. In one Hokianga district the people regard a 2000-acre block which has been held by the Department since 1937 as a stock-breeding farm, as stolen from them. Farmers consider themselves impoverished by the budgetary control or the fixed repayments by which the Department recoups its outlay.[7]

In the Far North, most of the thousand Maori farms are uneconomic: divided 30 years ago when 20 cows and 40 acres would keep a family, they cannot do so now, and farmers frequently leave their farms to wives and children and go out to work for wages. To quote P. W. Hohepa, who grew up in the district he is writing about, 'When the Department, the Dairy Company, the Hire Purchase firms, and the local store all take their share of the cream cheque, there is rarely anything left for the farmer. Most farmers in fact depend on Social Security benefits for the household's livelihood while the farming income acts as the debt eraser. Many still cannot make ends meet.'[8] Two years ago some were abandoning their farms. (It is typical of pakeha miscomprehension that a comment I heard at the time from a city dweller was that it was because they preferred to live off social security.) The solution would seem to be intensification of farming, but lack of capital or credit prevents it. At Auckland and Kaitaia, some delegates asked for more training of Maori farmers; others said that Maoris do not make full use of the schools existing. One-man dairy-farming, with its long hours and regular routine, does not suit traditional Maori work-patterns; some in Hokianga have solved this difficulty by working as teams on one another's farms in turn. Yet it seems to have produced a strain of individualism: in Panguru at least the idea has developed that 'he who farms should have full control of the land'.[9] In most of the farms there, the occupier has obtained from the joint owners either freehold ownership or a long-term lease. This development towards a European system of ownership is in harmony with the Department's theory of 'integration', but not with the attitudes of Maoris in sheep-farming areas.

More profitable has been the Maori initiative of incorporations, originated by Ngata among the Ngaati-porou, and working successfully not only on the East Coast but in Hawkes Bay, Rotorua and the King Country. Incorporations are an adaptation of communal ownership to a capitalist economy: run by committees of management and employing executive staff, they can (subject to the approval of the Maori Land Court) undertake farming, milling, reafforestation and quarrying. Bulk-buying and high post-war wool prices have brought wealth to some of the 180-odd incorporations in the Tai Rawhiti Land District; they have become more like private companies than communal enterprises. Some of the profits, however, are used for communal amenities: housing for workers and beneficiaries, scholarships, training of youths as farmers, the upkeep of maraes. At Tauranga-Taupo, it was recommended that incorporations be granted the freedom of private companies, even though at present they are taxed more lightly. They have been suggested as a source of credit for, say, the less fortunate dairy farmers of the Far North, but they are not empowered to reinvest. If this restriction is removed, one might see the development of Maori capitalism, the eventual emergence of an owning class. There would be sheer confusion if shares were freely disposable.

One vexed question for which administrators like Mr Corbett and Mr Hunn have proposed drastic treatment is the fragmentation of land holdings. This problem, attributed frequently enough to the growth in population, is in fact the direct consequence of the imposition since 1873 of a European system of individual ownership on traditional Maori land title, which, as is well known, was communal and hereditary. The owners of the land were its temporary occupants, 'trustees from the past and for the future'.[10] Under European law they were converted into individual shareholders, thousands of whom now own land assessed at only a few pence; the succession orders involve effort and expense costing more than the value of each share. The unsatisfactoriness of title divided among hundreds of scattered owners prevents any part-owner from taking the initiative and farming the land. Devices to meet this problem have not been successful. 'Consolidation', by which an owner of interests in several blocks can exchange them for several interests in one, is slow and laborious; and a consolidated holding fragments as its owner dies.

In 1953, Mr Corbett introduced 'conversion', whereby interests worth less than £25 can be bought by the Maori Trustee (a public servant) and sold to other Maoris; but there is a natural hesitancy on the part of other Maoris to offend the taangata whenua by purchasing land which is traditionally theirs. Since 1957 there has been 'the £10 rule' by which the Land Court can take from its inheritor an interest worth less than £10 and give it to another who already has more. There has been some voluntary use of the system of family arrangement by which a family agrees that one of them shall buy the others out and have freehold title. All of these go against traditional Maori attitudes (though the last indicates a change in attitude) and all work in the direction of sole ownership. Mr Hunn's proposal that the base-line be raised from £10 to £50 has been strongly opposed by the Presbyterian Maori Synod and by elders who discussed it in Auckland last July, as have his suggestions of primogeniture, or that fathers should nominate a successor by word of mouth. The reluctance to make a will is not superstition: it is a conviction that it is wrong to exclude any of one's children from his inheritance, that all one's descendants are entitled to inherit the land one has held in trust for them. Mr Hunn's alternative suggestion, however, has the inspiration of Ngata's conception of incorporations, and has been welcomed by the Synod: the incorporation of tribes as land-owning bodies, in which every member shares but has no rights of disposal. It is a return to the traditional conception of ownership. There would no doubt be administrative difficulties in defining a tribe and in working out whether or not some people are entitled to membership: but these difficulties would seem fewer than those that follow from fragmentation.

'Land is more than soil', the Synod says. The man who owns a penny-worth of land in his home district, even if he has moved to the city, has turangawaewae, a place to stand, which implies his right to speak on his marae, and gives him a sense of belonging. Maori adolescents may not bother themselves with questions of inheritance and may know neither their whakapapa (genealogical table) nor their hapuu (subdivision of a tribe); yet they frequently feel the need to return to their ancestral home, for consolation and renewal of security, to lick the wounds of the city. Without this sense of belonging and the certainty of a home to go back to, Maoris would feel alienated and dispossessed: the frustrations and privations of the city would cause more demoralisation and crime. Both the Whakarewarewa and Wairoa conferences opposed Mr Hunn's suggestion that ownership of an urban 'home' might be an acceptable qualification for turangawaewae: to a Maori a house is private property, but his land is not. This is assimilation with a vengeance.

Whakarewarewa delegates discussed the continued existence of the Maori Land Court and concluded that, in spite of its irritatingly slow and cumbrous processes, it should be retained as a protection of the remaining Maori land. The Court is empowered to prevent sales of land to non-Maoris but in practice for some years has contented itself with seeing that a fair price is paid. Maori land is still being alienated, since 1953 at an average rate, according to Mr Hunn's figures, of 17,000 acres a year; according to figures given at Waitetoko by his predecessor, T. T. Ropiha, of between 20,000 and 30,000 a year. Mr Ropiha added that if this rate continues a further million acres will have gone by the end of the century and there will be only the mountain-tops left. Land can be taken under the Public Works Act for roading, for public amenities and for urban development. It can be sold on the resolution of three owners, with the onus on the other owners (if they see the notice in the paper) to dissent and apply for a partition of their shares. Further, the transfer to sole ownership and freehold title, current in the four northern counties, increases the possibility of such land being sold to non-Maoris: it depends only on one man. It is not surprising that elders with their long memories of fraudulent buying and confiscation suspect such devices, and the suggestion that they be extended, as subtle new refinements of pakeha land-hunger.

There is dissatisfaction with rating of undeveloped land by local bodies: since 1953 land on which rates have not been paid can be leased or even sold by the Maori Trustee. There is understandable impatience on the part of County Councils at the difficulty of tracing multiple owners. Nevertheless, Maoris have real grievances. Tuwharetoa delegates at Tauranga-Taupo said that the Taupo County Council had raised the rates on lakeside land, valuing it as potential pakeha bach-sites. One owner, whose land adjoined a forest, had his rates raised because of the future value of the seedling pines that had sprung up on his property. Owners have been forced to sell in order to pay the rates.

Local bodies have often shown an unwillingness to understand that amounts to cultural arrogance. The Rotorua Town Council, ashamed of the ill-sanitated slum that confronts tourists at Whakarewarewa, has forbidden further building and has offered the residents resettlement at Koutu, but does not understand their reluctance to leave ancestral land. Twelve years ago the Auckland City Council compelled the Ngaati-whaatua (after about seventy years of confusing pressure from the Council, government departments and the Land Court) to leave their derelict shacks at Orakei marae and move into rented State houses on 'Boot Hill', as they called it; someone put a match to the meeting-house, no one can say who, but the Ngaati-whaatua are convinced it wasn't a Maori match. No doubt the people are materially better off, but for some time their resentment at losing their land caused a good deal of anti-social behaviour in Kitemoana Street. It is understandable that they did not warm to the City Council's offer to develop the old marae as a tourist display.* The site for a new marae is not taken as full compensation, since it has not the ancestral associations of the old one.

Last March a three-man board of trustees (with the approval of the Maori Affairs Department) ordered the demolition of sub-standard houses at Omahu near Hastings. People in their beds were wakened by bulldozers pushing at their walls. Their reluctance to act on the warning they had received may be explained by the fact that though they will have title to subdivided sections and will eventually have new houses, they will have to pay for both and were not given any choice.

Elders feel that the remaining land must be retained so that, as the Synod puts it, 'the old home of the people may remain a sheet anchor for the sons and daughters who go forth to make a life in a new world'. Maoris, it was said at Turangawaewae, are 'afraid of the unfamiliar',[11] and it may be some generations before migrants cease to feel the need for their old home, if they ever do. Nevertheless, it can only support a lessening proportion of the people. The absolute numbers of rural dwellers will rise, however, and they can only be supported by land development and more

* This incident is complicated by the fact that the offer was a keen councillor's perversion of a scheme of Maharaia Winiata's—a cultural centre set on the old marae. Dr Winiata himself did not consult the taangata whenua, a serious omission for which the Council cannot be blamed.

intensive farming. Several conferences have suggested the establishment of industries in rural areas, but they were not sanguine, and a Gisborne round table frankly admitted that the idea was unrealistic. Elders at the Auckland conference suggested that Maoris should set up co-operative industries, financed by the wealthy incorporations. They could cite the experience of an incorporation between Taumarunui and Tokaanu, which cut timber and milled it, and running into restrictive practices from pakeha companies, treated it and set up two joinery factories. But this incorporation has since sold its milling assets to a timber company and has turned to developing the land for farming.

It was possible for the 1939 conference to deplore the movement to cities and for I. L. G. Sutherland in 1935 to see no future for the race but a life based on the land. Now it is recognized that for a good proportion migration is inevitable. The 1956 census showed 30.7 per cent of male Maoris employed in 'agriculture, forestry, hunting and fishing', and 54.4 per cent in manufacturing, construction, transport, storage and communication. The latter proportion is likely to increase. The high proportion of juveniles means, as Borrie has said, that for every person for whom employment had to be found in the past, there will be more than two in the future. Finding a job is the first concern of the Maori who comes to a town, and the Auckland conference suggested the appointment of special placement officers and that the Department of Maori Affairs should set up a Labour Bureau. Most migrants go into unskilled labour, often seasonal; and those who come to the cities often shop around from job to job before they settle. Insufficient education and unfamiliarity with the range of employment keeps many Maoris of high intelligence in jobs that pakehas of the same intelligence would not be doing. One might expect this to lead employers to prefer Maoris as employees, but not many have woken up to it. Many employers are reluctant, fearing absenteeism, laziness, stupidity and difficulties of understanding. Girls find it hard to get any work except in factories, laundries, restaurants and hospitals: shopkeepers and banks often turn them down. At Whakatane it was said that in one South Auckland company town the company discriminated against Maoris; but I am told that since a take-over, the new direction actually prefers Maoris (as freezing-works do) because they are often stronger, develop physical skills quicker, are more confident with machinery, and, it is probable, are less conscious of union awards than pakehas, less suspicious of the management. The last can lead to occasional tension with non-Maori unionists. (The Maori ideal work-pattern is one of vigorous, efficient, co-operative team work for a purpose: and the Latter Day Saints were able to harness this in building the Temple and College at Tuhikaramea on subsistence labour.) Few lads are attracted to apprenticeships except, it was said at Gisborne, in the motor-trade, though a carpentry training-school in Auckland has been a success, and another has just opened in

Christchurch. The reason for this is not only insufficient education—Maoris are quick to pick up skills in handling materials—it is that living away from home, a youth cannot support himself on apprentice's wages, without subsidy from home, and that is usually not possible. The high proportion of Maoris in unskilled labour makes them vulnerable to any economic depression: queues for jobs would be mostly Maoris, and racial friction among the workless would be almost certain.

Youths migrating to the cities arrive often without permanent accommodation and without enough money: they probably have relatives to stay with till they find board, though the relative's house may be overcrowded. They may find one of those bed-and-breakfast places that 'welcome' Maoris and charge more for the privilege, or insist on their being out all day, even at weekends. They may prefer to go flatting with friends. They are likely to have pakeha neighbours complaining, and police interrupting, if they sing at parties. They keep shifting from place to place. They are removed from the restraints of their home district—the Tribal Committee, wardens, older relatives who sit and watch them at the youth club dances; and they are glad to be free of the parental nagging that descends at adolescence. They are exposed to the excitement and anxiety-ridden values of the films and popular music. They frequently get into trouble. In 1960, a fifth of magistrate's court convictions for 'distinct prisoners'* in arrest cases were Maoris, and 17 out of 100 prisoners sentenced in the Supreme Court; 31 of 100 prisoners received were Maoris. It is possible, as was argued at Whakatane, that the statistics give an inaccurate picture, since there are no figures for undetected crime, and it might well be that most Maori crime is detected. Maoris are less frequently represented be counsel and more often plead guilty. Delegates at Whakarewarewa claimed that adolescents under police interrogation confess to crimes they haven't committed in the hope of escaping an anxious and unfamiliar situation: the 1955 inquiry into the Ruka-Harris case confirms that this has happened at least once. Police are seldom willing to call in a welfare officer or the tribal committee. Magistrates in Hamilton and Rotorua have stated that Maoris are not obtaining proper counsel, but in other towns seem to be provoked into strictures: pakeha offenders are not called a disgrace to their race. A year or two ago, one magistrate took it on himself to deliver a misinformed attack on the Ringatu religion, and order a youth to abandon it. But if there is any prejudice in the magistrates' courts, the statistics show only a slight difference between the proportions of Maoris and non-Maoris who are not convicted.[12] Measures suggested at conferences were the provision of legal aid, and co-operation between the police and welfare officers or tribal committees. Since offenders will talk more freely to Maoris, more participation of Maoris in the processes

---

* i.e., prisoners as distinct from charges.

of justice is desirable: not only Maori policemen, but Maori J.P.'s. It is a pity there are so few Maori lawyers; consequently there is no immediate prospect of Maori magistrates. Maoris are excluded from jury rolls, but at present Maori leaders prefer to accept this as a restriction incurred by the right of a Maori who has committed a crime against another Maori to be tried by a Maori jury. But since most Maori offences are not against other Maoris, and the right is seldom invoked, I cannot see why the right to be tried by a Maori jury should entail the exclusion of Maoris from other juries.

Most of the crimes are against the person (assault, sexual offences) or against property, particularly theft, breaking and entering, and car conversion. At Kaitaia it was said that in a small community where everyone is related it is no crime to help oneself to another's property, and that Maoris do not take so serious a view of carnal knowledge. This defence is not a strong one, but it points the need for Mr Hunn's suggestion, supported by two conferences, that youths about to leave for the city should be instructed in 'permissible conduct'. But surely one factor in car conversions is the discrimination against Maoris (imposed by insurance companies) by rental car firms. For the rest the reasons for juvenile crime are boredom, insecurity, unemployment, frustration from overcrowding or from boarding where one is not welcome, and a desire for kicks. Several conferences suggested more provision for recreation and social life: in the country there are the youth clubs, in the cities there are the pakeha sports organizations and the Y.M.C.A., and Auckland has (for schoolboys) its police-run Boystown. Wellington has its Ngaati-Pooneke Club; Auckland's Community Centre is more of a hall for dances and talent quests than a true social centre—and factionalism has held up progress with the proposed Ngaati-Aakarana marae. Several conferences have seen the problem as one of reception of migrants as they reach the city. A Wellington soft-goods firm, with the help of welfare officers, found accommodation for twelve girls it was bringing from Wairoa, but obviously the possibility of this sort of arrangement is limited. Elders at the Auckland conference suggested tribal 'embassies' in each city, financed by tribal Trust Boards, as meeting-places and reception centres. Six-month transit hostels have been suggested. And the simplest and most radical suggestion, from the Tauranga discussion group who prepared a paper on employment for the Whakarewarewa conference, is that pakeha homes should take Maori boarders.

The Tauranga group's statement is worth quoting since it gives an insight into how Maoris see the problem. If the English is awkward, it should be remembered that it is a foreign language, and, further, that it would be unusual in European society to have a group meeting fortnightly to discuss a serious public question, consisting of secondary pupils, an apprentice, four clerks, a labourer, a telephone operator, a hotel domestic, three teachers and three farmers:

The whole situation requires fundamental thinking for, at the present time, where Maori youth must leave the spiritual security of their homes, and the society in which they have grown up, to live in an alien and not-understood environment, the guidance necessary in the growing up period of adolescence and early adulthood must be supplied. This is the very period when all humanity needs guidance but is least willing to accept it even from their own family. The problem is not so much the provision of board and lodging but the provision of those spiritual necessities which culminate in that feeling of 'belongingness' to the community from which stems self-respect. . . .

So here we put out clarion calls to both Pakeha and Maori. To the former we ask that you go out of your way to welcome us into your communities and into your homes and that you be not over-critical of those behaviour patterns which do not conform to yours. If at times we jar we shall at least be being given the opportunity to learn how to conform. Without your sympathetic co-operation we shall find the results of all our strivings to be in vain, consequently not worth the effort entailed. Take our youth into your homes as boarders, rent us your homes not your derelict buildings, give our families who come to live among you the courtesies of neighbourliness.

To the Maori people we say, if, as is now the case, you have for the economic stability of yourself and your family, to leave your home district and take work in towns then accept those unknown difficulties, so frightening because they are unknown, with the set idea that your inherent abilities and strength of character can overcome them; realise that it is a sad fact that the behaviour pattern of many of our race has over the years been such as to warrant condemnation, and determine to eschew them. The acceptance of those requirements on each side will do much toward the elimination of the necessity for so much hostel accommodation.

It is of course not only city Maoris who come before courts but it is in the city that the Maori is exposed to the greatest pressure to abandon his traditional securities; and consciously or unconsciously every Maori is engaged in a personal debate whether to assert or abandon some particular attitude or habit, whether to adopt or reject some new one. A similar situation may evoke from him a response differing according to whether it is in a Maori or a European or a mixed context. The new values and criteria that are most impressed on him are those for which European society tries to provide its own safeguards—those of the films, the comics and the teenage idols. Juvenile delinquency is not a peculiarly Maori problem; yet if a youth dresses like a bodgie or a girl sweeps up her hair and wears leopard-skin matadors, they are fundamentally different from their pakeha counterparts. They respond more spontaneously to friendliness; they respect old people; they are capable of enjoying themselves with no more artificial stimulation than a guitar. There is merit in Mr Hunn's proposal for segregated Borstals: Maori inmates would be more amenable to encouragement from welfare officers and clergymen if they were free from the sneers of pakeha inmates. From two sources I am told that racial friction is high in a maximum-security establishment like Invercargill where there are 35% Maoris; it probably reflects the different pressures and psychological tensions that motivated the two groups of prisoners in their crimes. The Presbyterian Maori Synod suggests short terms in strict-discipline reformatories, but this may be theological harshness. I would suggest that for Maori prisoners group counselling would be profitable.

When all is said on crime, it is sobering to remind oneself, not of the 5% who offend (1.5% pakeha) but the 95% who don't.

Few Maori offenders have been educated beyond Form IV, and in all conferences education was seen as the solution to problems of health, child-rearing, employment and crime. Maori elders have long seen education as the hope for their people; Trust Boards and incorporations provide grants and scholarships to pupils and students of their tribe; the Ngata and Ngarimu post-graduate scholarships are more generous than any other in New Zealand. Yet the paradox is that there are far too few Maoris in the upper forms at secondary schools and at university, and in contrast with the keenness with which Maoris 120 years ago learned to read and write, there is a depressed class of parents ignorant and apathetic to, or incapable of advising on, the future vocations of their children.

It is necessary to look at the schools Maoris attend. There are 155 Maori primary schools in rural areas, and 10 Maori District High Schools. The Maori primary schools are administered by the Education Department and have often been served by teachers not only aware of the special needs of their pupils, but dedicated to their work and likely to stay longer in the one place; nearly half of them now are Maoris. Parents look on the school as theirs, talk to the teacher about their children, and turn up with batches of scones when the inspector visits. Most Maoris who are in the professions were educated at these schools. At secondary level there are eleven church boarding-schools with a mainly Maori roll, which inculcate a pride of race, and half of the Maori graduates at Auckland University in the past four years have been to these schools.

But they cater for only a minority of the Maori school population: two-thirds of the primary pupils are in Board schools, and four-fifths of the secondary pupils are in public secondary schools. A great many Maori children at these schools, feeling that their teachers take no special interest in them, become apathetic and find themselves pushed into the lower streams. They are usually about a year behind pakeha pupils in attainment, and the gap widens. Pupils coming from Maori primary schools to public secondary schools are discouraged by the impersonal atmosphere, and some do not recover from the change. Many of their teachers look on them as dumb and their parents, shy of a pakeha institution, take little interest in the school. Measures taken to deal with the problem are inadequate. The Post Primary Teachers' Association has set up a committee on Maori education. In 1955 an advisory committee was set up to advise the Education Department. An officer of the Department has access to all primary schools where there are Maori pupils. The measures have not met the problem: the provision of that warm personal interest to which Maori children respond and without which they are lost. It has been noticed that the pupils become keener when they have a Maori teacher. Various suggestions have been made at conferences: that at Board schools with a high Maori roll, there should be a sympathetic teacher with special responsibility for them; that Education Boards should have advisers on Maori education; that Maori parents should participate in Parent-Teacher Associations; that there should be more Maori vocational guidance officers. As a result of the Marton conference, a voluntary group at Whanganui set itself up to advise Maori pupils on education and careers; another at Palmerston North; and the Whakatane group which prepared a paper on education for the Whakarewarewa conference has formed itself into a permanent Maori advancement group.

A Maori pupil suffers from a number of disabilities which have a cumulative and long-term effect. He may have to travel an hour and a half each way to school. He is not encouraged to be inside the house except to do chores which he may resent and which cut into the time he needs for homework. He cannot do homework in an ill-lit home where the only place is the kitchen table, perhaps already occupied by adult elbows and cards and flagons; where the tradition is that children should not distract adults from their occupations. He cannot discuss his homework with his parents, whose conversation is in any case limited to people and local preoccupations; there are no books in the house, and there is no tradition of reading to children at bed-time. Economic pressures may force him to be absent from school: perhaps Dad is away shearing, Mum is ill and he has to look after the younger ones; he may have accompanied Dad on his shearing trip; he may have had little sleep after a late adult function in the house or on the marae. The cost of his staying on at school is a real problem for his parents. He is greatly attached for emotional security to his age-group, and when they leave school, he leaves with them. There is money to be earned and he wants to be independent. He does not find it easy to defer immediate satisfactions for the sake of a distant goal: he has not been trained in the pakeha habits of foresight, thrift, patience. At Kaitaia it was said that some parents fear education as something that will take their children away from them.

Since they can only be removed by attention to health and housing and by education of the parents, these disabilities are not likely to disappear for some time. One delegate at Tauranga-Taupo said that Maori children will not perform as well as pakeha children till a generation of parents has had secondary education. Frequently it was said at conferences that parents must accept more responsibility, make more sacrifices, plan their lives around their children's vocational needs. A useful practice at Reporoa could be widely imitated: school certificate pupils use the local school for evening study.

Even at university level, in spite of the effect of boarding-schools, these disabilities have their effect. Most of the Maori students I have known are practical rather than imaginative; concentrate on passing rather than involve themselves in their subject of study. A good many of them fail because they are subject to more temptations: they have more friends than pakeha students and consequently there are more parties and outings. The Maori student has not the individualist incentives of the pakeha: according to Ausubel and the Ritchies he has a deep-seated fear of distinguishing himself for fear of attracting criticism, but I cannot say that I have noticed this; though it is true that he is afraid to ask questions in tutorials for fear of making a fool of himself. He is likely to say—and genuinely mean—that his aim is to help his people, then dismayed at his failure to apply himself, to retire from the effort. The 'Rakau' researchers would attribute his performance, among other things, to a deficiency in the use of imagination and fantasy;[13] Ausubel to an inability to handle abstract concepts. He may be right; all I would say is that in his first year a Maori is likely to feel his English vocabulary inadequate, and to be imprecise and unsure in his use of abstract concepts *in English*. Yet quite a few have managed to graduate; and, as far as I can see, the difference between those that have and those that haven't—apart from intelligence— is simply that the graduates have worked steadily, usually encouraged by their wives or friends or interested lecturers.

Most Maoris who have School Certificate go in for teaching. Those who enrol at university go mainly for arts courses; there are fewer in science and medicine; a few in fine arts, and only an occasional engineer, commerce student, lawyer or architect.

There has been pressure for the transference of Maori primary schools to Board control, a transference that the parents do not desire. James Ritchie has given an account of how, through disrespect for Maori methods of arriving a communal decisions (by which silence means dissent and a question is fully talked out till unanimity is reached), through restrictive chairmanship, through confusion and misunderstanding, a parents' meeting at Murupara apparently assented to a decision they actually disagreed with. Since then the Department has agreed in principle to the recommendation of the Advisory Committee on Maori Education that, while it recognizes that eventually the distinction between Maori and Board schools will disappear, no school should be transferred without the free consent of the parents. Nevertheless the Education Department shows signs of impatience to hurry the process. Pukekohe is a case in point.

Ten years ago a separate Maori school was established there as a result of pressure from parents and teachers who complained of the dirty habits of the children of Maoris working in the market gardens; they had already imposed segregation of toilets and shelter-sheds. The Maori parents deeply resented the Department's action, since they were not consulted; but since the school has been established, they have wholeheartedly and unanimously accepted it as a school where their children have self-respect. Department policy now is to integrate the three local schools, but the Maori parents are opposed and even financed the school bus when for a time the Department discontinued it, and will resent the transference if it is imposed in defiance of their wishes. They fear that their children will not get a fair deal at the Board schools.

It is often said that integrated schools are nurseries of good race relations, but it would seem to depend on the proportions, on the race relations outside the school, and probably other factors. It was said at Rotorua that relations between Maori and pakeha pupils are good where Maoris are in a majority of about 60%; they are probably good where pakehas are in a clear majority with only a few Maoris. Where there is a Maori minority of about 25%, it was said, relations are poor. It looks as if pakeha children resent an unassimilable minority. But all this must depend on the state of race relations in the district: in a church boarding-school the pakeha minority is popular with the Maoris; in Pukekohe there would be friction, whatever the proportions.

Advisory committees like the ones in Whanganui, Palmerston and Whakatane could identify bright pupils and encourage their parents to send them to boarding-school if they can afford it. The most spectacular outcome of the Hunn Report was the setting up of the Maori Educational Foundation with the aim of providing secondary scholarships and trade training for gifted pupils. Since the scholarships come only from interest on investment, the immediate prospects are limited, but they will grow. The board of trustees is weighted on the side of the Government, and there is some caution on the part of Trust Boards and incorporations about doing what Mr Hunn has urged, channelling all their educational grants into the Foundation: it is a question of control of their own money and a natural preference that it should be used for members of their own tribe. It is not possible to predict how the current drive for donations will proceed. All success to it, but it is being run like a grand charity, and I suspect there is a certain sales resistance (from pakehas) on the ground that the public is being asked to subsidise an undertaking that is usually considered entirely a Government responsibility.

Besides this Government action, there are from Maoris themselves signs of hope: at conferences a concern over absenteeism, proposals for starting supervised play-centres on the maraes for pre-school children, and this statement from the Tauranga discussion group: 'In spite of all the difficulties we see in the way, in spite of all calls for assistance which we have made in this evaluation, we admit that, in the final analysis, in all efforts made on our behalf to help us cope with economic circumstances, the primary and fundamental effort must come from ourselves.'

The currency of the Maori language cannot be accurately described. A recent Education Department 'survey', consisting of an on-the-spot questionnaire to headmasters of Maori schools, was worthless. On the East Coast, in the Urewera and in the Far North, Maori is spoken in the homes. There are districts where the children know no Maori. One hears of children in Maori-speaking areas who resist using Maori and answer their parents in English. In the cities there is the pressure of courtesy, by which Maoris in the company of a pakeha, use his language—and there is usually a pakeha around. No doubt, if it is indicative of a trend, this is pleasing to those pakehas who look on a non-Indo-European language spoken by fewer than 170,000 people as an anachronism and an irritating disconformity; one suspects that educational policy-makers would be happier if the language did not exist. The Pope policy for native schools, followed from 1877 to 1930, assumed that in order to prevent the disappearance of the race, rapid acculturation was necessary and only English must be used: the Ball policy from 1930 admitted some elements of Maori culture, but not the language as a teaching medium, on the grounds that Maori children should not speak inferior English.[14]

But after 85 years of compulsory English Maori parents and children often still speak a dialect of English with a limited vocabulary and range of constructions. And many teachers implemented official policy by strapping children if they spoke Maori—a thing for which a well-known kuia (old woman: a term of respect) told me she would never forgive my race. When they first come to school some children are taught in a language they either do not know or only partly know. In English-speaking districts the kind of English spoken is not standard New Zealand English. The question arises of the psychological effects of linguistic frustration: of not having a language in which to express one's most complex thoughts or most intimate feelings. And it is arguable that there is a connection between self-respect and knowledge of a language which expresses one's ethnic traditions. Language like land would seem to be an anchor against demoralisation. But until some reliable research is done, no one can accurately say how widely, or by what age-groups, Maori is spoken.

There have been, both at young leaders' and students' conferences and from the Gisborne Jaycees, a number of recommendations that Maori should be taught in schools. So far as one can distil the common agreement of all these motions, it would be that Maori should be available at all secondary schools with a good proportion of Maoris, and that Maori studies and correct pronunciation of place-names should be compulsory at all primary schools. A stronger proposal was that Maori language should be compulsory for all Maori pupils and optional for pakehas. The difficulty is to find the teachers. For the last few years, Maori studies has been taught at two training colleges, but not language: yet as far back as 1939 this very request was made by young leaders.

Desirable as these proposals are they will not transmit the language as a current medium of communication. Only Maori parents can do that. Frequently enough one speaks at morning-tea to a delegate who has supported such a proposal and finds that he and his wife use English at home. But whatever the Maori people decide to do with their language, we should at least not hamper their freedom in deciding.

The Council for Educational Research recently received a grant from the J. R. McKenzie Trust for research in Maori education. In its 85 years experience of Maori schooling the Department of Education has done no research and has conducted its policy by hit-or-miss methods and according to the personal theory of some administrative 'architect'. No one can provide an answer to such questions as would be of practical use to the Department's teachers, such questions as Bruce Biggs asked at Kaitaia: 'If a child is bilingual at school-entry, what will be the actual words he is likely to know in each language? Is his total vocabulary in both languages equal to the total vocabulary of a unilingual child? Does he distinguish conceptually between the two languages? Does he have different emotional attitudes to the two languages? Just what English constructions does he use? What constructions in English are unfamiliar to him? Does it help or confuse him to explain usage of one language by another? On exactly what points is his use of English unacceptable as New Zealand standard English?'[15] Suggestions made at a Wellington conference called to discuss how to use the McKenzie Trust grant were that an experiment be done in a Maori-speaking community in using Maori as a teaching medium to Standard II, and teaching English at first as a second language (as is done in Samoa); that there be research into methods of teaching Maori; a study of the factors behind the success of Maori graduates; evaluation of existing institutions like Maori District High Schools and boarding-schools.

There has been unofficially sponsored research into wider questions in the last few years. David Ausubel's chapters on race relations in *The Fern and the Tiki* are unique as a brief popular survey of mutual attitudes between the two peoples: his *Maori Youth*, though its testing methodology has been dismissed by a psychologist[16] remains a shrewd rough assessment of the Maori situation in 1958. More challenging to accepted ideas are the 'Rakau' studies by the University of Wellington Department of Psychology, studies of children and their parents in a forestry town. The methodology of these studies too has been dismissed by a psychologist.[17] I know nothing of the validity of the tests that were used, but the observations on family life contain many insights. Yet the hypotheses the researchers claim to have confirmed are suspect, and some of them I cannot reconcile with my experience of Maoris. Their picture of the 'Rakau' personality is of one determined by an infancy experience of extreme indulgence followed by a 'rejection' when the next baby comes, an unsatisfied seeking for security in the group of siblings and playmates, and a tenuous rapprochement with parents during adolescence. They delineate the finished 'basic personality' as insecure, anxious, full of unresolved aggression, conformist, afraid of involvement, craving love but unable to give it. I doubt if Freud can be applied to Maoris or that one can limit one's study of Maori children to the household family of Mum, Dad and the kids. I fear that we are being given a new stereotype, and one that has less relation to its model than the usual one of cheerful, happy-go-lucky Hori. The studies are admittedly ethnocentric, but I suspect that they may have the effect of carrying the pakeha sense of cultural superiority to the point of ceasing to envy the Maori his freedom from our obsessions and insecurities, since he is mentally in a worse case than we are. For years our administrators and urgers have been telling the Maori what is good for him: now we are probing into his personality and telling him *that* is out of order too.

How then does Maori culture differ from our own? It is not a matter of carving, and genealogies, mooteatea and patere, though the old people still sing them, or of pois and action-songs. It is a matter of a different kinship system, different values and aspirations, a different system of child-rearing. There is the attachment to the land; the sense that (unlike the pakeha) one's ancestors have lived here for nearly a thousand years and that this is the home of one's descendants. Beyond the household family there is the wider whaamere, which as Pat Hohepa defines it, consists of all the descendants (with their spouses and adopted children) of an ancestor who has died within living memory (usually the father of the oldest living member).[18] Beyond the whaamere there is the sense of belonging provided by his membership of the tribe. There is the preference for spells of hard, long group work for a group purpose which can be achieved in foreseeable time, rather than for sustained, regular work for oneself. There is the concern for the immediate, rather than for the distant future; the admiration of generosity and sociability and hospitality, the deliberately happy-go-lucky attitude to time and money, the high value placed on personal relations, and the consequent preference for the company of others who feel the same way, that is (usually) for other Maoris. There is the preference for sea-foods and food cooked in a haangi. And in spite of local factionalism, there is the loyalty to one's tribe, and then to other Maoris as against the pakeha. To be a Maori is to know and feel for each one of the hundred-odd members of one's whaamere, to expect a welcome when one visits them, wherever they are; to feel the obligations of aroha and feed and accommodate a guest and help any relative or friend in difficulty. At the present time too, it is to be more familiar with bereavement—since a number of one's relatives, even younger ones, will have died. It is to be more understanding towards the criminal, since one probably has a relative or two who have been 'in trouble'. There are, too, the ceremonial of the marae, the big huis, the religious hui toopuu, the opening of meeting-houses, the tangi, the formal meetings of representatives of two whaamere to arrange a wedding, and the distinctive character of Maori weddings, unveiling of tombstones, Maori church services, twenty-first birthday celebrations, and parties with their endless repertoire not only of action-songs but songs in English that everybody knows but few pakehas have ever heard of. What can be called Maori culture today is closer to European culture than to Maori culture at the time of European contact; in its informing spirit, however, it is quite distinct and is not likely to be 'integrated' away by administrators. Most Maoris participate in at least some of its expressions. It is made up, as Maharaia Winiata put it in a data paper prepared for the Auckland conference in 1959, of 'those things in the modern world to which the Maori clings to help him keep his sanity in what for him is a confused and confusing world'. It is a source of security and stability, and in districts where it is abandoned there is more drunkenness and demoralisation: if youths in the cities are bereft of it there will be more crime.

It is on this question that the Hunn Report has been most severely criticized—by the Presbyterian Maori Synod, by Bruce Biggs and by Richard Thompson, who called it 'essentially a European document'.[19] Mr Hunn sees no more of Maori culture than a few 'relics'—language, arts and crafts, and the institutions of the marae. He is in a hurry to promote integration by swifter urbanisation, but his conception of integration is close to assimilation. At Waitetoko marae he illustrated his view of its pace with the hypothetical case of a Maori girl who at 20 married a pakeha, whose daughter at 20 another, and her granddaughter likewise, so that the woman at 60 would have eighth-caste grandchildren. It is hardly a typical case. The Hunn Report is to be commended as the most important official statement in years on Maori inequalities in housing, health and educational achievement. It has resulted in increased housing allocation, a committee on Maori health, plans for more vigorous land development and the Maori Educational Foundation. In some of its suggestions on land title it overrides Maori sensibilities, though it contains the inspired suggestion for the incorporation of tribes. But in its theoretical basis it is confused and over-simplified and unacquainted with the spirit of Maoritanga.

It is a paradox in New Zealand that those least sympathetic to Maori aspirations often invoke an abstract equality as their sanction for wanting the abolition of Maori schools, the four seats, and the Department of Maori Affairs. A good many liberals and sympathisers are taken in by the slogan. An Australian socialist once accused me of being a racialist because I was 'stressing differences'. It is, as Dr Biggs has put it, something that has long been a bug-bear of New Zealand thinking, a confusion of equality with uniformity; and the most intelligent official statement for some years is Mr Hanan's: 'What suits one person or one race does not always suit another. To treat people equally you sometimes must treat them differently.' Even Mr Hanan was surprised at the opposition of the Maori M.P.s to his proposal on juries.

Pakeha resentment at 'pampering of the Maoris' was stimulated when Labour's majority was equal to the number of Maori seats held by Labour. But the post-war record of the Department of Maori Affairs, especially its pre-Hanan housing policy, can hardly be called pampering. The Department continues its role of mediator between the State and the Maoris, and Maoris still feel the need for it. Yet its attitude, at all levels, leaves a lot to be desired: one informed commentator has called it 'colonial'.[20] Mr Hanan's championship of Maori rights is unlikely to be translated into the day-to-day transactions at district offices. Further there is the paternal way in which the Department is represented on so many organizations set up and financed by Maoris—the Maori Purposes Fund Board, the boards that award the Ngata and Ngarimu scholarships, for example, or the way in which such organizations are often persuaded to leave crucial decisions to subcommittees made up of pakeha public servants. The Women's Welfare League had to resist attempts at departmental supervision. There is departmental control of the Maori-financed *Te Ao Hou*, and its timid, uncontroversial policy, even under Erik Schwimmer's editorship; the avoidance of controversy on the niggardly quarter-hour of news in Maori on Sunday evenings. It is arguable that continuation of the Department's paternalism will produce dependence on advice and assistance. On the other hand, sudden withdrawal of the Department's mediation would be leaving the Maori people to sink or swim, and most of them would sink. A progressive, even if leisurely, withering-away should be foreseen, and a necessary prerequisite is that Maoris should be allowed more control of their own affairs, and that where decisions (as they more frequently will) affect both races, their opinion should be consulted and given more than proportionate weight.

Peter Fraser's Economic and Social Welfare Act of 1945 provided for Maoris to police themselves through honorary wardens, to attend (within the limits of State direction) to their own welfare by the appointment of welfare officers, and to govern some of their local affairs through tribal committees and tribal executives. At Gisborne it was said that about a quarter of the 80 executives and the 440 committees were inactive: otherwise the system has worked well. Last year's Act completes the organization at a national level by setting up a Dominion Council of representatives elected by tribal executives. There will be a voice for the Maori people independent of political parties.

Before Apirana Ngata died he predicted that in ten years Maoris might be considering the need for the abolition of separate parliamentary representation. The question was brought up at the elders' round table at Turangawaewae, but a secret ballot showed that, though the elders thought it must come sooner or later, they did not want it yet. It was said that there were three possibilities: abolition of the seats; requests for one or two more seats to meet the increase in Maori electors; some elders of National Party allegiance advocated reduction of the number of seats so that the number of registered voters in any Maori electorate should be no smaller than the number in the average pakeha electorate. A motion at Gisborne to ask for more seats was lost. On the other hand, at several conferences, it was thought to be too optimistic to hope that on a single electoral roll, there would be four Maori members elected. It was said, further, that electoral areas are too large, many electors do not know their members and that Maori representation should not be tied to pakeha party politics, that some electors prefer to consult the local pakeha member. At present Maoris must register on the Maori roll, half-castes can opt to be on either roll, and less than half-castes must register on the European roll. But the system is flexible in that it is by one's own declaration that one is Maori, half-caste or European; and it was claimed that some Maoris prefer to be on the European roll, and some less than half-castes enrol as Maoris. A suggestion at Turangawaewae and Whakatane was that Maoris be allowed the same option as half-castes; and this might meet the needs of the urban Maori whose Maori member may be more concerned with rural problems.

In 1960, meeting a group of his electors on the All Black issue, Mr Anderton, member for Auckland Central, banged the table and said it was absolutely inconceivable that Labour could ever lose the Maori vote. The policy of the 1949–57 administration did not lose Labour any votes. Yet there is among more educated Maoris a general dissatisfaction with the alliance between Labour and Ratana and with the inactivity of their own representatives, except perhaps Sir Eruera Tirikatene. George Harrison standing for National, Arnold Reedy for Social Credit, did not represent endorsement of the total policies of those parties so much as opposition, in the only practical way, to the present representation. Perhaps the Dominion Council of tribal representatives will alter this. Whether post-Hunn policy can seriously reduce Labour's majority in the Maori vote in the short time before the next election is doubtful. It is possible that Cabinet's support of Mr Hanan is based on this hope, but it would be a pity if an enlightened policy were withdrawn because political calculations were not confirmed.

Not enough trust has ever been put in Maori initiative. It was Maori initiative that was ultimately responsible (at a Maori Labour conference in the thirties) for the 1945 and 1961 Acts; for the formation of the Maori Women's Welfare League; for the 28th Battalion Association and the leadership conferences that began in 1959. If the initial direction of such moves is withdrawal from the pakeha, it is only for the purpose of establishing identity: from this position pakehas are invited to share in activities.

There are pakeha members of Tribal Committees, of the League; the 28th Battalion's club at Opotiki is open to all ex-servicemen; pakehas have participated in the leadership conferences. There is no fear of Maori nationalism—Paul Robeson speaking at the Auckland Community Centre, pointing to inequalities of economic status, urging militancy, failed to strike a chord of sympathy. In some ways Paul Robeson was only saying what Mr Hunn has said. But militancy does not attract Maoris, because they have an ideal of racial harmony.

Maori policy is one of taihoa, by and by. On the one hand elders put up a passive resistance to the pace of 'integration', on the ground that Maoris are being asked to cope, in less than two hundred years, with an advance that took Europeans something like two thousand. On the other hand they meet European impatience with patience. Bay of Plenty elders did not make public protests when the magistrate condemned Ringatu, but invited him to a hui where they explained the tenets of their religion. In the harmonious New Zealand society that they envisage, they wish to retain their identity; what they seek is recognition, not just as individuals, but as a people made up of different tribes and with the right to disagree among themselves and with preferences of behaviour as valid as the European's.

Intellectuals and sympathisers often get impatient because of hesitancy of Maoris to interest themselves in wider public or international questions. It should be remembered that the Maori people are in deep confusion about the New Zealand pakeha world, let alone the whole world, or the stressful western pattern of living we are trying to impose on them. The local confusion may reflect simple unfamiliarity with pakeha institutions— a father wishing to decide on an atlas for his schoolgirl daughter visits a library but does not know where to look and does not ask for assistance because he doesn't know whether he has to pay.[21] Often they avoid confusion in relation to the world situation by a simple acceptance of the official doctrine. Soldiers volunteering to shoot Malayans whose quarrel with their Government is of no interest to them do not doubt that, as they are told, they are shooting bad men. (No doubt there are other attractions— as Erik Schwimmer has given them[22]—secure employment, a regular life, the presence of other Maoris, pleasant inter-tribal rivalry.) I remember a Maori who turned up at a committee meeting of the Citizens' All Black Tour Association and argued that since Her Majesty the Queen had said 'We are one people', the Rugby Union was defying her, and that if this were pointed out to them they would be horrified at their effrontery and immediately mend their ways. Maoris are not trained in the subtleties and sophistications by which we discount the hypocrisies we profess. Nor do any except the more educated appreciate the fact that there is not one 'pakeha way' but dozens.

At the conference on research into Maori education it was suggested that there should be a sociological study of a European village by Maori social scientists. The suggestion was not made in any spirit of smart alecry

—though it would be interesting to have 'Rakau' opinions on the way university psychologists bring up their children—but as a means of educating Maoris in the details of pakeha life. Maoris in general like pakehas—provided they are friendly. I am told, though I take it with a grain of salt, that in 1939 when the question of Maori support in the war was at issue, Sir Apirana Ngata told Peter Fraser that after long consideration the leaders of all the tribes had decided they would rather have him than the Japanese. There is something admirable in the calm and courtesy in which Maoris indiscriminately listen to Paul Robeson, teach action-songs to a Chinese theatre company, entertain an Indian diplomat, a Formosan or American Indian MRA man, Katherine Dunham and Rewi Alley.

The trend of Maori progress towards a cordial adjustment to the European occupation is in two apparently dissimilar directions. On the one hand, their freedom to withdraw for such affairs as they wish, to be Maoris among Maoris when they want to be. On the other hand, and this is less possible without the other, a greater participation in European activities at all levels—not only in employment, but in local bodies, voluntary organisations and in the arts and entertainment. There has been progress in this direction. Maori viewpoints are frequently expressed from positions in a pakeha social structure—a Presbyterian Synod, an article by a staff journalist, an adult education tutor-organiser, a women's welfare organisation. The changes and difficulties of contemporary leadership were represented in the apparent inconsistencies of Maharaia Winiata. Seeking ways to advance his people he chose the Methodist Church, anthropology, adult education and the King Movement, which he saw as symbolic of a possible national Maori identity—but which alienated him from tribes that traditionally did not recognise the Maori King. Seeking at the same time ways to bring about workable race relations he espoused Moral Rearmament, the Citizens' All Black Tour Association, visited China to study the treatment of minorities and it was possibly he who contributed informed notes on Maori affairs to the *People's Voice*. Maha alive made many enemies: dead he was unanimously praised. If he struck some pakehas as anti-pakeha, it was that pakeha arrogance and patronage made him angry. In his haste to achieve his goal, and his impatience with inter-tribal suspicion, he sometimes violated Maori protocol. He represented a change he himself theorised about, a change in the channels of leadership. Increasingly Maori leadership will come not from outstanding figures like Ngata and Te Puea, but from hundreds of smaller local people who are specialists in their own professions.

In the arts and entertainment there has been significant movement. Maoris have practically taken over popular entertainment. In the more sophisticated arts there have been stories in English in *Te Ao Hou*, the poems of Hone Tuwhare and Rowley Habib, the wood-sculpture of Arnold Wilson, the paintings of Ralph Hotere, Katarina Mataira and Muru Walters (it is difficult to imagine a prominent pakeha footballer who also paints). The work of all these artists is informed with a quality not European. Maoris have distinguished themselves in amateur acting and professional opera. If they have not entered other arts—symphonic music, few architects, no ballet dancers from a people so sure on their feet—it is because they are not familiar with these arts, as in the case of the father who didn't know how to use the library. From the other direction in the last few years there has been from pakeha artists and intellectuals an increasing interest in the Maori: there has been Noel Hilliard's *Maori Girl* and a greater number of short stories with Maori characters, two good children's books about Maori boys. And Bruce Mason's *Pohutukawa Tree*, for all its distorted view of race relations and its improbable Maori psychology, represented a gesture of pakeha conscience. More pakehas, partly dissatisfied with their own culture, have taken the role of what Erik Schwimmer calls 'mediators' and found Maori company enriching and satisfying. My guess is that, among the educated, intermarriage, especially between Maori men and European women, is increasing. It may be too much to hope that this movement, at educated levels of society, will be powerful enough to offset the unpropitious attitudes of a great many pakehas—the potential hostility, the impatience, the arrogance, the patronage and that kind of paternalism that is hostile to Maoris making their own decisions, the readiness of State-Advanced suburbia to condemn them in terms of its own inhuman values; the forces that made David Ausubel foresee a worsening of race relations.

The way of life we have been trying to 'integrate' on to the Maoris is a spiritually impoverished version of a deeply anxious, individualistic and often sadistic (and dirty-minded) Euro-American culture. If instead of forcing them into our uniform, we would allow Maoris to be themselves and recognise them as themselves, we could at once rid ourselves of our intermittent worry about what we are 'doing for the Maoris', and at the same time they could enter more confidently into bi-racial New Zealand activities, to our enrichment. If I may add a personal coda, if New Zealand weren't the home of the Maori people, it wouldn't be mine for long either.

Notes

1. For background to this article I am indebted to three or four dozen papers and articles too numerous to name, and to conversation with Bruce Biggs, Pat Hohepa, Hugh Kawharu, B. Kernot, Joan Metge, Erik Schwimmer and Matiu te Hau. I am also indebted to I.L.G. Sutherland's assessment of the Maori situation in 1951, published in the *Journal of the Polynesian Society*, 1952; to the 'Rakau Studies' by Victoria University of Wellington psychologists; and to David P. Ausubel's *Maori Youth*. My own claim to be able to present as far as possible a Maori point of view is six years' close association with Maori students, and my attendance at the young leaders' conferences organised by the Auckland Council of Adult Education in the Auckland and Hawkes

Bay Provinces since 1959. There was a national conference in Auckland in 1959; regional conferences in 1960 at Turangawaewae marae, Whakatane, Gisborne and Kaitaia; in 1961 at Tauranga-Taupo, Whakarewarewa and Wairoa. I have not seen the reports of similar conferences at Christchurch, Marton and Waitara.

I have doubled long vowels in Maori words except those in everyday use in English such as *Maori* and *pakeha*, and names of places and persons.

2. Ritchie, Jane, *Childhood in Rakau*, Wellington 1957, p. 26.
3. Report of Young Maori Conference, Auckland, May 1939, p. 18.
4. *Maori-European Standards of Health*, Department of Health, Wellington 1960, p. 4.
5. Borrie, W.D., 'Some Economic and Social Implications of Maori Population Growth in New Zealand', *Journal of the Polynesian Society*, December 1961, p. 410.
6. Report of the Waiariki Young Maori Leaders' Conference, Whakatane, August 1960, p. 30.
7. Hohepa, P.W., in a thesis subsequently published, *A Maori Community in Northland*, A.H. & A.W. Reed, Wellington, 1970, pp. 52, 66–7.
8. *ibid.*, p. 67.
9. Booth, John, 'A Modern Maori Community' in Freeman, J.D. and Geddes, W.R. (eds.), *Anthropology in the South Seas*, New Plymouth 1959, p. 242.
10. Maori Synod of the Presbyterian Church of New Zealand, *A Maori View of the Hunn Report*, Christchurch, p. 21.
11. Report of the Waikato-Maniapoto Young Maori Leaders' Conference, Turangawaewae, May 1960, p. 20.
12. It is possible that no conclusion can be drawn from the published statistics which show only a selection—arrest cases only (which are only a tenth of total distinct cases) and only about half of those, without any indication of how these cases were selected. For what they are worth, the percentages worked out from the selection of distinct arrest cases from the Magistrates' Courts in *Reports on the Justice Statistics of N.Z.* are: 2.84% fewer Maoris not convicted than non-Maoris in 1958; 3.52% in 1959; 3.64% in 1960.
13. Ernest Beaglehole and James Ritchie, 'The Rakau Maori Studies', *Journal of the Polynesian Society*, June 1958, p. 137.
14. Report of Young Maori Conference, Auckland, May 1939, p. 22.
15. Report of the Northland Young Maori Leaders' Conference, Kaitaia, October 1960, p. x.
16. Richard Thompson in *N.Z. Monthly Review*, September 1961.
17. Dugal Campbell in the *Journal of the Polynesian Society*, December 1958.
18. Hohepa, *op. cit.*, p. 93. Also Joan Metge, *The Maoris of New Zealand*, Routledge and Kegan Paul, London 1967, pp. 130–4.
19. In *Comment*, Winter 1961.
20. 'Hohere', in *Here and Now*, October 1957.
21. The incident is taken from 'Kaumatua' in *N.Z. Monthly Review*, July 1961.
22. *Te Ao Hou*, September 1961.

Frank Sargeson's Stories

Frank Sargeson's stories have been so long out of print that it has been difficult for younger readers to know at first hand the work of a writer early accepted as 'a pioneer and vital power'[1] in New Zealand writing, who was for a generation of writers of fiction something of what Gogol was to the nineteenth century Russian novelists. The sixteen signatures to a letter to Mr Sargeson on his fiftieth birthday (in which they acknowledge their debt to him)[2] are in fact a roll-call of New Zealand writers of fiction of the time: the only name missing is that of Mr Sargeson's senior in age and date of first publication, John A. Lee. And it can be said that even for those writers who have begun to publish since that date, their job has been made easier and their success more possible by Mr Sargeson's going before them.

It was in 1935 that, sorting a little incongrously with some of the confident leftist assertions of *Tomorrow*, Mr Sargeson's modest and deceptively inconsequential first sketches appeared with any frequency. By the end of 1939, that fortnightly had published about thirty sketches. There were two slim collections—a paperback of twenty-nine pages in 1936 and a hardback of little more than a hundred pages in 1940. The fuller collection of *That Summer and Other Stories* in 1946 ran to less than two hundred pages, and included many of the stories of the earlier collections. Leaving aside the three novels and the plays that have been written since, Mr Sargeson's oeuvre is small. Yet by his fiftieth birthday it had facilitated the publication of the books of Roderick Finlayson, Dan Davin, David Ballantyne, A. P. Gaskell, John Reece Cole and Janet Frame. In what lay the fertilising effect?

Before Mr Sargeson, those writers born into the imaginative desert of pre-depression New Zealand and unable to afford the release of expatriation, available to Katherine Mansfield and to Jane Mander, had been able to accommodate themselves to their situation only by finding expression

---

This essay was first published as an Introduction to Frank Sargeson's *Collected Stories 1935–1963* (Blackwood and Janet Paul 1964).

in free-lance or spare-time journalism, book reviews and the uncertain recognition of an occasional magazine story, and, if they were lucky enough, in books published in London. A newer generation of writers, driven by the depression to question the rigid but hollow orthodoxies of their society, was conscious of an outlook distinct from that of London, and was no longer content to see it either as their spiritual Hawaiki or as their spiritual Mecca. But if they were to write for a native readership, they were concerned to adopt a stance more dignified than that of, say, some of the contributors to the *New Zealand Artists' Annual* (1926–32)— alternately pretentious and apologetic, always self-conscious. They were concerned to do as the poets had done a few years earlier, establish a meaningful connection between their experience in the society they lived in and that of their compatriots who might read them. In Frank Sargeson they found a writer who, without map or other guide than the technical example of the American Sherwood Anderson and the inspiration of the Australian Henry Lawson, had cleared some tracks they might confidently follow. It was important to them—perhaps, it might seem now, unnecessarily so—that his stories had been accepted by the English *New Writing* and the American *New Directions*. But, more important, he had shown that imaginative truth could be reached by being true to his country. 'You proved,' the sixteen writers said in 1953, 'that a New Zealander could publish work true to his country and of a high degree of artistry, and that exile in the cultural centres of the old world was not essential to this end. One could be provincial, in the best sense, and of the world at the same time.' What Mr Sargeson had achieved was a sense of identity and of audience: he could speak directly without the mediation of London; he could write—as say Frank Anthony (in his novel) and John A. Lee had not been able—without that occasional self-consciousness and nervous tie-straightening that came of having to explain oneself to an English market; without the attitudinising that Robin Hyde picked up from her twelve years of journalism.

It needs little imagination to reconstruct the uniform crudity of popular sensibility which ran through all classes of pakeha New Zealanders from the beginning of the century to the thirties, a spiritual insensitivity disturbed not at all by the first world war but only by the depression; a crudity incarnated in the solid unimaginative flesh of Bill Massey, Prime Minister from 1912 to 1925, and continued in the solemn bumbling figure of George Forbes, Prime Minister from 1931 to 1935. It was the ethos of the hard-working small farmer impatient of all behaviour that did not self-evidently contribute to material gain or public decorum. Visitors like George Bell, an American consul, commented on the complacency, André Siegfried on the distrust of the intellect, Sidney Webb on the vulgarity. In 1929, J. B. Condliffe could note that 'the middle-class conception of cultural education for children rarely goes beyond lessons on the piano-forte'. It was a cultural climate in which reading was a waste of time, imagination an impractical self-indulgence, morality a programme of self-denial and the masking of personal passions except, perhaps, those of righteous envy and anger. Blanche Baughan celebrated its virtues, even wishfully supplying what she herself missed most, an appreciation of the arts. But though the head of her Active Family playing Schubert at the end of a long week's work may well have been true, he was hardly typical; and one suspects that it was the social code of the Active Family, bent on breaking in that farm with no better object than to sell it at improved value and break in another, that eventually dried up the considerable talent that created its lasting image. It was a social code that had driven Katherine Mansfield back to London; Alice Webb attempted no more than to question the complacencies of its surface; Jane Mander and Jean Devanny made their feminist protests against it; Robin Hyde felt its essential injustice. Even though the code owed a lot to the temperance feminists of the nineties who had reduced the men to half the vote and shut them out of the bars at six o'clock, it was a crude and unfeeling ethos, and it was women writers rather than men who were moved to challenge it.

Yet if the political victory of the urban worker in 1935 gave the first decisive blow to the small-farmer outlook, some of its attitudes continued. The new hopes that the Labour victory opened for the worker reflected themselves mainly in increased spending: his outlook remained little less conformist; if originality and non-conformity amused rather than angered him, he was no less distrustful of them. Frank Sargeson noticed the new combination of increased consumption and old uncouthness. 'That's the point about these days,' he wrote in 1937. 'They're a combination of frightful crudity and even more frightful refinement. But luckily BOTH are somewhat spurious.'[3] At least the threat to the spirit was less. But a political change had not brought a moral change.

What Mr Sargeson sought to do was to comment on New Zealand society in the light of his more humane, more tolerant and compassionate vision of man as a loving, suffering animal who often mutilates himself and others in propitiation of false gods. He did so not by frontal attack or by broad comprehensive survey, but by close and sympathetic spotlighting of parts of the under-surface of society. He sought to expose and isolate the dead tissue in the minds of those who like Uncle 'can't suppose', to pause where there were unnoticed growing-points in the unvoiced thoughts or intuitions of social underdogs and outcasts, to show them as they respond to warmth and light or come to nothing in a frosty atmosphere.

In a story that Mr Sargeson did not wish to include in this selection, Harry discovers the secret of the permanence of his landlady's squally marriage when she tells him that her husband 'loves beautiful'. Harry goes on:

Everything you did you ought to do beautiful. If you did that, Harry said, you'd always have a sort of core inside you that nobody would be able to touch. It wouldn't matter what you had to go through, whether you had to go on relief or anything, nothing would be able to touch you. If you loved beautiful and hated beautiful and did everything beautiful, then you'd live beautiful. Right inside, in that core inside you, you would.[4]

It is this core of beauty in his characters that Mr Sargeson is interested in, a core so vulnerable to attacks of the worm. The work of the borer, however, is only too visible and it is any form of rigid principle imposed on and inhibiting the vitality of the lonely human soul, capable, if not interfered with, of making its own satisfying relationships with others. Ultimately he saw that life-denying principle as deriving from the Protestant ethic of Success and the doctrine that Time is Money, a doctrine that he feared would corrupt before birth such an earthly paradise as Michael Joseph Savage might hope to set up.[5] Repeatedly, his stories involve a conflict between the beauty of the human spirit and some doctrine or dogma that inhibits it and contorts its expression.

Father Doyle's kindliness is preferable to granpa Munro's scrupulous bigotry. Miss Briggs and Frances, in the midst of life, are made mean by their own narrowness; they and Uncle in his hard knocker are both victims and enforcers of a life-denying code. More harmful, because it is more generous in its provision for the claims of the flesh, is the sober philosophy of the Scot who finds his calling as an undertaker, since it drives his protégé to a devotion to duty that kills his baby and kills his marriage. In the Department, humanity or what is left of it survives only in the basement, in the failures, Mr Birtleberry and the pathetic Mr Flyger in love with a girl too young for him. Jones has enough charity to feel guilty at walking past a man in need of help and he knows that in doing the right thing he has done the wrong thing. Mrs Bowman's greed reasserts itself over her grief and she drives Sally back to the explosives factory that nearly killed her. The inhumanity of an economy that operates like a machine forces a workless old man to begging to warm his hands in a bucket of soapy water. The pressures of a production system whose rewards reflect the fluctuations of supply and demand, drive the Man of Good Will, with his appreciation of labour and growth, his feeling for his crops and the soil, to stage a futile strike, and they reduce him to a paralysis both literal and symbolic. It is in a seizure of righteousness that the Good Boy kills his girl-friends. It is in disgust with his own randiness that Victor burns the tom cat. Myrtle's guardians, with their sense of the fitness of things, can see only dirt in the adolescent love of their ward and old Bandy. If cunning beats strength in the Rangitoto Channel, it is Fred's envy of Ken's success—his body, his prospects, his education, his success with girls—that tempts him to murder. It is the inroads of European spuriousness that are corrupting the remnants of vitality in Maoris in the place up north. And there is irony in a rationalist acknowledging irrational forces that are beyond the comprehension of his reason. To the Colonel's daughter, her home town was 'a very proper little town. No place for anybody with spirit.'

In contrast to the inhibiting forces, there are the points of growing. Children know things that adults have forgotten. There is the warm and comforting memory of being a boy with tooth-ache in granma's protective watchfulness. There is Boy feeling his way to terms with a half-understood adult world. There is the full humanity of the author's paternal grandmother.

There is the Unitarian youth's discovery that the navvy in the bar and his little girl with her rag doll are more profoundly alive than the girl at the church social. The Maoris in the dump up north are more sensitive and generous than the pakehas who are taking their money. Nick, no longer Dalmatian but not yet New Zealander, is more sensitive than his neighbours the Crumps; his tender groping adaptation, the narrator dimly senses, is his own situation and that of all New Zealanders, not yet grown into their time and place. Ted's affections, finding no outlet in his marriage, go out to a dog and a canary. The youth at the beach guest-house under the Norfolk pines finds no satisfaction in the pointless activity of his mother's sporting friends, and would rather emulate the aimless adventurous life of the old rolling stone, Fred Holmes, who is still free in spirit. The old man recalling the innocent love of Myrtle and old Bandy remembers that it taught him that up till then he had 'somehow managed to get life all wrong'; from that revelation he is appalled at the savagery of court sentences for sexual offences. It is the naked freshness of a reminiscence of the old man on the park seat that wakens the stranger into recognition, behind the mask of a cadging old man, of a boyhood hero, and into shame at the initial hardening of his heart. It is high spirits that lead Daisy Willoughby to what is, in the eyes of the town, her fall, and high spirits inspire the Colonel's daughter to lead Clem from respectability to his liaison with a piano. The writer of the Letter to a Friend, alert and sensitive himself, sees the contrast between the sensitive youth and his unresponsive, respectable father; the question is raised in the reader's mind, will the son turn into a copy of his father, or has a younger generation escaped the uniform?

When the forces of constriction are in direct conflict with living impulses, usually—depressingly—it is constriction that wins. Many of the characters like Bill in 'That Summer' or the narrator in 'The Making of a New Zealander' play it by ear and intuitively steer clear of conflict; outwardly they conform, inwardly they lie low, 'hang on', waiting for some gesture of loyalty or affection to which they will readily, if shamefacedly, respond. But whether they conform or not, it is, as Robert Chapman has said, 'with a purposelessness more horrible, not only because it is subconscious, but also because they could not mentally grasp the problem were it presented to them.'[6]

But for those characters whose wills take sides in the conflict there can only be violent solutions. Fred envying Ken's possession of those qualities that bring success in the world can make no gesture more positive than drowning him. Victor, resenting Elsie's standoffishness and his own lust, burns the tom-cat and symbolically does violence to himself and to life. George, vain and homosexual, takes it out on the society that rejects him by mocking its orthodoxies and killing Tom who upholds them.

A number of Mr Sargeson's characters seek security in emotional relationships with men or with men as well as women; it is this desire, unrecognised in their society, that is starved in George and in Fred, that Tom cannot comprehend. It is such a desire that explains the narrator's regret when Ted's canary escapes and he goes back to his wife, or another narrator's when his gift of a pair of socks to Bill costs him his friendship with Fred. And it is in their taking for granted the monopoly of their men that most of the wives in these stories are so insensitive. Ted gets more satisfaction out of his dog and his canary. Jack would rather be outside digging his hole and his wife can't see the point of it anyway. Big Ben might have adapted himself to his new country, but his wife made no effort.

Occasionally the tables are turned, however, and in these stories the author allows his sympathies an ironic victory. Jack's wife isn't satisfied till the hole is filled in again and then complains that he will dig shelters for other people but not for his own family. Ben and his wife had left England to make a better future but they head straight back to the growing certainty of war. The milkman meets, in the woman with the piece of yellow soap, someone tough enough to extort exemption from the code of debtor and creditor. Aunt Emily, in a story not included in this collection, insists on weighing her feathers before she entrusts them to the man who will make her eiderdown, and she never knows that he stuffs it, not with her feathers, but with some cheaper material. Hilda and her girl-friend think they've worked it nicely with the two strangers but they are left waiting for the phone-call. The Colonel's daughter made it her business to break up a stuffy and loveless marriage, though Clem's second marriage can hardly be more to her liking.

At times indeed the author's sympathies get the better of his compassion. There is a hint of satisfaction when Fred defeats Ken. Wives are nags who give foolish advice and sensitive husbands like Ted and Jack have developed a kind of defensive taciturnity. The teller, if not the author, sneers at the nostalgic Englishwoman abroad, but in her kindliness she is a more attractive personality than the two French girls who are rude to her. Even the man who has lost his pal feels that Tom's self-righteousness was provocative. But in two of these stories compassion wins: in Mrs Potter crying over her knitting we suddenly see the pathos, not the irony, of the situation and we are reminded that the story is titled not 'Three Women' but 'Three Men'. The youth may have chosen to lead an adventurous life, but seeing Fred Holmes's coffin bouncing on the back of the truck, he realises that whatever sort of life he lives, there's always death at the end of it. And in 'An Affair of the Heart' if Mrs Crawley's devotion to her son is a terrible thing it is also a beautiful thing.

Mr Sargeson's view is a compassionate one, but in his view humanity is perverse. In 'Tod' there is a small allegory of the human situation, mankind quarrelsome and affectionate in turn, calling on Tod, waiting for Tod to set things right.* In 'Cats by the Tail' it is sensual pleasure and the perverse pleasure of power that people seek. In 'An Attempt at an Explanation' there is a vision of life as a chain of parasitic relationships, a compassionate paradox of living hungry things preying on other living hungry things. The boy goes on:

> If I'd been older perhaps I would have made a picture for myself of the earth as just a speck of dirt drifting in space, with human creatures crawling over it and crouching down and holding on tight just as the lice had done on the back of my hand.

It is, as H. Winston Rhodes has said,[7] a universe of loneliness and indifference, in this respect like that of Arnold's 'Dover Beach', where the only thing that can make existence tolerable is human warmth; and those who are spiritually alive in Mr Sargeson's stories are those who are dimly aware that they are lonely and rootless and those who have warmth to offer. The dead ones are the staid ones—my Uncle, Ken, Tom, the clerks in the Department, the Methodist minister, Myrtle's guardians, granpa Munro, Jack's wife, Big Ben's wife, the undertaker—who could not conceive of the abandonment of man in the cold deserts of space, who do not recognise their own or others' need for affection and loyalty. It is essentially a view of life to which we have become accustomed in some post-war European writing.

The cold indifferent universe is actualised in the winter world of 'That Summer'. Bill is a type-figure of the displaced persons who inhabit so many of the stories: he chooses displacement, planning to kick around in the city for so long as his money lasts; and Auckland under siege of the slump is an appropriate landscape. Even the improbable partnership of Bert and the transvestite Maggie is part of a world too peculiar to make sense to Bill, a world of the slightly grasping Cleggs living in squabbling partnership, of avenging detectives, impersonal labour exchanges, lonely strangers who have to be taken on trust though they are as likely to turn out spongers or thieves as decent blokes; a world in which to survive one has to be fertile in dodges like stealing money from milk-bottles or telling a hard-luck story to a parson or putting it across a medical board. In such a world the supreme consolation is the loyalty of a mate: 'A man

---

* *Tod* of course suggests *God*, and there is a striking affinity in theme and title with *Waiting for Godot*. But more than this, *Tod* is German for death.

wants a mate that won't let him down.' Bill chooses Terry because he is the sort 'that'd go solid with a joker'. Bill is faced with his one challenge, the only big decision of will he is called on to make: being loyal to Terry; and in his unrationalised way he makes it his one mission. For the sake of loyalty to Terry he turns down another offer of mateship from a stranger in the park, a farm job in the country and an offer from a girl. Yet, at the end, when he has sent for the priest, he doesn't go back to Terry. Terry is left to die without his mate while Bill goes looking for a sheila. He plays it by ear and death is something he ducks away from. And the horrible thing is that all the experience of that summer will be no more to him than things that happened that summer: he will drift to another job, another mate perhaps, and he will have learnt little from it all that he didn't half-know already. That is Mr Sargeson's vision of man as the little man, kindly, fumbling, stoic and resourceful, submissive but independent; with feelings of his own though without the words to express them or the will to enforce them if the pressure against them is too great; compliant but indestructible.

But even if in these stories we have, as Professor Rhodes has said, not a realistic representation of New Zealand life and society, but an artist's personal vision of life, it is nevertheless true that Mr Sargeson is writing from a particular time and place, that he is writing of a local variant of the human situation. In *Up onto the Roof and Down Again*, a diary of a brief return to the King Country, he recalls life on his well-read pioneer uncle's farm when he was a boy, 'a life that was nearly all work while the daylight lasted, but work that was rarely hurried and never scamped or ill-done, that was related to the seasons and the weather, but not to the day of the week or the time of the day, that had results you could see under your hands, and a meaning that had little to do with the money it brought.'[8] He imagines he sees on a ridge of the Mamaku plateau a native honeysuckle that his uncle had identified for him (which he came to contrast with the tame English honeysuckle planted by a nostalgic old lady); and for him it stands 'not for New Zealand as it is, *but New Zealand as it might worthily have been.*' His uncle's brave vision has been lost, so has the warm humanity of his Cockney paternal grandmother; the New Zealand that is he measures in terms of that lost Eden. Mr Sargeson's stories are as much a comment on State-Advanced suburbia, on the pursuit of status-symbols, and the rejection of human comradeship in contemporary society as they are on the human situation; they are a comment on what he called, reviewing Janet Frame, 'the mental sleep from which there is no awakening, ... the emotional strangulation that is slow but sure, and as deadly as death.'[9] This personal vision Mr Sargeson has, with a patient and dedicated craftsmanship, pursued in his later work.

In his sketch 'The Last War' Mr Sargeson quietly excludes cliché sentiments and classroom chauvinism to consider honestly how the 1914–18 war had affected him at the time. In the same way the vernacular in which so many of the characters in this collection talk and think is chosen to exclude falsity; and it is artistically appropriate also in that it represents the limits of their understanding of the forces that move them. Mr Sargeson's sensitivity in using it has been made more obvious by bad imitation in some of the apprentice work of other writers. There is considerable variation in style—more evident in the later stories—according to its aptness to each narrator, who is a different person in each story.

Notes

1. James K. Baxter in *Canta*, 7 July 1948.
2. *Landfall*, March 1953.
3. *Tomorrow*, 18 August 1937, p. 656.
4. 'Conversation with a Landlady', *Tomorrow*, 7 August 1935, p.16.
5. *Tomorrow*, 3 August 1938, p. 625.
6. *Landfall*, September 1947, p. 222.
7. *Landfall*, March 1955, p. 28.
8. *Landfall*, December 1951, p. 250.
9. *N.Z. Listener*, 18 April 1952, p. 13.

The Recognition of Reality

I found when I began to think about New Zealand writing in terms of inheritance and adaptation that the metaphor was rather inflexible. It was not, to extend the metaphor, a question of a shifted plant having to adapt itself to new soil and climate; but a question of the shifted people and their descendants having to reorient their own consciousness, drop old assumptions about themselves and have the courage to make new ones, a question of their learning to recognise themselves in the limitations of their time and place and in their new relation to neighbouring peoples. I assume that collectively it is the function of a nation's artists, modifying Stephen Dedalus's words, to forge the conscience of their race, to provide a moral and imaginative context in which their people can feel, think, and behave. New Zealand's development towards an independent literature has been marked, like I suppose that of any other, by false trails, difficulty, personal suffering, and sweat. The hardest thing has been the recognition of reality.

I do not propose to trace this development; it has already been done in E. H. McCormick's survey, and in the introductions by D. M. Davin, R. M. Chapman, and Allen Curnow to their anthologies.[1] All I intend to do is to provide some illustrations that I find illuminating in this emergence of the conscience of a people.

The settlers who arrived in their hundreds of thousands in the later nineteenth century, were mainly British men and women of the working and lower middle class whose minds had been formed in the middle nineteenth century. Inheritance in the form of the *mores* they brought with them has been a hindrance rather than a stimulus to writing, but as Robert Chapman has shown,[2] it determined the themes of fiction for the first half of this century. The settlers, by means of Government buying and by

This essay was originally written as a talk given at a conference on Commonwealth literature at the University of Leeds in September 1964, and was printed in *Commonwealth Literature*, ed. John Press (Heinemann Educational Books, London, 1965).

persuasion and force and fraud had by the end of the century expropriated most of the usable land from the indigenous people who had occupied it for at least eight hundred years. By the end of the century they had established an economic relationship with the mother country by which New Zealand was an outlying farm providing food and wool to the metropolis. It is only in the last few years that there has been any threat to this relationship. The energies of the settlers went into the conversion of untilled land to pasture that would carry crops of butter, meat, and wool; other pursuits were considered inferior and some of them even harmful to material prosperity.

To some extent New Zealand began without a literary inheritance because—apart from very early settlers like Samuel Butler and Lady Barker, who did not stay—these land-hungry settlers were not a reading lot. From the 1890s until the accession of a Labour Government in 1935 their values dominated the country—the values of the puritanical hard-working small farmer. It was a morality hostile to the imagination, to art, even to reading since reading wasted time; it was embarrassed by the exhibition of emotion, except perhaps righteous envy and anger; it valued the practical man, even the handy man, more than the thinker. It wasn't a good time for a writer to be born, yet it is out of this time that the first signs of an assured and distinctive note in New Zealand writing emerged.

In some ways the atmosphere worked against clarity of vision; the truth couldn't be faced without sentimentality or deprecation and often enough was better ignored. Some examples of this I can illustrate from stories from Mr Davin's anthology:

[In this story a boy and his parents call on a neighbouring spinster whose mother has just died. There is a horse tied outside and they know she has taken a lover.]

'I did see the horse,' insisted Walter, and felt that like all older people his parents were in some sort of conspiracy against his finding things out. 'I did see the horse.'

'Of course you saw the damned horse,' said his father suddenly. 'Shut up about it, that's all.'

Jim was walking past, carrying a bottle with a straw stuck in it. They looked away and pretended they hadn't noticed but Auntie Laurel said quietly to Mum, Fancy bringing it out here, where everyone's having their lunch.

'Mother, mother, I know why the little boy hasn't got a father. It's 'cause he was killed at the war.'

'Margot, go inside at once.'

Mrs Chatterton stamped her foot, her voice broke shrilly.

'Margot! Do as I say, at once! And don't have so much to say for yourself.'

A people made up of Walter's father, Auntie Laurel, Mrs Chatterton and their like would hardly welcome a fiction which might display them in action and invite them to self-analysis.

One can see the oppressiveness in Blanche Baughan's story, 'An Active Family'. Miss Baughan came to New Zealand in 1900 when she was thirty. She was a sensitive and cultured woman, uneasy at the materialism of her new home and eventually she turned her energies from writing to championship of penal reform. In this story she celebrates the virtues of the very people whose ethos (I suspect) discouraged the creative impulse in her: her subject is a fanatically hard-working family—self-contained, independent, affectionate within the group—breaking in a farm. It is obvious that Miss Baughan is anxious not to be 'critical': almost every adjective, even the nouns and verbs, carry their load of approval or apologia. She even wishfully supplies what she missed, an appreciation of the arts, when Dad after his furious week's work sits down at the piano to play Schubert. Yet there is a question she does not ask: what is all this activity *for*? The family is breaking in the farm with the sole aim of selling it at improved value so they can buy another and break that in and presumably continue doing this till they sell up and retire in comfort— if they have lived long enough.

What I am saying is that Miss Baughan could imaginatively handle some of the reality around her but not all of it. A contrast with Lady Barker's sketch in the same anthology will make this clearer. She was in the country three or four years and because she knew she was returning and because her position as the only gentlewoman on her husband's sheep-station gave her an assurance almost aristocratic, she was able to see more clearly than writers of fifty years later. For example, she could notice without embarrassment or fear of accusations of vanity that the shepherds at her open-air Christmas dinner were uncomfortable while she remained, yet would be offended if she went away. I think Miss Baughan would have parried off such a thought.

Alice Webb was a writer who tried in a quiet and earnest way to consider moral and social problems as they presented themselves to women inclined to philosophize over a cup of tea, such problems as whether mothers' helps were overpaid, whether English war brides were as worthless as rumour said, whether clergymen had a soft job. Her most searching examination of conscience is 'The Patriot', and she asks the question whether the farmer who volunteered with his horse to fight in the First World War had made as great a sacrifice as his partner who stayed behind to manage the farm, doing two men's work without glory or complaint. As far as it goes it is a judicious question. But what she does not question is the rightness of '14–'18 jingoism and because of this her story is denied the breadth that might have made it less parochial. One aspect of reality that the earlier writers did not examine was themselves and their own assumptions.

If Katherine Mansfield had stayed in New Zealand it is possible that her writing, in keeping with the moral climate of the country, would have been harsher and more austere, as it is in her early story, 'The Woman at the Store'. Expatriation was the price she paid for self-realisation as a writer, but imaginative repatriation is the impulse of some of her best later stories, those she wrote in homage to her young brother, killed in the war. 'I can't say how thankful I am to have been born in New Zealand, to know Wellington as I do, and have it to range about in', she wrote in her last year. It is these stories that have most attraction to New Zealanders and yet if she is still probably the best-known of our writers outside New Zealand, she had little influence either on her contemporaries or on subsequent writers. She found a way for herself, but it was one that others could not follow.

Some tried, or hoped for, emigration. It was almost impossible to get an imaginative book published at home—the population was not much over a million—and space for stories and verse in newspapers and magazines was limited, and sometimes unpaid. A generation of writers grew up who could only accommodate themselves to their situation by free-lance journalism and the hope of a book published in London, a market seen through a haze of outdated notions. If England had been home to Butler and Lady Barker, it became Home to a generation fifty to seventy years later, even though they were born in New Zealand: their spiritual Hawaiki and, if they could make it, their spiritual Mecca. Of those who emigrated it is only those who either returned or maintained their imaginative connection with New Zealand who achieved anything—Jane Mander, Alan Mulgan, D'Arcy Cresswell, A. R. D. Fairburn, M. H. Holcroft. Those who stayed away—John Guthrie is the most distinguished of them—did not fulfil their promise: it was a mistake to think that their modest talents could transplant. Yet the dilemma was real enough, and there is ambiguity in Fairburn's comment on it, written after it had passed:

I'm Older than You, Please Listen

To the young man I would say:
Get out! Look sharp, my boy,
before the roots are down,
before the equations are struck,
before a face or a landscape
has power to shape or destroy.
This land is a lump without leaven,
a body that has no nerves.
Don't be content to live in
a sort of second-grade heaven
with first-grade butter, fresh air,
and paper in every toilet;
becoming a butt for the malice

of those who have stayed and soured,
staying in turn to sour,
to smile, and savage the young.
If you're enterprising and able,
smuggle your talents away,
hawk them to livelier markets
where people are willing to pay.
If you have no stomach for roughage,
if patience isn't your religion,
if you must have sherry with your bitters,
if money and fame are your pigeon,
if you feel that you need success,
and long for a good address,
don't anchor here in the desert—
the fishing isn't so good:
take a ticket to Megalopolis,
don't stay in this neighbourhood!

The difficulty for the writer who stayed at home was to achieve imaginative integrity; working alone in an atmosphere of discouragement it was not easy to relate his literary inheritance to his actual experience, to sort out what experience was important to him and his neighbours, even to know how he felt about his experience. It is not surprising that a number of minor talents with only their talents and a desire to write to sustain them were tempted into poses and pretensions—attitudinizing, sentimentality, trick endings, whimsy, fantasy: Ngaio Marsh and M. H. Holcroft (in their early writing) were not immune. Of a collection of twenty-five stories published in 1930 I find only four, none of them good, which strike me as reflecting anything real about New Zealand at all; of a collection of twenty published in 1938 again only four.[3] I will illustrate. In one of them the driver and fireman of a train carrying the Governor-General get drunk and hit top speed for the boast of having given the Governor a fright. There is a colonial egalitarianism about it that rings true. In another, a Scots settler takes his bride to a sod hut on a farm, neglects her for the farm; she is bitter and is tempted to run off with his mate, who when he returns to claim her a year later finds her content and engrossed in a baby. In another, a young farmer's efforts to break in land are not appreciated by his family who want a town life; they leave and he stays to marry a local girl who he thinks will help him but her plans are to persuade him to sell up and move to town. In the fourth, a man in the backblocks longs for escape to sea but is loyal to his responsibilities first to his mother and when he marries, to his wife and family. When his family grow up, he runs away as far as the Auckland waterfront, takes fright and goes home to find that his wife too has dreamt of freedom and left. I have said that these are not good stories, but they are the only ones in this collection in which the plot derives from some reality in New Zealand life and is not a cliché or arbitrary construct set against a New Zealand background.

The greatest indignity, to my mind, was *The New Zealand Artists' Annual* (1926–32) produced by an unlikely combination of writers and cartoonists; alternately pretentious and apologetic, always self-conscious, it strikes a modern reader as wanting to demonstrate that the writer was a philistine like anyone else but he must be allowed his moments of soulfulness. Yet three years before this publication had started, one poet working alone and without audience had stoically achieved the miracle of dignity and integrity. He had not left the country, had in fact written, 'I think I have no other home than this'. He had written some of these poems before he was nineteen, and he published them himself. The difficulty of his achievement is apparent in this poem; so is the fact that his allegiance was to an inheritance quite foreign to his immediate community:

Song of Allegiance

Shakespeare Milton Keats are dead
Donne lies in a lowly bed

Shelley at last calm doth lie
knowing 'whence we are and why'

Byron Wordsworth both are gone
Coleridge Beddoes Tennyson

Housman neither knows nor cares
how 'this heavy world' now fares

Little clinging grains enfold
all the mighty minds of old . . .

They are gone and I am here
stoutly bringing up the rear

Where they went with limber ease
toil I on with bloody knees

Though my voice is cracked and harsh
stoutly in the rear I march

Though my song have none to hear
boldly bring I up the rear.

New Zealand now had the beginnings of a poetic inheritance of its own. Mason's example and that of Ursula Bethell—brought out by an obscure London publisher—and the fact that the depression of the 'thirties made young intellectuals question the hollow orthodoxies of their community, made it comparatively easy for a younger generation of poets to follow: A. R. D. Fairburn, Allen Curnow, Denis Glover, D'Arcy Cresswell Charles Brasch, Basil Dowling. One of them set up the press, the Caxton, that was to publish them. A national inheritance of verse had been established by 1940, and if since 1950 a group of younger poets has challenged it, their position is still in relation to it. This group which includes James K. Baxter, Louis Johnson and Alistair Campbell and younger poets, see the development not as Mr Curnow has presented it, as a search for reality culminating in Mason and the Caxton poets who have made the younger poets possible, but as a growth towards maturity and freedom from the preoccupations of time and place evident in those older poets. They have concerned themselves more with urban and international themes and with urban personal relations. And yet I feel there has always been something unreal about the argument, except the spirit of gang warfare in which it has sometimes been conducted. It misrepresents Mr Curnow's performance both as editor and poet to say that the verse he admires or writes is concrete only in a local or regional way, or that the themes of Mason, Fairburn, and Glover have no more than local relevance; on the other hand, many of Baxter's and Campbell's poems are fairly precisely 'located' in the backblocks and some of Johnson's in suburbs of the welfare state. There has, in any case, been no obstacle to publication. Since the inception of state patronage of literature after the war and Mr Johnson's foundation of the *Poetry Yearbook*, which he has edited since 1951, poetry, if only because production costs are cheaper, has become the least difficult form of writing to publish; certainly easier to publish than it was in Mason's time.

Almost contemporary with the political defeat of the small farmers' party in 1935, Frank Sargeson's sketches and stories began to appear in a left-wing journal *Tomorrow*, which ran for five years. Mr Sargeson's first sketches were modest and deceptively inconsequential. What strikes one about them at first is their unpretentiousness, their apparent artlessness; yet Mr Sargeson is a man deeply versed in an inheritance European, American and Australian. Seen against the stories in the collections I have mentioned the distinction of his is that they never overreach. He set out to undermine respectability by exposing the dead tissue in the minds of the spiritually dead and revealing points of growth in the minds of the spiritually alive, whom he most often found among social outcasts and underdogs. He had travelled, and returning had worked single-mindedly as a writer. He was more fortunate than Mason in that he soon found an editor and later a publisher (the Caxton Press) willing to publish him. In *A Man and his Wife* (1940) he had achieved a sense of identity and of audience; he could write for his community without the mediation of London, without the occasional self-consciousness one finds say in Robin Hyde or John A. Lee. However, it was reassuring that he had been accepted by the American *New Directions* and John Lehmann's *New Writing*.

Mr Sargeson had done what Katherine Mansfield had not, had cleared some tracks that others might confidently follow: only his senior in age and date of first publication, John A. Lee, and his more-or-less contemporaries in first publication, Roderick Finlayson and John Mulgan, can be said to be independent of him. Those who to a greater or lesser degree are indebted to him include Dan Davin, A. P. Gaskell, John Reece Cole, David Ballantyne, Janet Frame, O. E. Middleton, Maurice Duggan, Phillip Wilson, and Bruce Mason. Mr Sargeson I think established—or at least extended—a tradition in New Zealand fiction of liberal humanism, tolerance, sympathy for the little man and an intolerance of pretension. An outsider could say 'Well, you'll find all that in Fielding'. But it had to be done in local terms. A more recent group of writers of fiction—Ian Cross, Sylvia Ashton-Warner, Maurice Shadbolt, Noel Hilliard, M. K. Joseph, Marilyn Duckworth, Maurice Gee—have grown up independently of him, but it would be fair to say that their success would have been less possible without Frank Sargeson's break-through. There has not been among prose-writers the same polarisation into generations and factions as among the poets and Mr Sargeson's eminence is generally recognised.

I was surprised to find that the number of New Zealand writers of fiction of merit who have appeared since Sargeson is more than thirty. In the last seven years the market within New Zealand for New Zealand novels and stories has grown considerably. It reflects the fact that the country is going through an introspective phase, one of self-analysis and self-criticism. I find this a hopeful sign. It is good for us that our readers and critics are of our community, that we don't stand or fall by the chance notice of a reviewer in one of the half-dozen London quality journals, coping with his weekly batch. A good many of the books that are important in our history have not been noticed in London, and often it is obscure publishers who have brought them out. But the only thing surprising in this is that it took us so long to learn to stand on our own feet.

Expatriation is no longer a problem. All writers have felt the need to get out for a while to see the wider world. Of recent writers who have stayed away longer than others, almost all—James Courage, Dan Davin, David Ballantyne—have kept up the imaginative connection with home; Rewi Alley in China would be the only exception I can call to mind.

One aspect of New Zealand experience that I have deferred is the relationship of the European occupiers to the six per cent minority of Maoris. If it was a tenet of critical theory in the 'forties that New Zealanders had yet to come to terms with a landscape alien and unfriendly, it was overlooked that the pre-European Maori had in myth and settlement already come to terms with it. If M. H. Holcroft could see the landscape as without history it was because the landscape he was looking at was in the comparatively unsettled south: in many parts of the Auckland Province the hills are topped by the sites of old fortified villages whose history, forgotten even in Maori tradition, is accessible only to archaeological excavation. In the *Poetry Review*, summer 1964, Howard Sergeant quotes Miss M. J. O'Donnell's remark that 'the life and history of the Maori people, with its ancient romantic legends and mythology' is 'as yet unexplored'. Mr Sergeant says she is wrong because Allen Curnow and others have dealt with Maori mythology. But neither is quite right. Allen Curnow's play *The Axe* deals with culture-contact in Mangaia, one of the Cook Islands, several thousand miles from New Zealand: otherwise his contribution in this respect has been confined to collaborating in translating a number of pieces of traditional Maori poetry. Miss O'Donnell is wrong in describing Maori traditions as 'romantic'; it was one of the false tracks of the nineteenth-century poets to romanticise such Maori myths as appealed to them—particularly the story of Hinemoa and Tutanekai. But it is regrettable that to most pakehas the traditional Maori myths, prettified and bowdlerised, have no higher status than children's reading.

The recognition (in something like its political sense) of another contiguous culture has not been easy for pakehas generally, let alone their writers. The early colonists, for obvious reasons, were not prone to examine their attitudes to the people they had dispossessed. Double standards were apparent: Alfred Domett could turn his literary character Tangi-Moana into an epic hero, 'a God-made King of men', but as a politician speaking in the New Zealand Assembly in 1860 he could describe an actual chief as a 'marauding cannibal and free-booter'. Alfred A. Grace certainly had human sympathy for the Maori and preferred Maori ways to the self-righteousness of pakeha ways, and in this vein he could write of the Maori as a lovable good-humoured cunning rogue. But in another work he writes a sentimental and romantic love-story of pre-European Maoris, and in yet another he started the comic stereotype, still with us, of shrewd, simple-minded, happy-go-lucky Hori. The three attitudes do not easily fit. Between Grace's last (1910) and Finlayson's first (1938) most pakeha writers turned their attention away from Maoris as many of them were living at the time, withdrawn in rural slums, dispossessed and without much hope or interest in pakeha society. Yet fundamentally in most of the writing about Maoris from after the land wars to the depression, there is a feeling of guilt about and a distaste for the contemporary Maori. The novels of the land wars that show him as fierce and treacherous or fierce and brave seek to justify his current condition: either he deserved his defeat or he lost in fair fight. Only Satchell's *The Greenstone Door* (1914) sees the tragedy of the conflict. Those who wrote about the pre-European Maori looked away from the present to a noble past, interpreted according to nineteenth-century European literary attitudes, seeing him as a heroic but pathetic victim inevitably sacrificed to Progress. Those who saw him as a comic figure saw him as a kind of pet and implied that his current condition was the way he liked to live. The Australian Henry Lawson's one story of Maoris states clearly that universal brotherhood is all very well, but you can't extend it to Maoris.

After Grace, Roderick Finlayson was the first to see in Maori life an alternative to the coldness and selfishness of pakeha society, though it is interesting to note that this theme, like several others, is prefigured in

Katherine Mansfield, in her story 'How Pearl Button was Kidnapped' (1910). But in Mr Finlayson the Maoris become symbols of a simpler and more 'natural' life. In his story 'The Totara Tree', where electric power board officers try to cut down a tree that is sacred to an old woman, Mr Finlayson is objecting not only to pakeha disrespect for Maori sensibility but to electrification itself, an objection not in fact shared by Maoris. Mr Finlayson is best when he is describing, observing sympathetically; he is less successful when he tries to enter the minds of his characters; their thoughts are too trite and simple, and since their passions are simple he solves their problems by simple, violent solutions—suicide, murder, revenge. His attitude implies a lack of sympathy for what has happened since, the migration of young Maoris to the cities in search of employment, a mixed attitude to the advances in health and education, greater participation of Maoris in the general life.

This migration has enabled a number of writers of short stories to write sympathetically of Maori individuals they have met. There is still, however, an incomplete appreciation of the distinctness of Maori communal life and of cultural features that Maoris prefer to retain—a different kinship system, a sense of belonging to an extended family of 100-odd members rather than to a 'nuclear family' of Mum, Dad, and the kids; a sense of the obligations of aroha (fellow-feeling) towards friends and relatives in need; the desire to congregate; the admiration of courtesy, generosity, sociability, and hospitality; the distaste for pakeha stinginess and coldness, greed and calculation. But the stereotype of the Maori as feckless, jolly and without complexity or stress is becoming less frequent in writing.

Of contemporary writers Noel Hilliard is the only one to realise all of these features and to catch the spirit of Maori life. Like Finlayson he is best when he is sympathetically observing. Netta in *Maori Girl* is a pathetic victim of social forces, but to prove his point he denies her the victory over circumstances that it was in her character to achieve, and he is not always convincing when he enters her mind. It is significant that Sylvia Ashton-Warner in *Spinster* is convincing in her Maori children, less so in her Maori adults; and that among the best imaginative writing about Maoris in recent years are three or four children's books about modern Maori children.

Of course the only authentic expression of a Maori view can come from Maoris themselves, and in recent years there has been the emergence of a a group of Maori painters and some writers in English. The difference in attitude can be illustrated by quotation.

Noel Hilliard in this passage is comic, sensitive, and accurate:

Later the children were sent out while the grown-ups discussed whether Wai should wear white or not. Mum and the other relations wanted white but some of the older women, and the vicar's warden were insisting on a colour. 'What's it got to do with all them what

Auntie Wai wears?' Bubby asked. 'It's something you'll find out by and by,' Mum said. So they sat on the veranda playing Last-card while the voices hummed on in the sitting-room for nearly an hour. Towards the end they could hear Dad, and he sounded as if he had his temper up: 'She can get married in her pyjamas if she wants to!' When Bubby was called in to take around the cakes for supper, she could tell from Mum's smile that white had won.[4]

Mr Hilliard, to some extent an outsider, has recognized his limitation in making the observer a small girl, only partly privy to adult deliberations. In this passage from a Maori writer, Rowley Habib, there is a sense of belonging. It is after a burial:

By the apple-trees a group of women were busying themselves with their shawls. Two of them were lifting their babies onto their backs, and they bounced them around a little to settle them more comfortably in the blankets. Down by the Hepis' fence the priest was talking with old Doc and Tita. He was gesturing slowly with his hands and now and then he would look across the paddock at the sun. Everyone was talking about the beautiful day, everything except the burial.[5]

A pakeha writer—though not Mr Hilliard—describing the same scene might have been arrested by aspects unfamiliar to him and have sought a metaphor for the women with the babies in their shawls, an image that would make them memorable and fix them, like a tourist's camera, so that no deeper meaning could be penetrated.

And if pakeha writers in the 'thirties and 'forties saw the landscape as alien and without a past, Hone Tuwhare's attitude, always deeply attached, is very different. Mr Tuwhare is indebted technically and personally to R. A. K. Mason, who introduces his first collection, about to be published in New Zealand. In this poem he returns to his ancestral homeland in Northland, seeing land once covered in forest now scarred by soil erosion. I have to provide a few glosses: manuka is a scrub, rather like a tall heath and has white or pink blossom something like a small apple flower; its leaves often have a reddish tinge. Mana means something between authority and prestige: high standing. The marae, here deserted through depopulation, was the open-air site of communal gatherings; it is always adjoined by two halls for accommodating guests and feeding them: it is these that have the rotting eaves.

Not by Wind Ravaged

Deep scarred
    not by wind ravaged nor rain
    nor the brawling stream:
    stripped of all save the brief finery
    of gorse and broom; and standing

>   sentinel to your bleak loneliness
>   the tussock grass—
>
>   O voiceless land, let me echo your desolation.
>   The mana of my house has fled,
>   the marae is but a paddock of thistle.
>   I come to you with a bitterness
>   that only your dull folds can soothe
>   for I know, I know
>   my melancholy chants shall be lost
>   to the wind's shriek about the rotting eaves.
>
>   Distribute my nakedness—
>   Unadorned I come with no priceless
>   offering of jade-and-bone curio: yet
>   to the wild berry shall I give
>   a tart piquancy; enhance for a deathless
>   space the fragile blush of manuka . . .
>
>   You shall bear all and not heed.
>   In your huge compassion embrace
>   those who know no feeling other
>   than greed:
>   of this I lament my satisfaction
>   for it is as full as a beggar's cup:
>   no less shall the dust of avaricious men
>   succour exquisite blooms with
>   moist lips parting
>   to the morning sun.

Natural elements in Mr Tuwhare's verse are humanised and dramatised in a way that would be false in pakeha convention. (The sea-egg is the sea-urchin; the paua a shellfish.):

>   and the sun's feet
>   shall twinkle and flex
>   to the sea-egg's needling
>   and the paua's stout kiss
>   shall drain a rock's heart
>   to the sand-bar's booming.

That his themes are not confined to his situation in his country is evident from the title-poem of his collection *No Ordinary Sun*, which is the Bomb, and from this poem which needs no gloss:

Time and the Child

Tree earth and sky
reel to the noontide beat
of sun and the old man
hobbling down the road.
Cadence—

of sun-drowned cicada
in a child's voice shrilling:
. . . are you going man?

Where are going man where
The old man is deaf
to the child.
His stick makes deep
holes in the ground.
His eyes burn to a distant point

where all roads converge. . . .
The child has left his toys
and hobbles after the old
man calling: funny man funny man

funny old man funny
Overhead the sun paces
and buds pop and flare.

I have spent so much time on Mr Tuwhare not as a culmination or as a prize exhibit but because the entry of a viewpoint of different inheritance will be important to us. The Maori writer will have to draw on reserves of strength and integrity to resist the pakeha image of him, difficult enough amidst the confusions resulting from the pressure of pakeha society, in the name of 'integration', to assimilate him, turn him into a brown pakeha in outlook and aspiration. I once thought that the Maori writer would have difficulty reaching a Maori audience (I do not suggest that he will, or should, write exclusively for Maoris) but having observed the attentive and warm response to Mr Tuwhare's reading from an unprepared and unliterary Maori audience, I no longer think this is so—though he is less likely to reach them through print than through speech. New Zealand life will be greatly enriched if we can learn to see the country and its life through the eyes of a number of Maori writers.

I hope I have shown that as I see it the problem in New Zealand has been the recognition of truths about ourselves, both pakeha and Maori, and about the country; an acceptance of our time and place as a prerequisite to writing that can, if it wishes, take it for granted and forget it.

Notes

1. E.H. McCormick, *New Zealand Literature: A Survey*, 1959; D.M. Davin (ed.), *New Zealand Short Stories*, 1953; R.M. Chapman and Jonathan Bennett (eds.), *An Anthology of New Zealand Verse*, 1956; Allen Curnow (ed.), *The Penguin Book of New Zealand Verse*, 1960.
2. 'Fiction and the Social Pattern', *Landfall*, March 1953, reprinted in Wystan Curnow (ed.), *Essays on New Zealand Literature*, Heinemann Educational Books Ltd, 1973.
3. O.N. Gillespie (ed.), *New Zealand Short Stories*, 1930; C.R. Allen (ed.), *Tales by New Zealanders*, 1938.
4. 'Auntie Wai's Wedding', *A Piece of Land*, 1963.
5. 'The Burial', *Te Ao Hou*, vol. 5, no. 2, 1957.

The Reluctant Bushman

The only Australian writer to have a State funeral and a statue in the Domain, Henry Lawson has never been fully collected between hard covers. Lawson criticism has been haunted by biographical issues. His venerators, insisting on the Noble Bushman or the tireless champion of the working man, have been embarrassed by his later less heroic years or by his violent insularities. If his biggest readership outside Australia is probably in Russia, there must be uneasiness at his racism and his yellow-peril jingoism. His mates in defence insisted on 'the real Henry', a gentle sensitive man with brown searching eyes.

One can't ignore the biography because it contributes so much to his subject-matter. And it is necessary to sift him because at his best he is in the line of the great English comic humanists.

The clue to Lawson's contradictions is his loneliness: it gives passion to his recognition in others of his own humanity. It was a loneliness extending to desolation. Deaf, neglected as a baby, pushing a plough at ten, victimised by his workmates as a youth, the young man who tramped, often hungry and workless, for six months in the Darling Country, felt the loneliness and desolateness of the great outback in which every nomadic labourer needed a mate (and the Union) to survive. His most revealing personal discovery was that booze was a way to communication with his fellow-men.

Cecil Mann begins this new selection with Lawson's 'Fragment of an Autobiography'—for the first time (except for a few sentences) published in full. A deprived childhood recollected in self-pity, it is as Mann says satisfying, because (whether his account is true or not) the pity extends to the mother who hurt him, to the narrow community that thought him peculiar, even to his persecutors at his first job in the city. His strength

This essay was first published in the *New Zealand Listener*, 1 October 1965, as a review of *The Stories of Henry Lawson* (3 vols.), ed. Cecil Mann (Angus & Robertson).

originates in his weakness: from self-pity to understanding and love. The strip of New South Wales running north-west from Sydney to Hungerford in Queensland is almost the whole of Lawson's Australia; it can be read as a hostile world in which individuals are beaten unless they have the defences of personal courage or sad delusions or the protection of a mate.

Lawson's attitude to his fellow men is ambiguous. The Union buries its dead, but the funeral is a farce and most of the mourners never get out of the pub. He could see the bushman as narrow and selfish, the city worker as brutish and corrupted by sport, yet he could write of the splendid type of bushman he had known out West, and on a letter from a shearers' union secretary seeking permission to use his lines on a tombstone for a shearer killed in the '91 strike, he wrote that this made him 'prouder than anything'. He knew he idealised his bushmen and in one place, cancelled and stetted, he said so.

His idealised bushmen are apostles of mateship; the cult is sentimentalised in yarns of men who fight if their mate's name is traduced, who each carry in their swag a personal grief their mates never inquire about. The code is at odds with domesticity, and two men owe it to their boss to lie to his widow about his death in the d.t.'s. It is hard to admire the martyrdom of the 'hero' whose secret is five years' hard for attempted bank robbery, willingly suffered rather than sully the name of the bank manager's niece he had been visiting by night.

At the other extreme there is the bitterness of 'A Rough Shed' and 'The Little World Left Behind'; it is less offensive than the sentimentality or the agonies of 'The Selector's Daughter', with death and suicide. Lawson occasionally uses a death to shame the reader into bowing his head. One suspects that the crucial incident in the Sydney stories of Arvie Aspinall, the death of the overworked exploitee of industry, is a sort of retrospective revenge on the mother who sent Lawson to the carriage-works where he was persecuted.

But in genial mood Lawson is pleasant, if undemanding, company. The wry ambling humour of 'Coming Across' and 'The Darling River' fully employs his intelligence and observation. There are the yarns of practical jokers, of jackeroos and city coach-passengers taken down by simple bushmen, the confidence tricks of the New Zealander Steelman. There are the generous human sketches of Baldy Thompson the squatter, Peter McKenzie the digger and the wild Irishman of the West Coast, of Brummy Usen who couldn't convince anyone he was alive because the bush telegraph said he was dead; there is the genially ironic sketch of Mr Smellingscheck; the yarn of the retriever with a mouthful of explosive and burning fuse that sent the diggers scattering; of Jimmy Grimshaw's cool winning of the desirable widow who owned a shanty.

In the best of the stories there is harmony between human nobility and human smallness. Character, setting, irony and pathos are admirable in 'The Bush Undertaker'. In 'The Drover's Wife' he celebrates the toughness of one of those 'leathery women with complexions like dried apples' but there is a metaphysical context as well. The dog shakes the snake 'as though he felt the original curse in common with mankind'; 'the sickly daylight breaks over the bush.' There is pity and admiration for suffering and strength in 'Water them Geraniums' and 'No Place for a Woman'.

There is little development in Lawson. There is a calm dignity and honesty in the Joe Wilson stories but they are ultimately disappointing. Mann imputes the intermittent stiffness of style to Lawson's writing for a British publisher; the reason might rather be that Lawson was breaking new ground, trying to examine his own faltering marriage and imaginatively set it right again. But the self-analysis and self-knowledge demanded were beyond him.

Lawson was twice in New Zealand. Each time he intended to settle, but was back in Sydney in less than a year. 'This intensely cautious country' he called it and, 24 years later, 'Toadyland'. His 1897 visit was productive, but of the romantically conceived Maori sketches, there remains only the embittered 'Daughter of Maoriland'. Poor Sarah, helping herself to the groceries of the teacher who is kind to her catches the full outcry of the affronted paternalist. Steelman carried off bigger loot with no more than a wink from the writer, but his victims were mugs and Steelman was white. The indulgent tone limits the kindly sketches of Black Joe and Ah Soon, humanity tussles with prejudice, but if Lawson protests in 'Madame Bong Fong' that he cannot hate the Chinese, one recalls 'His Mistake', a joke about an Aboriginal who killed a Chinese shepherd mistaking him for some new pest.

This edition contains the 137 stories of the *Prose Works* reprinted frequently since 1935; besides the Autobiography what is new is 500 pages of a selection of prose (artificially grouped into 'books') taken from periodicals from 1893 to 1923, but most of it from Lawson's latter days. The criterion has been 'fair-average-quality Lawson'; but the later prose is less assured. The vision is retrospective while Australia goes to the dogs; he tries to catch his earlier effects, and his attempts to write of England don't succeed. There are several essays by and about Lawson, including those of A. G. Stephens and H. M. Green.

Cecil Mann knows his Lawson, but his notes are long-winded, repetitive, contradictory and concern themselves with superannuated issues. There has only been random collation of the text with the manuscripts, typescripts and corrected clippings in the Mitchell Library: but one error, Aliaura for Ahaura on the West Coast (which has been appearing since 1894) seems to be Lawson's own; if he knew of the error he did not correct it. Lawson usually took pains to get his Maori names right.

This is probably the fullest collection we shall ever have. Besides the outstanding stories, what one remembers is a rich impression of a period and place; a scattered society of shearers and rouseabouts, drovers and bullockies and swagmen, shanty-keepers, struggling selectors and diggers, spielers and hatters and tough uncomplaining women. Lawson's subject is loneliness, the consolation and comedy of comradeship, the beauty of courage in the face of suffering. In the best stories the 'real Henry'—a gentle, kindly realist—is attractively present.

Recent Maori Writers

In this attractively designed book, for which Reeds and Miss Orbell are to be congratulated, the general impression of the best writing is of singing that is at once party song and hymn. Traditional European categories do not fit: comic and tragic modes can blend or succeed each other without sentimentality; satire and lyricism are not mutually exclusive, or didacticism and self-mockery. Witi Ihimaera in several pieces published last year in the *New Zealand Listener* and *Landfall* (too late, I suppose, to be considered for this volume) is poignant, sensitive, clownish, with a controlling current of feeling that is warm and—dare one use the word in 1971?—good. It is rare for our writers to reveal themselves so trustingly, or (if you prefer) create so disarming a *persona*. S. M. Mead, a deeply serious man, tells a cautionary tale that if it were read aloud to a Maori audience would fill the air with their laughter. The many-sidedness of response to experience is one of the attractive features of the stories and in some cases runs counter to a single-purpose 'line' of development that has probably been picked up from European models. It is nevertheless no less than their due that the contributors to this volume should be judged by the same ultimate aesthetic criteria as other writing is judged by.

All of these poems and stories are concerned with the experience of being a Maori in contemporary New Zealand or seeing New Zealand life through the eyes of a Maori. If I say little of Hone Tuwhare it is because his work is well known, but one is reminded of his unique combination of gentleness (that is not softness) and durability (that is not toughness) in a tone that claims ready respect and trust. In several stories the theme is the contrast between the old small farming community, its life centring on the whanau, the church and the marae, and the debut, heady, frightening and often hurtful, into the aggressive impersonality of the pakeha city; and these stories can be seen as allegories of the fall or of temptation or of

---

This essay was first published in *Landfall*, March 1971, as a review of *Contemporary Maori Writing*, selected by Margaret Orbell (A.H. & A.W. Reed Ltd).

challenge. Memory—the warm tears of aroha that give joy to the slow hongi with the cousin not seen for years—is a mental operation that older Maoris value more highly than pakehas. Rora Paki who must be nearly seventy recalls her youth in prose that is both narrative fiction and meditative essay. Riki Erihi remembers with warmth and scepticism the currents of religious factionalism and one-upmanship that played in his village; there is a slyness and compassion that recalls the comedy of Chaucer's fabliau tales and of Fielding. There is a story about the conflict between a boy's doctrine and the evidence of his senses when he observes the healing of a sick youth by a tohunga in whom he is forbidden to believe.

Witi Ihimaera, the youngest of the contributors, born in 1944, is a voice one wants to encourage. His 'Tangi' is moving because it is about bereavement, an experience more frequent in any one person's life, more fully encountered and more shared among Maoris than among pakehas, and there is a skilful counterpointing of the memory of an earlier tangi on two separate phases of the one that is the subject of the story. If I qualify my praise it is because Mr Ihimaera has done much better with the same material in last September's *Landfall*. Perhaps it is pakeha (or personal) defensiveness that makes me slightly uneasy that there is a tone in this story that is vulnerable to an irreverent refusal on a reader's part to be awed by a death. The bereft youth, reminded of an earlier bereavement when his favourite nanny died, is presented as a child left alone in the dark and so the story ends; but one knows that he is of working age and lives in a city and will survive. The tone is not self-pity, it is bewilderment, apparently compounded of guilt at having been away when his father died and a fear of being inadequate to his new role as head of the family. But this is not sufficiently identified or distinguished from self-pity; the mood seems over-simplified and one leaves this story (as one does not leave the *Landfall* piece) with a feeling that an effect has been achieved at the expense of part of the truth.

Rowley Habib's stories have appeared over the past fourteen years or so and it is a disappointment that the promise of his early work has not strikingly matured. His two stories are competent, but in 'The Boss' it is the incidental detail of life in the linemen's camp that is more interesting than the 'point' of the story which is a sentimental cliché—the tough boss who clumsily reveals a compassionate heart when one of his men is killed. I wonder if Mr Habib has been inhibited from following the trustworthy impressions of felt experience and from exploring contradictions and their implications (as he did in 'The Visitors' in *Te Ao Hou*, November 1957, and in his moving verse incident 'The Home Welcoming' in *Arena* in 1962) by some preconception about the attitudes he should take or conclusions he should reach or the role he is expected to fulfil. If so it is the conflict between observation and ideology that Riki Erihi's proper little devil had. Mr Habib for all this is a writer with a good deal of promise, but he needs to settle down quietly with the truths that only he can tell, wherever they lead him, and to start writing to please himself.

Rose Denness, who has published only one story, is also less interesting in the 'point' of her story—the old man's decision to make a leader out of the illegitimate boy of combined European and Maori ancestry—than in the incidental effects, the unfeelingness of the boy's mother, the comedy of the boy and the old man in the runaway gig, the vulnerability of the boy. Hirone Wikiriwhi's strength is his compassion for the girl who has had a baby from a man she does not want to marry; his weakness his faith in a ready-made solution, that the girl needs the support of a restrictive religion. Katarina Mataira tells a neat moral fable and finds a synthesis of aroha and the economic pressures of city family life. Patricia Grace is economical and amusing.

It was a pleasure to discover that the pseudonymous author of a story I liked when it appeared in *Te Ao Hou* was Arapera Blank whose alert feminine appraisal of experience is as conscious of the attractions of the old rural life as of those of the city and of the civilised values of Europe. Mrs Blank whose personal perspectives include growing up as one in a large family in the heart of Ngati-Porou country and living in a European city, has a quiet and lively talent I hope we will see more of. Mason Durie's stories were written when he was a student; he has since concentrated on medicine and he may have given up writing. His stories have pathos and some of the sense of strangeness of a modern self-conscious Maori youth in the face of older values. Harry Dansey's poem conveys a sense of being a stranger on his own ancestral land.

No editor can expect every reader to concur with his choice, and if Miss Orbell's is not entirely mine the field from which she had to choose is small, perhaps eighty prose pieces and a handful of verse. I would have omitted Nick Karaitiana's 'Lest We Forget' which (like an Australian war shrine with its coloured glass saints in uniform) manages at the same time to make war beatific and regrettable and to lift us like the old Warner Brothers' Celestial Choir to higher and holier spheres far beyond all human strife. One can see too that the slightly hectoring tone of Rowley Habib's poem 'The Raw Men', earthier though it is, is the consequence of having been written in answer to a foolish question from 'an Englishman not long in New Zealand'—how came these survivors from a destroyed culture to fight so well in the second world war? The real objection to these two pieces, whose motive I think is to remind pakehas of their debt to Maoris, is that they swallow false premises, official premises. The Maori right to social justice rests on claims older and more permanent than a willingness to fight in overseas wars.

It is clear that a question that must engage the Maori writer in English is the choice of moral values, discriminating between the genuine and the spurious in the pakeha world as well as recognising and protecting what is to be preferred from his own, and in a time when internal policies in this country have been allowed to become increasingly vulnerable to the whims of the stock exchanges of Sydney and Tokyo and New York he is likely to find the track a treacherous one. Most of these stories and poems reflect the optimism of the decade in which they were written, a period when pakeha goodwill and interest were more fashionable than now, when official policy was to encourage 'integration', when in a series of hopeful regional leadership conferences many intelligent young Maoris accepted the 'new world' ideology of adaptation to an urban society that would guarantee an equal place to the hard-working Maori of good will and would value him for his cultural contribution. It came to a disenchanted end about 1966 when Maoris recognized that few pakehas were even aware there was such a contract, that the Education Department was no less concerned than before to undervalue Maori language and culture and the Maori schools and that against almost unanimous Maori protest the Government was determined to push through the land grab of the Maori Affairs Amendment Act of 1967. The mood of the youngest leaders is activist and distrustful and there is a new generation, urbanised, under-educated and culturally deprived who may be more representative of Maori attitudes in the future. They have few of the cultural strengths that sustain the writers of this volume, and it is questionable whether, if any of them choose to express themselves in verse or fiction, they will write with the good will, the confidence in traditional Maori values, the lyricism and the celebration of being alive that distinguishes this collection. If they do not only they but we will have been saved. It is to be hoped at least that the contributors to this volume will continue to write, not only for the strength they can give their people but for the delight they can give us pakehas and the enrichment of seeing our surroundings through Maori eyes.

Home

There was one day three years ago when I crossed from Australia, from the brisk blue mornings of Canberra, with rosellas flashing and the loud calls of peewit and pardalote and magpie and currawong, to the seagulls and sparrows of the Manukau, to the showers and lead-pencil skies of Auckland in May. And walking down seedy old Symonds Street, in spite of the bland temperature, the rain and the grey I had a sense of being home such as I had not felt in all the bright and dust and heat and cold of the Monaro. So that when I am asked (as the N.Z.B.C. has asked me) why I live in New Zealand, the answer is that I was born here and it is only at home that I feel at home. I have enjoyed living in London and Australia but in those communities I was a guest; to use Maori terms, here I am tangata whenua, a native, and I hope I have turangawaewae, my native earth beneath me and the right to stand forward and speak.

I was born in 1922. I was 13 when the Savage government came in, dramatically marking the end of the lean years. For me, the new economic security of the early years of Labour opened possibilities like university which my parents couldn't have afforded earlier; and it released us all from the harsh old doctrine of work and thrift that had ruled the country for so long. The spending on libraries let in new ideas on education and psychology and politics as well as the imaginative literature of the twenties and thirties. It was possible to see our home experience in the light of the freshest thinking from outside. We also had a glimpse of an independent national policy, we could take pride in our health services and education and old Maori grievances were listened to.

I recall this past only to measure the present. Because with the new prosperity came the trend that has taken over and turned us into a very different society. I mean the lust to acquire the possessions the advertisers are always wheedling us to buy. If I wanted to point to two opposite

This piece was written for radio and was broadcast on the National Programme, 18 May 1972, and abridged in the *New Zealand Listener*, 12 June 1972.

poles in pakeha society—not the only ones—I would point to the comfortably-off blue-rinsed widow in her home unit, busy with her rituals of ownership, stoking her rubbish tin with the righteous wastes of her modest consumption vaguely disturbed that the world outside is not as it was when she went to school—comfortable for old ladies and kept in order by white Anglo-Saxon military alliances and occasional wars which we always won. At the opposite pole I would point to the demonstrator in his dirty jeans, his head in the cloud of his own hair, with a contempt for the value most of us set on possessions and status. He too is concerned to see his country's behaviour in the light of what is happening in the world and, so far as the world is aware of us, it is he who will retrieve the reputation of his country.

Which is not high. Look at our international position. Twenty years ago in England I wanted to tell people I was a New Zealander; in recent years I have waited till I am asked. In the one area where our help could be of real service, the South Pacific, we have given, but too stingily to win the goodwill that would follow if we were generous. We have taken part in a most callous gang attack on the people of Indo-China, their crops and soil and water, their very sources of life; and we did it for the sake of American protection and a bigger share of the American market. At the same time our envoys have been running around the capitals of Europe like beggars saying, Please be sorry for us; expecting Europeans to forego their economic advantage for the sake of *our* comfort. Wouldn't it be better to turn our smallness to advantage and develop a policy of neutrality and self-reliance?

At home the large rewards go to the aggressive and the quick off the mark, to the selfish and the lucky. We have given power to men who measure the value of an activity by the profit it turns in, who undervalue education and have let our health service run down, who are still filching from Maoris the last of their land if it can be turned to profit. If we let them they will turn our landscape into private parks for millionaires and industrial waste heaps. Other countries are finding there can be a terrible price for concentrating on production and consumption, on exports and markets. We are fortunate in what we still have the opportunity of avoiding the extremes of pollution and biological disturbance that have been reached overseas.

But our most important domestic concern is race relations. One of the prides of Auckland, some would say its best one, is its large Polynesian population, not only Maoris from all the tribes of the North Island, but immigrants from the diverse villages of Western Samoa, from Niue and Tonga and the Tokelau atolls, from Rarotonga and Mauke and Mangaia and Aitutaki and Pukapuka and Manihiki. I dwell on these names to suggest the cultural diversity whose value we don't appreciate; not simply a diversity of language and song and mime and dance, but of ways of relating to one another, of the ceremonials of welcome and mourning, of codes of giving and receiving. In their readiness to smile and love, in their sense of what things are important in living, Polynesians know a great deal that we have forgotten or perhaps never learnt.

Yet so many of the Polynesian faces one sees on the streets in Auckland are hard and unfriendly, nagged by time payment or the fear of unemployment or the coldness of pakeha or palagi neighbours or landlords. It would be sentimental to expect all the virtues of the rural family village to survive the shift to a working-class suburb in an industrial city. But it is a great pity that Polynesians should be made to live as we do, behind walls and within the code of behaviour that the blue-rinsed widow approves, expected to be quiet and not have too many visitors. Because what we are likely to see as Maoris and Islanders are urbanised is a replica of ourselves; not as we see ourselves, but as they do, as we have treated them. And it may not be a good likeness; it could be a terrible one. We have already had warning from the violence of some of the first generation to grow up in the city, those adolescents who could find no better way of asserting an identity than gang violence. It is encouraging that in a recent example that was given a lot of publicity, a Maori gang from South Auckland, we did not fall back on the authoritarian streak that lies in us or on the hysteria with which we legislated against narcotics. In this case reason prevailed: a number of urban Maori leaders talked to the youths and looked for the causes, the Minister of Maori Affairs went to one of their functions. It is something that gives me pride in my country that a potentially destructive force has been converted to constructive social work in the suburb in which it developed. Where else in the world could an apparently anti-social gang be enlisted to raise funds for a church boarding school? But we have to be prepared to spend money on more profound and imaginative measures than this, because there are other gangs and will be more. And spending money on education and social work means rearranging our priorities.

In our relations with Maoris there is a much deeper issue that takes me back to the point I started with. What right have I to claim turangawaewae in this country? We have to face up to history. For several centuries it was Europeans who moved in on the rest of the world, invading, defeating, annexing, settling. In a post-colonial world we are likely to see an extension of readjustment to those parts where the original people were outnumbered and reduced to a politically ineffective minority. We are likely to see a reassertion of ancestral claims, some demand for re-negotiation of the mutual rights of descendants of the occupiers and the occupied. New Zealand will not escape this process, though it has a great advantage in that Maoris were not denied political rights. But there will not be inter-racial stability until we pakehas have recognised the unjustness of our position—that we are living here by virtue of the violence and fraud that our ancestors practised on those whose land it was, and the descendants of those Maoris will not be put off by the argument that their ancestors were content with a few axes and blankets or muskets or even several hundred thousand pounds paid in later compensation.

We might have avoided this if we had treated Maoris as partners and not wards, had allowed them to use their own initiative and co-operated with them in meeting their needs and aspirations. But Maoris are now putting our professions of good will to the test. We have rested our belief in our happy race relations on two lies that we tell our children at school. The first is that in practice we honour the Treaty of Waitangi; the second is the myth that the Maoris themselves were preceded by an extinct people called Morioris—we have known for years that it is not true, but we preserve it as a way of projecting onto Maoris our own uneasiness about our right to be here.

In this context we can see that the young activists who call themselves Tamatoa, the young fighters, are helping us to see the truth. They may not have the whole of the truth and there are Maoris who do not agree with them. But Maoris are better than we are at talking things out and reaching unanimity. We have to recognise that most Maoris are agreed in wanting for their people a recognised and valued place in a society that allows room for their language and their own ways of behaving and feeling.

So that if I were asked to make up an honours list of those to whom a future generation will owe most, it would not include many whose names get into the front page headlines; it would include rather a great many people I will never meet and whose names I don't know. It would include those who volunteer their time and energy for peace and civil liberties or the human dignity of prisoners or to save the landscape and our flora and fauna; it would include those who turned out on the streets for peace in Vietnam, who have campaigned to save Lake Manapouri, and teachers who have upheld the values of their profession. But especially it would include those who are contributing to racial harmony: Maoris and Islanders who have accepted the challenge of maintaining something of their way of life while they raise families in a new environments; pakeha students who have been helping Polynesian children with their homework; Maori academics who have worked hard to develop community self-reliance in the new outer suburbs of West Auckland; teachers who have raised the performance of Maori pupils; pakeha women members of the Maori Women's Welfare League, members of organisations called Hart and Care.

Outside the arts and literature our national distinctions are fewer than we think. But those in which I take pride are first, the presence of so many Polynesians whose different values and aspirations provide a continual and fruitful criticism of our own; and second, the good proportion of pakehas who care about good race relations.

Two Tributes

H. Winston Rhodes

Harold Winston Rhodes retires at the end of this year after thirty-seven years teaching in the English Department at the University of Canterbury, a career that brought to New Zealand something of a phase of Australian intellectual life and left a mark on New Zealand letters and the climate in which they are produced.

It would not surprise those who know him to learn that Winston Rhodes, after an outstanding record which took him to the Medical Faculty, switched to a course in arts. Graduating Master of Arts at the University of Melbourne he tutored in English, both privately and at Ormond and Newman, the Presbyterian and Catholic colleges of the university until 1933 when he was invited to join the staff of the English Department at Canterbury University College.

The professor who had succeeded Arnold Wall in the previous year was Frederick Sinclaire, a New Zealander who had returned from an appointment with Walter Murdoch, directing adult education in Perth. In the 1910's and 20's Sinclaire had been a leading figure in the intellectual life of Melbourne, as a Unitarian parson and then the leader of a breakaway group, the Free Religious Fellowship. He conducted classes of the old W.E.A. type, where literature was discussed along with the ideas of a number of social philosophers of the preceding half-century—Orage, the Fabians, Chesterton, Shaw and Marx. Sinclaire was then an energetic and inspiring figure; his part in the development of Australian writers' conception of their social role is only now being investigated; besides his following of trade unionists, Unitarians, students and pacifists, his classes were attended by Louis Esson, Frank Wilmot and Vance Palmer, who with his wife Nettie, was to lead the Australian writers' social scene throughout the thirties and forties.

When he came to New Zealand Sinclaire had the mellowness of an old-fashioned book-lover, content to draw spiritual sustenance from his

This piece was first published in *Landfall*, December 1970.

Chaucer, his Spenser and Shakespeare—he made them 'his'—from Milton, Wordsworth, Hazlitt and Browning, especially Browning: he had his own 'great tradition'. The English Department at Canterbury College had a hundred odd students then, and one lecturer. When that lectureship fell vacant, Sinclaire asked the council to write to Winston Rhodes in Melbourne.

Rhodes was 28 when he came to Christchurch in 1933, the year after the worst period of the depression in New Zealand, the year in which Frank Sargeson first published, the year of the fuss about *Oriflamme* at Canterbury College. He made the acquaintance of members of the Caxton Club; and he and his wife in their Papanui Road flat had weekly discussion evenings for radical students. In a time when this year's novel is on next year's course it is perhaps not easy to imagine a time when (since the English course stopped at 1910) students were grateful to a lecturer who put on voluntary lectures on 'modern literature' and (when the Caxton Press began to publish) New Zealand verse. It was Winston Rhodes who introduced me to my first undergraduate literary passion, Virginia Woolf.

He readily made connexions with his new community. He lectured for the W.E.A.; with Sinclaire and Mrs Rowlatt he helped to initiate a travelling library service, a scheme later adopted by G. T. Alley as the Country Library Service. Denis Glover was taken on for a time as a junior lecturer, and with Sinclaire, Glover and Kennaway Henderson, Rhodes helped found *Tomorrow* the fortnightly that first gave repeated space to Frank Sargeson. When Sinclaire, disheartened by the renewal of war in 1939, turned rapidly and prematurely old, Rhodes quietly took on the administration of the department.

In Melbourne he had organized classes in English for Jewish refugees from Fascism; in New Zealand he joined, founded, chaired, addressed or sat on committees of a dozen or two left wing organizations, the League against Fascism and War, the Left Book Club, Friends of the Soviet Union, the Spanish Aid Committee, the Rewi Alley Aid Committee and during the war, the China Aid Committee. He met Alley in the thirties, and he soon met his Auckland counterpart Willis Airey, with whom he enjoyed a warm friendship until Airey's death.

If some of the positions he took have been betrayed by their outcome, they are none of them positions he need repent. He has not regretted his choices and they were not made in idealisation: he did not expect that the Soviet Union would escape its passage of complacent mediocrity any more than England in the eighteenth, or France in the nineteenth century. It was the fulfilment of the common man he stood for, and he was prepared to suffer for his stand. His political involvements, briefly respectable during the war-time alliance with Russia, became suspect when the cold war struck. Academic enemies saw that his merits were not seriously considered when Sinclaire retired in 1948. There was, however, a student round robin expressing the fullest confidence in him. In 1950, on his first sabbatical, he visited Europe, including the Soviet Union for the first time; there were to be two later visits, and one to China.

With his new professor, John Garrett, and Lawrence Baigent who had been appointed lecturer after the war Rhodes helped to organize the Writers' Conference in 1951, an occasion in which for the first and only time all the generations of writers met, argued and pooled and rejected ideas—Pat Lawlor, Sargeson, Curnow and Glover, Baxter and Louis Johnson. Vance Palmer was fittingly the guest speaker. For New Zealand writing it was an event in self-discovery. In the late 1950s, with Wolfgang Rosenberg, Rhodes, disappointed at the demise of *Here and Now*, founded the *New Zealand Monthly Review*, with an aim of finding common ground of interest for trade unionists and left-wing intellectuals; a journal that has some likeness in its spirit and the unpaid dedication of its writers in the Sydney two-monthly *Outlook* edited by Helen Palmer, daughter of Vance.

Rhodes's way has been to work with others, with their names up front; his influence has been by his voice rather than by his pen. It is not surprising that North Islanders do not know him well or that his position has been misunderstood. His critical position has never been the Zhdanovism he has at times had the reputation for. His one critical pamphlet reflects something of the concerns of Arnold and Leavis: that literature can restore and correct and can protect one against the depersonalisation of modern life, and the artist is the natural enemy of the Philistine, the bureaucrat, the technocrat, the efficiency expert and the computer.

But fundamentally in his fairmindedness, in his belief in good sense, that literature should be comprehensible to the common educated reader, in his preference that novels and plays should be life-like, in his belief that art should make the world better, his position is that of Samuel Johnson, the critic he once confessed he would dispense with last. It is a moral position, not a moralistic one; he is out of sympathy only with the currently more fashionable élitist theories, and sceptical of theories that make too sharp a distinction between art and life. It was a shock as a simple first-year student with an ambition to be an 'author' to hear that living was more important than writing. One never left a lecture of Rhodes's with one's preconceptions intact. But far from preferring socialist realism, Rhodes was one of the first to write in praise of Janet Frame and to write seriously of Sargeson. In his *Monthly Review* editorials he has repeatedly prodded the narrowness, the puritanism and smug assumptions of the orthodox left, and he has opened its columns to the fresh light of Keith Buchanan's essays on non-European literature.

It is characteristic of him that he has been prodigal of his time and energies on committee work, on pamphlets, on W.E.A. lectures and courses. A modest man himself, he has put much of his effort into facilitating expression for others—his edition of *Verse Alive* (a selection from *Tomorrow*), of several volumes of verse and prose of Rewi Alley. But when a second chair in English was created in 1964, John Garrett recommended his appointment from a field of candidates that included scholars of more respectable and carefully groomed reputations. It was a wise and creditable choice.

He introduced the first full paper in New Zealand literature in a New Zealand university; an effort that will have its effect in an alert and critical audience emerging from secondary schools. His two booklets on New Zealand novels, intended as suggestive rather than sufficient, are aimed at the sixth former and the common reader. Probably Winston Rhodes has done as much as any one man in this country to prepare for its writers the milieu in which they must work: an alert critical native audience which understands their intentions. I don't know if other writers have their mental critics whose voices are heard when they are revising. I think Winston Rhodes and Lawrence Baigent have been mine.

In latter years Professor Rhodes found time for his extended study of Frank Sargeson. In retirement he will be able to follow his interest in Australian literature and, a subject that has engaged him in recent years, the writing of African novelists. We can hope now to see more of his own work.

James K. Baxter: A Personal Memory

There were three of us with choices of conscience to face who left a training college picnic at Brighton beach south of Dunedin in 1941 to make a call of homage to Archibald Baxter in the township. The Baxter family had one son in military defaulter's camp and accepted philosophically that they lived in a state of partial siege. Archie heartened us; Mrs Baxter talked proudly of 'Jum' who came in from school before we left. I recall the sharp, sensitive profile, the soft pale complexion and an odd impression of a boy snug in his parent's affection but at a distance from it and from all of us.

He had not remembered that visit when we met again in 1948, students at Canterbury; eventually he was literary editor and I editor of *Canta*. He gave up his studies and I have forgotten how many jobs he had: proof-reading at the *Press*, stoking a hospital furnace, living on milk and invitations out when he was not working. We saw a lot of each other for that year; we were fond of each other and confided freely. If I had been in such a forcing house of outward conformity as the army while he had grown in the freedom of a Quaker household and sown a reputation at Otago University as a wild man with women and alcohol, we shared not only a taste for beer but a dismay that the times which in our memory had seen Stalin's purges, world war, Guernica, Belsen and Hiroshima offered

---

This piece was first published in *Islands* 3, March 1973.

neither peace nor likelihood of accommodating the idealist hopes we thought we had lost. He had (he said it like an older man forgiving the errors of his youth) believed in the natural virtue of the working man and I had thought communism could eliminate injustice and war. We remembered *Darkness at Noon*, and read Graham Greene, talking in terms no longer in vogue of natural man and original sin and of eros and agape and caritas and the sin of sloth or despair to which he felt especially prone and called by its medieval name *accidie*. The truths that we were finding out were old ones, and humbling: that the seeds of oppression and violence lay in the nature that we had in common with other men, and a recognition of the supreme value of compassionate love—truths that explain the compassion Baxter could feel not only for the victims of authority but for its agents. We were drawn to the security and conviction that religious orthodoxy offered, envying the Middle Ages their simplicity of belief. I was attracted sentimentally to Catholicism but Jim who read C.S. Lewis was happier with Anglicanism. He was received into the Church of England, but it did not surprise me later (though by then I had less faith in the religious solution) that he turned Catholic. It was a logical step and if I could have believed in it I would have taken it myself.

We often put in time in pubs, frequently on a Saturday night in one of the several Christchurch bars that would serve you after hours if you rang three times and kept your voice low. If it was day I might find Jim at the bar reading *Deaths and Entrances* which lived, with the notebook in which he wrote in tall sloping print-script like stands of bamboo the first fair copies of his poems, in one of the deep pockets of a long gray overcoat that he wore rain or shine buttoned to the neck and with his pale face made him look like someone just out of hospital; or perhaps explaining to a bookie he had got talking to what it was to be a poet. I was impressed that he could sustain such a conversation and hold the bookie's respect. It was a privilege I imagine hundreds have shared to be the first to see a new poem. 'To my Father' and 'By the Sumner Clock Tower' I first read in bars in that thick little notebook with hard glossy black covers. He read the manuscript of everything I wrote then and I can understand the attraction he has had for young writers because he could take your new work in all its gaucheness and see the grace of the impulse in which it was conceived. From his own adolescent practice he remembered what it was to write badly. When I tried to write verse he told me I didn't harden my heart enough. I valued his sympathy and insight, his tolerance and common sense, his heavy oblique humour and his endless image-spinning talk.

There were aspects that puzzled me. He had moods of depression he did not talk about. I did not understand why he should feel guilty when he saw a policeman or why at his age he was so concerned at the thought of death. I was embarrassed when a barman at the Shades turned us out because he had violated the after-hours protocol and climbed a high gate rather than go through the ritual of knocking to be readmitted from the urinal which was down a back alley; or again when in broad sunlight he turned to a suburban hedge to piss. Even his flow ran dry when a rock-faced matron stepped off her bicycle behind him.

In the late forties there was in Christchurch a group of writers and artists that included Denis Glover, Allen Curnow and Colin McCahon, with Charles Brasch as a quarterly visitor and Fairburn and Mason coming from Auckland. (It was in Christchurch in 1948 that Baxter first met Mason, not in the sixties in Dunedin as he said in his memoir of Mason in *Landfall*.) Jim with the achievement of one book of verse behind him and another in press had a wide round of acquaintance with whom he was welcome, likely to turn up at any hour, a bottle hauling on one of his pockets. Pale, coughing and hung over he knocked up Lawrence Baigent at six one Sunday morning, asked for a bottle of milk and sat down to write, without need for revision, a piece on Frank Sargeson that was overdue for *Canta*.

When I first knew him he was recuperating from a broken love affair with a Dunedin medical student; he was badly hurt. A little later in the year Jacquie Sturm who had been a friend in Dunedin came to Canterbury College. She wrote verse over the initials J.C. and sometimes appeared in the same issue. When they married at the end of the year they went to Wellington where they found a good friend in James Bertram. I remember Jim writing to me that love was suffering and so many of New Zealand's unrecognised tragedies were in the Flats Wanted column. They rented a bach or cottage at Belmont above the Hutt river and I stayed with them the following Easter.

I went to England and we corresponded for several years; but the Korean War had returned my thoughts to a political direction and I had less sympathy with Jim's later phases. In later years if I met him with a group it seemed that his talk was directed to a sounding board and that he deflected attempts to re-establish the old relationship. But it was easy to talk to him if he was alone or with Jacquie and his family; it was like that at Messines Road and Karori in the mid-fifties when he was teaching; at Westshore on holiday in 1963 (he and Jacquie liked an essay I had written in *Landfall* on the current position of Maoris, and I am grateful for the disinterested good sense of the advice he gave me on a personal problem I put to him); and at Dunedin in 1966 when the news came of his appointment to a second year of the Burns Fellowship. At Dunedin I thought him as settled and content as I had seen him and didn't recognise the 'money dungeon' that had been stifling him and he had broken from, as he told me, barefoot in May and wearing dungarees like tents, when we sat down together in the Kiwi Hotel three years later and talked with the old directness and intimacy and on an impulse he gave me his advance copy of *The Rock Woman*. I only saw him once again and then he was in a mood to taunt me, unjustly, with having backslid on my old leftism.